"As a fanboy of both the Focolare and thei
Communion I am so pleased that we now ha... ...
chapters written by serious scholars who can take this vision to a new
level. We have been in desperate need for a new playbook when it comes
to speaking about ethics in business. And now we have one."

Charles Camosy
Bioethics Professor at Creighton School of Medicine.
Author of *Resisting Throwaway Culture*

"The volume is a welcome addition to the literature on Economy of Communion, to which it brings an original sensitivity due to its American origin
and to the fact that its editors (and also several contributors) are not part
of the first circle of scholars, most of them European, that have started it."

Benedetto Gui
Sophia University Institute

"*Finding Faith in Business* accomplishes the difficult and important task
of carrying out a rigorous scholarly engagement with the Economy of
Communion (EoC) movement while also offering insights for living
out EoC principles in daily life and business in many different cultural
contexts. In an age of social, economic, political, and environmental
challenges, these are the challenging voices we need to hear as we seek to
discern how businesspeople can live out their faith at work and home in
a way which contributes to the common good. I look forward to sharing
these essays with my business students and incorporating many of these
practices in my own life."

Elisabeth Kincaid
Legendre-Soulé Chair in Business Ethics & Director of the Center
for Ethics and Economic Justice at Loyola University New Orleans

"If someone wants to get a comprehensive picture of one of the most
interesting movements related to business, this book is the place to look.
Andrew Gustafson and Celeste Harvey have provided an important
collection of essays from some of the leading thinkers on the Focolare's
Economy of Communion. In light of the increasing distrust of our modern
institutions today including business, this book is a pathway of *finding
faith in business* once again."

Dr. Michael Naughton
Director of the Center for Catholic Studies
University of St. Thomas, St. Paul, MN
Author of *Managing as if Faith Mattered*

"This volume on the Economy of Communion should come with a warning: 'If you take its ideas seriously and to heart, you will be turned upside-down and inside-out. You will have to let go of the idea that business is the work of autonomous selfish actors who compete to have more in a zero-sum economy and accept in its place the radically opposed metaphysical idea that business is a love of persons at play in the communion of being. In a word, this volume calls you to a greater understanding of the human truth, beauty, and good of business.' My counsel to you, dear would-be reader, is to be brave; be ready to be changed; buy the book, and tell all your friends."

Lance Sandelands
Professor of Management and Organizations and
Professor of Psychology at the University of Michigan
Author of *Being at Work* and *God and Mammon*

"We often hear the slogan 'Bring your whole self to work!' The faithful know that their religious dimension, their personal relationship with God, is not just a part or even the most important part of their identities, but that which gives integrity, purpose, and meaning to their lives. This book clarifies the theory and explores the practices behind the Economy of Communion. It is useful to those who have already received the good news, as well as to those who still haven't."

Alejo José G. Sison
Professor of Business Ethics at University of Navarra

"Andrew Gustafson and Celeste Harvey have collected essays which together constitute an excellent introduction to the Economy of Communion. Here you will find insightful essays on its nature and its implications for how we think about the economy, business, and policy. It is a great place to start if you are not yet familiar with the Economy of Communion, and an important resource for those already engaged with its ideas and insights."

Andrew Yuengert
Professor of Economics at Pepperdine University
Author of *Catholic Social Teaching in Practice: Exploring Practical Wisdom and the Virtues Tradition*

FINDING
FAITH
IN BUSINESS

FINDING FAITH
IN BUSINESS

An Economy of Communion Vision

Edited by

Andrew Gustafson
and
Celeste Harvey

NCP
NEW CITY PRESS

Published by New City Press
202 Comforter Blvd.,Hyde Park, NY 12538
www.newcitypress.com
©2024 Andrew Gustafson and Celeste Harvey

Finding Faith in Business
An Economy of Communion Vision
Andrew Gustafson and Celeste Harvey

Layout by Miguel Tejerina

Library of Congress Control Number: 2024932407

ISBN: 978-1-56548-597-6 (paper)
ISBN: 978-1-56548-598-3 (e-book)

Printed in the United States of America

This, our first book, is dedicated
to our first child
Amos Gustafson
(born October 8, 2022)

Contents

Acknowledgments

This book would not be possible had not the here-published scholars initially been willing to prepare papers to present at our Symposium on Business, Faith and the Economy of Communion, put on in the fall of 2018 by the Business, Faith and the Common Good Institute, with generous support from Heider College of Business at Creighton University. These papers were initially published by the Kripke Institute in their *Journal of Religion and Society* by editor Ron Simkins, whose encouragement and editing work are much appreciated. We are also grateful to New City Press for their willingness to publish this book, and the editors who helped us along the way. We do hope that the publication of this book will further the aims and vision of the Economy of Communion and help plant seeds of further thought, study, and practice of the Economy of Communion's values and vision. Finally, we especially want to thank John Gallagher, who initially introduced both of us to the EoC, and John Mundell, Nick Sana, and Paul Catipon, whose lives of lived-out EoC values have been a constant inspiration to us.

Introduction to the
Economy of Communion

Chapter 1

Introduction

Andrew Gustafson and Celeste Harvey

The Economy of Communion (EoC) is an entrepreneur-driven group with a very practical vision and purpose: to practice business in a way that promotes human dignity, especially by helping the poor. The words *economy* and *communion* are not usually found together. Upon first encounter, their conjunction may even be perplexing: What can this phrase possibly intend? The first word, *economy*, is clear enough: Economy concerns the way we provide for our material needs. Our modern market economy relies on private property, specialization and division of labor, and an advanced monetary system to facilitate exchange of goods and services. *Communion* is used here in the sense of "sharing or holding something in common with others" and thus "being associated or linked" (OED). Communion brings together *union* and *community* to indicate harmonious relationships and cooperation. Its opposite would be an economy of conflict, a way of providing that produces divisiveness and faction, driving people apart rather than pulling them together. The *Economy of Communion* says business need not be "every man for himself" and a "dog-eat-dog" world. Business can bring us together around a common vision. It can overcome divisions between the "haves" and the "have-nots." It can bring unity between all people, even the rich and the poor.

The EoC is rooted in a deep spirituality and informed by Catholic thought, so there are many different aspects to consider. We initially brought this group of scholars together to use their unique expertise to shed new light on the many aspects of

EoC, in hopes of developing a rich understanding of the power of EoC values and vision. As one of the entrepreneurs said at the symposium which prompted this publication: "Listening to these thinkers explain the Economy of Communion has really helped me realize why I practice business the way I do. It has enriched my vision for my business." That is our hope for this book—that it will help businesspeople and entrepreneurs, as well as academics, to more fully understand and appreciate the Economy of Communion approach to business.

In bringing these essays to print, our hope is that this collection will enhance the richness of the EoC movement and help inspire others to investigate Economy of Communion principles and business practices. First, we hope it will help spread the EoC way of thinking about business in general, but we also hope it will help the entrepreneurs associated with the EoC, as well as like-minded entrepreneurs outside the EoC, to think about the themes central to Catholic social teaching which are also central to uniting faith and business. In addition, we hope that by being easily accessible to students and faculty, this collection will prove a useful resource for the classroom, helping the students who are future business leaders to catch a new vision for business while suggesting to faculty possible connection points with current academic scholarship and their own research.

We hope that as the reader comes to understand the Economy of Communion approach to business, the double meaning of the title of this book, *Finding Faith in Business: An Economy of Communion Vision*, will become clear. In the first sense, the Economy of Communion helps us to *find faith in business* in the sense of believing in the positive potential of business to help society. Economy of Communion entrepreneurs have faith that with a focus on human relationships and a special attention for the poor, business enterprise can be a powerful positive force and a means of transforming culture and society for the better. In an age of cynicism about the purpose and effects of business, this faith that business can be used to bring about good is encouraging. Second, doing business in this way is an exercise of *finding faith in business* in the sense that business itself can be a means of spiritual exercise and development. The Economy of Communion offers a way of thinking about how business itself can be a spiritually enriching activity. Frequently when people think about faith and business they primarily consider what faith has to say to business, how faith should inform, direct, and transform business practices. That is, of course, valuable. But the Economy of Communion also sees another aspect of this relationship which is often overlooked: that when we practice business with an aim of promoting communion, business practice itself can become a spiritual exercise. The struggles, aims, hopes, and disappointments which arise through practicing business in this way can become part of the spiritual development of the entrepreneurs and others engaged in the business relationships. In this sense, the Economy of Communion vision of business sees it as a sanctifying practice—business practices can be a means of achieving higher transcendent and also humanizing purposes. When this happens, it is no longer just faith speaking to business, but business practiced in this manner is edifying and nurturing to our faith as well. As Pope Francis says,

> By introducing into the economy the good seed of communion, you have begun a profound change in the way of seeing and living business. Business is not only incapable (sic.)[1] of destroying communion among people, but can edify it; it can promote it. With your life you demonstrate that economy and communion become more beautiful when they are beside each other. Cer-

---

1.   Since business is clearly capable of destroying communion among people through injustice and exploitation, it seems clear the sentence should be read as saying: "Business is not only capable of destroying communion among people, but can edify it; it can promote it."

tainly the economy is more beautiful, but communion is also more beautiful, because the spiritual communion of hearts is even fuller when it becomes the communion of goods, of talents, of profits. (Francis 2017)

When business is conducted with a goal of promoting communion, it becomes a more beautiful activity, and communion and one's spiritual life also become more beautiful. And this is why Economy of Communion entrepreneurs have faith in the power of business to transform the world for the better.

What is the Economy of Communion?

a. Spiritual Origins of EoC in the Focolare

The Economy of Communion was started by the Focolare (pronounced foh-koh-LA-ree), a lay religious movement within the Catholic Church whose goal is to advance the cause of unity amongst the human family. The Focolare takes its name from the Italian word meaning "hearth." The hearth is the symbolic heart of the home, a place of familial intimacy, love, and security, a place of togetherness and warmth. The Focolare's ideal is a world where all people can join together around a common hearth in peace and unity, and in universal brotherhood, as if a family.

The Focolare trace their origins to the summer of 1943 when Italy was under Nazi occupation and the Northern Italian city of Trent was a target of sustained bombing by the Allied Forces. In the midst of widespread suffering, a young woman began to see God "present everywhere with his love" (Lubich; quoted in Gold 2010, 65). Inspired by her belief in God's abiding love and presence in the midst of this suffering, she and some of her close friends collected whatever they could spare and began sharing with their neighbors and anyone they discovered with dire needs (Gold 2010, 65). The example they set inspired others, and soon they were not only pooling what they had personally in excess but also taking donations from many others who wanted to do the same. In this way Chiara Lubich found herself the leader of a movement. The Focolare have steadily grown and expanded around the globe with over 2 million members worldwide (https://www.focolare.org/en/mariapoli/) and with significant concentrations of Focolare in Italy, Brazil, Argentina, and the Philippines.

There are many initiatives and projects of the Focolare—the Economy of Communion being just one—but all of them "share one principle aim and objective: promoting greater unity within the human family at all levels," overcoming social divisions based on race or ethnicity, or tribe or politics, or wealth or class, or sex, or age, or religion (Gold 2010, 40). Throughout the life of the movement, an especially important focus has been overcoming the kind of social barriers that arise from material inequality between different groups, where some enjoy material abundance and have more than they need, while others lack basic necessities. Recalling the founding experience of the movement, those involved in the community have a regular practice of making a personal inventory of their needs and their belongings and giving away whatever they now regard as unnecessary, so that others who are in need might make use of them (Gold 2010, 74). In this way, the Focolare practice the "communion of goods" with the goal that, as with the first Christian community written about in the Acts of the Apostles, there will be no one in need among them (Acts 2:45; Lubich quoted in Gold 2010, 70). The Focolare live for exceptional and demanding ideals, but in Lubich's view this is the only way to find true fulfillment and happiness. Speaking of the "culture of giving" that the Focolare seek to realize, Lubich says: "Human beings, made in the image of God, who is Love, find their fulfillment in loving, in giving. This is a need which is at the center of their being, whether believer or not" (Lubich 2001, 51; cited in Gold 2010, 65).

The adoption of this mentality gives rise to a unique perspective on need:

> Within the Focolare, the person in need is accorded a high position. [. . .] Need is not something inherently negative, something of which to be ashamed, but rather a situation that allows sharing to be put into practice among the community. Offering a need to the community is therefore a positive action; people are encouraged to "offer" their need in order to give others the opportunity to help. This in turn empowers the community, creating greater solidarity among the members. The act of receiving is therefore transformed into an act of giving. (Gold 2010, 76)

This desire to create solidarity between people and overcome the divisions that so easily separate different groups—especially divisions based on material inequality, from which a sense of inadequacy on the part of the poor and superiority on the part of rich so easily emerge, causing divisions and resentments between people—forms the backdrop of the creation and development of the Economy of Communion.

b. The Beginning of the Economy of Communion

The beginnings of the Economy of Communion can be traced to Brazil. In 1991, while on a trip to São Paulo to visit the Focolare community there, Lubich was particularly troubled by the stark contrast of symbols of wealth and poverty: the skyscrapers, climbing to the sky and gleaming in the sun and, not far from these, the *favelas*, spread out far and wide with their ramshackle dwellings. There were many Focolare living in the *favelas* without the basic necessities of life. When she asked about this troubling reality, she was told that amongst the Focolare community, they did what they could to help their neighbors in need, but the needs were never-ending, and so many people were so very poor. To Lubich it was becoming clear that sharing was not enough. They needed a way to *generate* funds for sharing, and the poor themselves needed employment and a path out of poverty. In this way, the idea of starting businesses as a way of providing employment and generating profits that could, in turn, be shared with those in need was born (Gallagher and Buckeye 2014, 19–21; Gold 2010, 84). The initial goal was to generate enough money to provide for the basic needs of the poor within the Focolare.

> Upon its launch in Brazil in 1991 the EoC had one principal aim: to create businesses that would produce profits to share in common. The documentation relating to the launch of the project comes back to this point—the EoC is about making money to distribute to the poor and for the promotion of a culture of giving. (Gold 2010, 117)

As Lubich put it, the culture of giving needed to become productive. Thus a vision emerged for using the potential inherent in the for-profit business model to provide for basic human needs through the sharing out of profits generated in the business. Many people came forward with ideas for new businesses. Others offered their savings to provide the capital needed to get these initiatives started. After its beginning in Brazil, the initiative spread rather quickly to many countries around the world, and new businesses were founded and a number of established businesses joined (Gold 2010, 87). In developing this model, the EoC recognized three legitimate purposes for profit: (1) direct assistance to the poor, (2) promotion of a culture of giving, and (3) re-investment in the business.

While the goal of producing profits for the purpose of sharing was a principal driver in the creation of the EoC, and the three-part division of profits is certainly distinctive, it has become apparent over time that the spiritual values of fraternity, gratuity, and reciprocity which originally motivated the creation of the Economy of Communion have far-reaching implications for the daily operations of business and economic activity more generally.

c. The Scope and Mission of the Economy of Communion Today

In 2017 Pope Francis spoke to an invited audience of EoC members at the Vatican. At that time he said of the EoC:

> *Economy and communion.* These are two words that contemporary culture keeps separate and often considers opposites. Two words that you have instead joined, accepting the invitation that Chiara Lubich offered you 25 years ago in Brazil, when, in the face of the scandal of inequality in the city of São Paulo, she asked entrepreneurs to become *agents of communion.* She invited you to be creative, skillful, but not only this. You see the entrepreneur as an agent of communion. (Francis 2017)

As an *agent of communion*, the entrepreneur is someone called to business for a purpose—as a vocation—to help the poor, to benefit the common good, and to use business to bring about improvement in people's lives and a transformation of society for the better. In the document *Vocation of the Business Leader*, the Dicastery for Promoting Integral Human Development describes the challenge given to business leaders to *enter into communion with others*: "The Church calls upon business leaders to *receive*—humbly acknowledging what God has done for them—and to *give*—entering into communion with others to make the world a better place" (Dicastery 2018, §5). The act of accepting what we have as a gift (gratuity) is what enables the entrepreneur to then reciprocate by practicing business in light of that grace (reciprocity) (Bruni 2017). In the words of Bruni and Hejj:

In the EoC, entrepreneurs are inspired by principles rooted in a culture different than what prevails in conventional practice and theory of economics. We can define this "culture" as a "culture of giving," which is the antithesis of a "culture of having." (2001, 378)

While typically the economics of business lead us to a vision of acquiring and having (profit) through business, the EoC vision is one of intentionally giving to others through business activity (giving grace, communion, dignity, and freedom through empowerment, for example).

Leo Andringa finds the EoC to be a prophetic voice putting forward an alternative to the kind of business mindset which led to the 2008 financial crisis. For example:

Many studies in the economic field confirm that, with the growth of wealth, happiness has diminished great-ly—above all in rich countries. We are all experiencing that a financial system based only on profit fell without an enemy. It was an implosion. It is the conviction of many that this type of crisis developed because society and the market lost their ethical reference and the au-thentic sense of their existence for the common good. ... The Economy of Communion ... shows a way that is sustainable for businesses and it can give a contri-bution to correct the unjust and wrong distribution of goods and give back meaning to economic practice and culture. (Andringa 2010)

In this vision, business itself helps "correct the unjust and wrong distribution of goods" rather than relying solely on government welfare-distribution policies. Additionally, rather than settling for the quite thin purpose of simply "making as much money as possible" and the consequent commodi-fication of culture which typically ensues, EoC aims to "give back meaning to economic practice and culture" by seeing our business ventures as meaning-producing activities which enhance the state of human beings and improve the common good. When Pope Francis addressed the EoC at the Vatican, he similarly challenged the EoC to be "agents of communion" and to resist the current dominant economic logic. He said:

> But you can share more profits in order to combat idolatry, change the structures in order to prevent the creation of victims and discarded people, give more of your leaven so as to leaven the bread of many. May the "no" to an economy that kills become a "yes" to an economy that lets live, because it shares, includes the poor, uses profits to create communion. (Francis 2017)

Stefano Zamagni describes the EoC with three words: generativity, reciprocity, and gratuity. Generativity is "the capacity to generate new forms of doing business, new modes of organizing the productive process, new ways of realizing the specific role of entrepreneurship" (Zamagni 2014, 46). EoC has an alternative view of business which does not see entrepreneurship primarily as a pursuit of profit, but rather, as a pursuit using the practice of business to contribute to the common good, especially by providing employment to the poor. The original vision of EoC was to create profitable businesses which would be able to employ many poor people, which in turn gives them dignity, freedom, and sociality in relationship to others as they take a place in society through productive work and contribution. Entrepreneurship in this EoC mode is not merely a seeking for profit; rather, EoC entrepreneurship has a vision of transforming lives and society for the better by bringing people into community. By reciprocity, Zamagni means not merely an exchange of equivalents, but rather:

> According to the EoC perspective, the firm is visualized as a community, not as a commodity that can be bought and sold in the market according to the conveniences of the moment. We know that a community

to function presupposes that its members practice the principle of reciprocity. (Zamagni 2014, 46)

This model of the relationship between company and community is different from what we frequently see today. Frequently a company may be bought or acquired, the local office is shut down in the acquisition, and the local workers are simply laid off or asked to uproot and relocate. The reciprocal model takes more seriously the relational aspect between the company and the community, and the company and the workers and customers. In fact, the relational aspects are the central part of the company. Far from a transactional this-for-that approach, this view of reciprocity sees business as a communal practice where everyone is committed to the good of the whole, and each is willing to sacrifice and give to the other. This is not a guarded relationship, but a free relationship of real trust which risks my well-being in the hands of others without caveat. When reciprocity is the principle of economic behavior, "transfers cannot be dissociated from personal relationships" because "the objects of exchange are not detached from the subjects who create them, with the result that the exchange that takes place within the market ceases to be anonymous and impersonal" (Zamagni 2014, 50). This is why the statement "It's nothing personal, it's just a business decision" is antithetical to an EoC way of thinking about business and life.

Finally, "the ultimate challenge that EoC invites us to take up is to strive to bring the principle of gratuitousness back into the *public* sphere" (Zamagni 2014, 46). For Zamagni, gratuitousness is not merely giving or getting something for free, but "the content of gift as gratuitousness is the specific interpersonal relation that goes to be established between the donor and the donee" (46). When one gives receives a gift, a relationship can be formed. Of course in business there are contractual expectations. This is a matter of justice. But in business, at times, a company exceeds the expected contract, or an employee goes above and beyond their job requirements. This is the sort of gratuity which leads to a sense of loving obligation to the other. "Gratuitous goods on the other hand—such as relational goods—create an *obligation* that is based on the special ties that bind us to one another" (53). Ethics deals in the realm of justice. Gratuitousness is beyond justice: "It has more to do with the supra-ethical sphere of human action; its logic is that of superabundance" rather than mere equivalence (this for that) which is the domain of justice and ethics (ibid.).

In a spirit of gratuitousness, EoC was begun as a way to especially help the poor and to bring about communion through business, using private enterprise to develop businesses which could not only provide a living for people but could also provide dignity, community, and even communion with one another and with God. This is a high calling for business—much more than the more simple goal to make money.

Situating EoC in the Political-Economic Landscape

EoC certainly thinks that business should serve the common good. But so do some other forms of free-market capitalism and, alternatively, anti-capitalist socialist proposals. It is useful to consider EoC as a healthier form of economic thinking, an alternative to both unfettered capitalism and anti-capitalistic socialism. EoC sees business and free enterprise as a means for bringing about societal well-being, especially for the poor. Bruni sketches the variety of ways in which business can bring about the common good, and the place of business in doing so, situating EoC between free-market capitalism and socialism (2012, 39). Bruni first describes the "capitalist approach." In the capitalist view, business actively contributes to the common good, but does so indirectly and unintentionally. Companies must respect the law and pay taxes, but beyond that businesses need only act prudently and responsibly to promote their own self-interest. In doing so, they unintentionally produce the common good as the invisible hand of the market propels them forward. Similarly, individuals need only contribute to the economy by prudently and responsibly seeking their own self-interest within the bounds of the law. In doing so, they too benefit all of society. Bruni explains:

> The common good as considered by economics today, then, is essentially an unintended result of the actions of individuals; as has been indicated, the purpose of a person who makes a contract to effect an exchange is neither the common good nor the good of the other, but that individual's own good or self-interest. (2012, 54)

Under capitalism, then, we achieve the common good not by intentionally considering the good of the whole, but by simply considering our own good, and the market forces help things to work out for the collective good. So this first approach to the common good is somewhat paradoxically rooted in self-interest. Another important characteristic of the "capitalist" approach is that it attempts to prevent the human interaction and concern which would lead to wounding: "Basically, economic personnel theory and agency theory are worthy attempts to foresee, mitigate and minimize the 'wounds' that face-to-face encounters cause" (Bruni 2012, 35). While the motivation is understandable, this has dehumanizing effects on business. Capitalist business also often renders and reduces the relationship between individuals to purely contractual relations and relations within the firm to primarily hierarchical relations.[2]

In contrast to the individualistic and hierarchical capitalist approach, there are two cooperative traditions: "The French

---

2. Since Coase's 1937 "The Nature of the Firm," Bruni claims, contracts (which are typically of an exchange between equals) have been strangely mixed with the hierarchical notion of the manager-agent relationship, so that this market system leads to an oxymoronic hierarchical contract situation, which is not a contract between equals, but a contract between a superior and subordinate (Bruni 2012, 32).

tradition was essentially anti-capitalist and anti-market, whereas the Italian tradition, in continuity with the civil economy… was more positive toward the market as a place for the exercise of civil virtues" (Bruni 2012, 34–35). Advocates of the French anti-market view, such as Louis Blanc's anti-market and anti-capitalist thought, "can be summarized in the motto 'competition is the disease; association is the cure'" (35). In Blanc's view the market is "simply uncivilized and dehumanizing, because—despite the apparent freedom and apparent equality—it conceals a lack of freedom and relational inequality" (35–36). We can see this negative assessment of business and the free market in the "Occupy Wall Street" movement and other recent movements critical of the effects of capitalism (e.g., Alain Caillé's Anti-Utilitarian Movement (Caillé 2003)).

The French social economy tradition sees market capitalism as being oriented around the interests of one individual (or a small group of individuals) who then make their money by establishing unfair contracts and relationships with employees, suppliers, and other businesspeople. Business interests in this view are anti-social and self-concerned, not societally concerned. No corporation can be civil because no corporation can be responsible—on this point Louis Blanc agrees with Milton Friedman, who argues that companies have no social responsibility because only humans can be held responsible (Friedman 1970).

The Italian type of cooperative tradition is what Bruni refers to as a civil economy, a third way which depends on private enterprise working within the free-market economy (not socialism) but by which the practice of business itself helps society in intentional and humane ways.[3] As Bruni says,

---

3. Although Antonio Genovesi (1765) is considered a grandfather of the civil economy, later theorists like Fedele Lampertico, Ugo Rabbeno, Luigi Luzzatti, Vito Cusumano, Ghino Valentini, and Leone Wollemborg continued this work into the late nineteenth century. Today theorists like Bruni and Zamagni continue the tradition (Bruni & Zamagni 2016).

"From this point of view, economics and the market are not inconsistent with genuine relationality; rather, economic activity is an expression of civic virtues" (Bruni 2012, 36). This civil economy perspective, which values the market but also rejects radical individualism and embraces a concern for community, fits the EoC model. The anti-market advocates of the French social economy tradition find this civil economy position absurd, since in their minds it involves the paradoxical view that an inherently anti-social entity (the company or corporation) should be responsible to society—not unlike saying that sociopaths should always practice altruism. Yet Bruni claims that the famous Italian economist Antonio Genovesi and even John Stuart Mill are in the civil economy cooperative tradition. Proponents of this civil economy cooperative tradition do not see cooperation and the market to be in contradiction, like the French thinkers. Rather, they see that the market and the company can be reformed through cooperation, synthesizing the capitalists and workers together (such as through worker-owner movements, among other approaches) (Bruni 2012, 37). In this civil economy view, the marketplace is a self-interested arena and the market forces help direct our activities to remain civil, for the sake of future market activity: "If in fact the market is seen as a place in which to practice the civil virtues, then there is no need to socialize it at a later time, because it is so from the outset" (Bruni 2012, 44). Bruni sees the EoC clearly in this third tradition, saying:

> Economy of Communion, although socially focused, is open to the market; in this sense it is not heir to the French-inspired radical tradition . . . but precisely to this Millian and Italian cooperative tradition. (2012, 38)

This, we think, is a very useful way to conceive of the Economy of Communion, and to understand the method and values which direct those of us who attempt to practice business in the EoC way. EoC businesses are in many cases designed for the sake of employing the poor and thus providing them a means to dignified work which is more respectful to their humanity than keeping them in an underprivileged position through our charity which assists with their living but does not substantially improve their condition. There is certainly a concern for cooperative work and *subsidiarity*—the notion that every person should be encouraged to exercise as much of their own autonomy as possible—which pushes decision-making to the proper level of those most affected (Naughton et al. 2015). There is a reason why the movement is often called "The Economy of Communion in Freedom" and that is because this is far from some sort of socialist or communist vision (although that mistaken identity has been given to the group, simply due to the use of the unusual word *communion* in the name).

So the EoC model is this: within the free market, without centralized government planning but rather with a positive view of the power of business to bring about the common good alongside profit in this market system, poor people are helped, community is established, humanity is enhanced and redeemed, and the vision of Christ that we should love one another becomes a central driving force in the very way we think about business activity and practice. This is a vision of business that inspires us and helps us to live integrated lives.

The Essays and Contributors of this Volume

A diverse group of authors has contributed to this collection, some of whom have a longstanding relationship with the Economy of Communion, and others who have become more familiar with it during the course of this project. All of the authors here have given serious thought and consideration and in many cases have written books and essays on issues concerning faith and business and/or Catholic Social Thought and the economy. The essays were presented at Creighton University at the Business, Faith and the Common Good annual symposium in the fall of 2018, put on by the Business, Faith and the Common Good Institute at Creighton's Heider College of Business. The topics vary, but each author has brought their own expertise and interest to bear on the EoC. The result is that we have expanded the scope of EoC thought and research and hopefully provided some new avenues and opportunities of research for the future.

Greg Beabout, who has written on Catholic Social Thought, business ethics, and economics, provides "Ownership and Business Succession: Considerations from Catholic Social Teaching and the Economy of Communion," which raises significant points about how business owners who have a vision for their company to serve the common good can sustain that vision and purpose even as they retire and transfer ownership of their company.

David Cloutier has written extensively on consumerism and the vice of luxury. Here his essay "Simplicity of Lifestyle as a Goal of Business: Practicing the Economy of Communion as a Challenge to Consumer Society" explores how entrepreneurs and businesspeople might take seriously the challenge to live according to a consistent set of values in both their private life and work life, and, assuming a commitment to simplicity in private life, how we might also implement policies and practices that resist the excesses of consumerism in the operations of the business.

Angus Sibley, who has written extensively on Catholic Social Thought and economics, provides "Economy of Communion: A Different Attitude to Work," pointing out the very positive view toward work which is found in Catholic Social Thought as well as the Economy of Communion.

Andy Gustafson, who has written on the EoC and business and the common good, provides "The Economy of Communion: Catholic Social Thought Put to Work," in which he brings together the theories of Economy of Communion and Catholic Social Thought with his lived experience as an EoC entrepreneur.

Jesús Morán and Amy Uelmen live and breathe the EoC life and have written extensively on the Focolare, Pope Francis, and the EoC. Their contribution, "Pope Francis and the Economy of Communion," illuminates the ways in which the economic vision and values of Pope Francis parallel those of the Economy of Communion.

Celeste Harvey, who has written on virtue, concerns of women, and business and the common good, here provides "A Person-Centered Theory of the Firm: Learning from the Economy of Communion" in which she contrasts the EoC model with that of the traditional stockholder and stakeholder models of the firm as well as other socially concerned business movements such as B Corps, social entrepreneurship, and corporate social responsibility.

John McNerney, whose work has centered on the human person and the personalist tradition of Pope John Paul II, provides here "The Business of Business: Recapturing a Personalist Perspective," in which he points to the uniquely person-centered nature of the EoC.

Jeanne Buckeye has written books on both the EoC and subsidiarity. In her essay "Exploring Subsidiarity: The Case of the Economy of Communion," she explains subsidiarity and how it permeates Economy of Communion practices.

John Gallagher, co-author with Jeanne Buckeye of *Structures of Grace*, one of the definitive books on the Economy of Communion in the U.S., contributes "The Economy of Communion as an Exercise of Prophetic Imagination." Drawing on the concept of the prophetic imagination as developed by Walter Brueggemann, Gallagher makes the case that the Economy of Communion offers a prophetic vision of business, and he highlights the challenges of this calling to practice business in an alternative way.

In addition to these original scholarly works, we are delighted and grateful to be able to reproduce here Pope Francis's comments to the Economy of Communion participants at the

Vatican in 2017; Chiara Lubich's short essay "For an Economy Based on Communion"; and renowned EoC scholar Luca Crivelli's previously unpublished essay "Economy of Communion, Poverty, and a Humanized Economy," which is a talk he gave at Geneva, Palais des Nations, in 2004.

Bibliography

Andringa, Leo. 2010. "The Economy of Communion." *EdC Online*. https://edc-online.org/en/publications/conference-speeches/6000-economy-of-communion.html.

Bruni, Luigino. 2012. *The Wound and the Blessing: Economics, Relationships, and Happiness*. Translated by N. Michael Brennen. Hyde Park, NY: New City Press.

Bruni, Luigino. 2017. "The Era of Partial Gifts." www.Luiginobruni.it (29 March) Oikonomia/On the Border and Beyond/10--The Era of Partial Gifts. https://www.luiginobruni.it/en/ok-sco/the-era-of-partial-gifts.html. Translated from *Avvenire* March 25, 2017. https://www.avvenire.it/opinioni/pagine/sul-confine-e-oltre-10-luigino-bruni.

Bruni, Luigino and Tibor Hejj. 2011. "The Economy of Communion." In *Handbook of Spirituality and Business*, edited by Luk Bouckaert and Laszlo. Zsolnai, 378–386. London: Palgrave Macmillan.

Bruni, Luigino and Stefano Zamagni. 2016. *Civil Economy: Another Idea of the Market*. Translated by N. Michael Brennen. Newcastle upon Tyne: Agenda Publishing.

Caille, Alain. 2003. *Critique de la Raison Utilitaire*. Paris: Le Decouverte.

Dicastery for Promoting Integral Human Development. 2018. *Vocation of the Business Leader: A Reflection*. St. Paul, MN: University of St. Thomas Press. Available online at https://www.stthomas.edu/media/catholicstudies/center/ryan/publications/publicationpdfs/vocationofthebusinessleaderpdf/FinalTextTheVocationoftheBusinessLeader.pdf.

Ferrucci, Antonella. 2010. "Business Operations in an EoC Firm: The Experience of Bangko Kabayan." *EdC Online*. http://www.edc-online.org/en/publications/conference-speeches/5938-business-operations-in-an-EoC-firm-the-experience-of-bangko-kabayan-en-gb-1.html.

Francis. 2017. *Address of His Holiness Pope Francis to Participants in the Meeting "Economy of Communion", Sponsored by the Focolare Movement*. https://w2.vatican.va/content/francesco/en/speeches/2017/february/documents/papa-francesco_20170204_focolari.html.

Friedman, Milton. 1970. "The Social Responsibility of Business is to Increase its Profits." *The New York Times Magazine*. September 13, 1970.

Genovesi, Antonio. 1765. *Lezioni di Commercio, o sia d'Economia Civile*. Naples: Appresso i Fratelli Simone.

Gold, Lorna. 2010. *New Financial Horizons: The Emergence of an Economy of Communion*. Hyde Park: New City Press.

Lubich, Chiara. 1978. *May They All Be One: Origins and Life of the Focolare Movement*. London: New City Press.

Naughton, Michael, Jeanne Buckeye, Kenneth Goodpaster, and T. Dean Maines. 2015. *Respect in Action: Applying Subsidiarity at Work*. St. Paul, MN: University of St. Thomas. https://www.stthomas.edu/media/catholicstudies/center/ryan/publications/publicationpdfs/subsidiarity/RespectInActionFINALAfterPrinterProof.withcover.pdf.

Oxford English Dictionary (OED). 2023. "Communion, n." *OED Online*. March 2023. Oxford University Press. www.oed.com/view/Entry/37318. Accessed May 25, 2023.

Zamagni, Stefano. 2014 "The Economy of Communion Project as a Challenge to Standard Economic Theory." *Revista Portuguesa de Filosofia*, T. 70, no. 1:44–60.

Chapter 2

Address of His Holiness Pope Francis to Participants in the Meeting "Economy of Communion", Sponsored by the Focolare Movement[1]

Pope Francis

Abstract: This speech was given by Pope Francis to a large audience of EoC members from around the world who came to hear him at the Vatican. In the speech he highlights the importance of bringing economy and communion together. He provides three key challenges to the EoC: 1) It is essential that the EoC share its profits and use them for the poor. 2) The EoC must stand in solidarity with the poor and help to create an economy which not only helps victims, but does not create victims in the first place. 3) EoC entrepreneurs must do all they can to share their vision of how the economy can bring about communion with everyone, especially with the young.

Dear Brothers and Sisters,

I am pleased to welcome you as representatives of a project in which I have been genuinely interested for some time. I

---

1. This speech by Pope Francis was given to a large group of EoC members from around the world who came to the Vatican to hear it on February 4, 2017. It can be found online at the Vatican website and is published here with permission of the Vatican: http://www.vatican.va/content/francesco/en/speeches/2017/february/documents/papa-francesco_20170204_focolari.html.

convey my cordial greeting to each of you, and I thank in particular the coordinator, Prof. Luigino Bruni, for his courteous words. And I thank you for your testimonies.

Economy and communion. These are two words that contemporary culture keeps separate and often considers opposites. Two words that you have instead joined, accepting the invitation that Chiara Lubich offered you 25 years ago in Brazil, when, in the face of the scandal of inequality in the city of São Paulo, she asked entrepreneurs to become *agents of communion*. She invited you to be creative, [skillful], but not only this. You see the entrepreneur as an agent of communion. By introducing into the economy the good seed of communion, you have begun a profound change in the way of seeing and living business. Business is not only [capable] of destroying communion among people, but can edify it; it can promote it. With your life you demonstrate that economy and communion become more beautiful when they are beside each other. Certainly the economy is more beautiful, but communion is also more beautiful, because the spiritual communion of hearts is even fuller when it becomes the communion of goods, of talents, of profits.

In considering your task, I would like to say three things to you today.

The first concerns *money*. It is very important that at the centre of the economy of communion there be the communion of your profits. The economy of communion is also the communion of profits, an expression of the communion of life. Many times I have spoken about money as an idol. The Bible tells us this in various ways. Not by chance, Jesus' first public act, in the Gospel of John, is the expulsion of the merchants from the temple (cf. 2:13–21). We cannot understand the new Kingdom offered by Jesus if we do not free ourselves of idols, of which money is one of the most powerful. Therefore, how is it possible to be merchants that Jesus does not expel? Money is important, especially when there is none, and food, school, and the children's future depend on it. But it becomes an idol when it becomes the aim. Greed, which by no coincidence is a capital sin, is the sin of idolatry because the accumulation of money per se becomes the aim of one's own actions. It was precisely Jesus who defined money as "lord": "No one can serve two lords, two masters." There are two: God and money, the anti-God, the idol. Jesus said this. At the same level of choice. Think about this.

When capitalism makes the seeking of profit its only purpose, it runs the risk of becoming an idolatrous framework, a form of worship. The "goddess of fortune" is increasingly the new divinity of a certain finance and of the whole system of gambling which is destroying millions of the world's families, and which you rightly oppose. This idolatrous worship is a surrogate for eternal life. Individual products (cars, telephones . . .) get old and wear out, but if I have money or credit I can immediately buy others, deluding myself of conquering death.

Thus, one understands the ethical and spiritual value of your choice to *pool profits*. The best and most practical way to avoid making an idol of money is to share it, share it with others, above all with the poor, or to enable young people to study and work, overcoming the idolatrous temptation with communion. When you share and donate your profits, you are performing an act of lofty spirituality, saying to money through deeds: "you are not God, you are not lord, you are not master!." And do not forget that other philosophy and that other theology that led our grandmothers to say: "The devil enters through the pockets." Do not forget this!

The second thing I would like to say to you concerns *poverty*, a central theme of your movement.

Today, many initiatives, public and private, are being carried out to combat poverty. All this, on the one hand, is a growth in humanity. In the Bible, the poor, orphans, widows, those "discarded" by the society of those times, were aided by tithing and the gleaning of grain. But most of the people remained poor; that aid was not sufficient to feed and care for everyone. There were many "discarded" by society. Today we have invented other ways to care for, to feed, to teach the poor, and some of the seeds of the Bible have blossomed into more effective institutions than those of the past. The rationale for taxes also lies in this solidarity, which is negated by tax avoidance and evasion which, over and above being illegal acts, are acts which deny the basic law of life: mutual care.

But—and this can never be said enough—capitalism *continues to produce discarded people* whom it would then like to care for. The principal ethical dilemma of this capitalism is the creation of discarded people, then trying to hide them or make sure they are no longer seen. A serious form of poverty in a civilization is when *it is no longer able to see its poor*, who are first discarded and then hidden.

Aircraft pollute the atmosphere, but, with a small part of the cost of the ticket, they will plant trees to compensate for part of the damage created. Gambling companies finance campaigns to care for the pathological gamblers that they create. And the day that the weapons industry finances hospitals to care for the children mutilated by their bombs, the system will have reached its pinnacle. This is hypocrisy!

The economy of communion, if it wants to be faithful to its charism, must not only care for the victims, but build a system where there are ever fewer victims, where, possibly, there may no longer be any. As long as the economy still produces one victim and there is still a single discarded person, communion has not yet been realized; the celebration of universal fraternity is not full.

Therefore, we must work toward changing the rules of the game of the socio-economic system. Imitating the Good Samaritan of the Gospel is not enough. Of course, when an entrepreneur or any person happens upon a victim, he or she is called to take care of the victim and, perhaps like the Good Samaritan, also to enlist the fraternal action of the market (the innkeeper). I know that you have sought to do so for 25 years. But it is important to act above all *before* the man comes across the robbers, by battling the frameworks of sin that produce robbers and victims. An entrepreneur who is only a Good Samaritan does half of his duty: he takes care of today's victims, but does not curtail those of tomorrow. For communion, one must imitate the merciful Father of the parable of the Prodigal Son and wait at home for the children, workers and co-workers who have done wrong, and there embrace them and celebrate with and for them—and not be impeded by the meritocracy invoked by the elder son and by many who deny mercy in the name of merit. An entrepreneur of communion is called to do everything possible so that even those who do wrong and leave home can hope for work and for dignified earnings, and not wind up eating with the swine. No son, no man, not even the most rebellious, deserves acorns.

Lastly, the third thing concerns the *future*. These 25 years of your history say that *communion and business* can exist and grow *together*. An experience which for now is limited to a small number of businesses—extremely small if compared to the world's great capital. But the changes in the order of the spirit and therefore of life are not linked to big numbers. The small flock, the lamp, a coin, a lamb, a pearl, salt, leaven: these are the images of the Kingdom that we encounter in the Gospels. And the prophets have announced to us the new age of salvation by indicating to us the sign of a child, Emmanuel, and speaking to us of a faithful "remnant," a small group.

It is not necessary to be in a large group to change our life: suffice it that the salt and leaven do not deteriorate. The great work to be performed is trying not to lose the "active ingredient" which enlivens them: salt does not do its job by increasing in *quantity*—instead, too much salt makes the meal salty—but by saving its "spirit," namely, its *quality*. Every time people, peoples and even the Church have thought of saving the world in *numbers*, they have produced power structures, forgetting the poor. We save our economy by being simply salt and leaven: a difficult job, because everything deteriorates with the passing of time. What do we do so as not to lose the active ingredient, the "enzyme" of communion?

When there were no refrigerators, to preserve the *mother dough* of the bread, they gave a small amount of their own leavened dough to a neighbour, and when they needed to make bread again they received a handful of leavened dough from that woman or from another who had received it in her turn. It is reciprocity. Communion is not only the *sharing* but also the *multiplying* of goods, the creation of new bread, of new goods, of new Good with a capital "G." The living principle of the Gospel remains active only if we give it, because it is love, and love is active when we love, not when we write novels or when we watch telenovelas. If instead we possessively keep it all and only for ourselves, it goes mouldy and dies. The Gospel can grow mouldy. The economy of communion will have a future if you give it to everyone and it does not remain only inside your "house." Give it to everyone, firstly to the poor and the young, who are those who need it most and know how to make the gift received bear fruit! To have life in abundance one must learn to give: not only the profits of businesses, but of yourselves. The first gift of the entrepreneur is of his or her own person: your money, although important, is too little. Money does not save if it is not accompanied by the gift of the person. Today's economy, the poor, the young, need first of all your spirit, your respectful and humble fraternity, your will to live and, only then, your money.

Capitalism knows philanthropy, not communion. It is simple to give a part of the profits, without embracing and touching the people who receive those "crumbs." Instead, even just five loaves and two fishes can feed the multitude if they are the sharing of all our life. In the logic of the Gospel, if one does not give all of himself, he never gives enough of himself.

You already do these things. But you can share more profits in order to combat idolatry, change the structures in order to prevent the creation of victims and discarded people, give more of your leaven so as to leaven the bread of many. May the "no" to an economy that kills become a "yes" to an economy that lets live, because it shares, includes the poor, uses profits to create communion.

I hope you continue on your path, with courage, humility and joy. "God loves a cheerful giver" (2 Cor 9:7). God loves your joyfully given profits and talents. You already do this; you can do so even more. I hope you continue to be the seed, salt and leaven of another economy: the economy of the Kingdom, where the rich know how to share their wealth, and the poor are called "blessed." Thank you.

Chapter 3

For an Economy Based on Communion[1]

Chiara Lubich

Abstract: Here Chiara Lubich, founder of the EoC movement, provides a brief explanation of the origins and key characteristics of the Economy of Communion. Among those characteristics are: 1) That we should practice business with the same personal values that animate the rest of our life, and that the economy can be a place for human and spiritual growth. 2) The EoC proposes that we practice business inspired by gratuitousness, solidarity, and care for the poor. 3) The poor have a "gift of need" which can be given to others—they are essential members of the EoC project. 4) Every EoC enterprise is part of a greater reality: the worldwide movement.

Typical of our Movement is the so-called *economy of communion* exercised in freedom, which is a particular experience of solidarity in economy. As an authentic expression of the spirituality of unity in the sphere of economy, it can be understood in its entirety and complexity only if considered

---

1. This speech was given by Chiara Lubich at the ceremony when the honorary degree in economics was conferred on her by Sacred Heart Catholic University (Milano, Italy). It can be found in the EoC North America website archives: https://eocnorthamerica.files.wordpress.com/2015/11/chi_19990129_en.pdf.

from the spirituality's viewpoint of the human person and social relationships.

It began in Brazil in 1991. The Movement, present in that country since 1958, spread to all its States, attracting people of every social category.

However, some years ago—because of the rapid growth of the Movement (there are approximately 250,000 of us in Brazil)—I realized that we were unable to cover even the most urgent needs of our members, notwithstanding the intense communion of goods. It seemed to me, then, that God was calling our Movement to something new.

Although I am not an expert in economic problems, I thought that our people could set up firms and business enterprises so as to engage the capabilities and resources of all, and to produce together in favour of those in need. They would have to be managed by competent persons who would be capable of making them function efficiently and derive profits from them. These profits would be put in common freely. One part would be used for the same goals of the early Christian communities: to help those in need, to give them something to live on until they find work. Another part, to develop structures to form "new people" (as the apostle Paul calls them), that is, people formed and animated by love, suited to what we call the "culture of giving." Finally, one part would certainly be used for the growth of the firm.

An entrepreneurial sector would have to spring up in our little towns of witness—we have twenty of them throughout the world. They are modern townships with all the expressions of modern life. Thus the presence of business enterprises is also required alongside schools of formation, houses for families, a church, handicraft industries and other activities that have risen up for the maintenance of its inhabitants, besides all of this a real productive industrial park should have arisen.

The idea was welcomed enthusiastically not only in Brazil and in the rest of Latin America, but in Europe and other parts of the world. Many new businesses came to life and many existing ones have adhered to the project by modifying their way of operating a business.

Adhering to this project today are some 654 companies and 91 minor productive activities. It involves enterprises operating in different economic sectors, in more than 30 countries: 164 operate in the commercial sector, 189 are industrial businesses and 301 operate in other services.[2]

The experience of the *economy of communion*, with the specific characteristics it draws from the spirituality, takes its place alongside the numerous individual and collective initiatives that have sought and seek to "give a human face to economy," as well as the many entrepreneurs and workers, often unknown, who envision and live this economic activity as something more and different from the pure pursuit of material benefit.

In fact, as it is in many other ideally motivated economic realities, the adherents of this project—entrepreneurs, managers, employees and others in the work force—are on the front lines in focusing, in all aspects of their activity, on the needs and aspirations of the person and on the well-being of the common good.

In particular, they seek: to establish loyal and respectful relations animated by a sincere spirit of service and collaboration with clients, suppliers, public administrators and also with competitors; to show appreciation for employees by involving them, to various degrees, in management; to maintain a way of operating the business which is inspired by a culture of legality; to be very attentive to the workplace and respect for nature, also by meeting the expenses of costly investments; to cooperate with other business and social

---

2.   These numbers were accurate at the time that Chiara wrote this (1998) although today there are closer to 1,000 EoC companies worldwide.

realities in the area, with a look to solidarity towards the international community.

The *economy of communion* presents other characteristics, which are very significant for us, because they are directly connected to our spirituality's vision of the world. Here are a few:

1. Those involved in the business enterprises of the *economy of communion* seek to follow, albeit in the forms required by the context of a productive organization, the same style of behaviour that they live out in all ambits of life. We are convinced, in fact, that we must imbue every moment of life in society with the values we believe in, therefore also economy, so that it too may become a place for human and spiritual growth.

2. The *economy of communion* proposes modes of behaviour inspired by gratuitousness, solidarity and care for those in need—attitudes normally considered typical of non-profit organizations—even in businesses which naturally seek a profit. Therefore, the *economy of communion* does not present itself so much as a new form of enterprise, alternative to those already existing. Rather, it intends to transform from within the usual business structures (whether they are shareholding corporations, cooperatives, or other) by establishing all relations inside and outside the companies in the light of a lifestyle marked by communion. Everything is done in full respect for the authentic values of the business and of the market (those pointed out by the social doctrine of the Church, and in particular, by John Paul II in *Centesimus Annus*).

3. Those who find themselves in economic straits, the recipients of a part of the profits, are not viewed simply as persons who are "assisted" or as "beneficiaries" of

the business. Instead, they are essential members of
the project, within which they give their needs as a
gift to others. They too live the culture of giving. In
fact, many of them renounce the help they receive
as soon as they recuperate a minimum of economic
independence, and not rarely, they share with others
the little they have. All this is an expression of the
fact that in the *economy of communion*, although it
underlines the culture of giving, the emphasis is not
put on the philanthropy of a few, but rather on sharing,
where each one gives and receives with equal dignity,
in the ambit of a substantially reciprocal relationship.

4. In addition to the support provided by a profound
understanding among the promoters of each business,
the *economy of communion* enterprises feel that they
are part of a vaster reality. They put in common the
profits because they are already living an experience
of communion. This is why the business enterprises—as I already mentioned—develop within small
(at least for now) "industrial parks" in the area of the
Movement's little towns, or, if geographically distant,
they are ideally "linked" to them.

Many people ask how these businesses, so attentive to the
needs of all the subjects they deal with and of society as a
whole, can survive in a market economy. Certainly, the spirit
that animates them helps to overcome many of those internal
contrasts, which obstruct and in some cases paralyze all human organizations. In addition, their way of operating attracts
the trust and benevolence of clients, suppliers, and financiers.
Nonetheless, we should not forget another essential element—
Providence—which has constantly accompanied the development of the *economy of communion* during these years. In the
economy of communion, we leave room for the intervention
of God, also in concrete economic activities. And we expe-

rience that after every choice that goes against the current of usual businesses procedures, he gives that hundredfold which Jesus promised: an unexpected income, an unhoped-for opportunity, the offer of a new collaboration, an idea for a new leading product. . . .

This, in brief, is the *economy of communion*. In proposing it I certainly did not have a theory in mind. Nonetheless, I see that it is drawing the attention of economists, sociologists, philosophers and scholars of other disciplines, whose interest in this new experience and in the ideas and categories underlying it, go beyond the Movement in which it developed historically.

In particular, in the "trinitarian" vision of interpersonal and social relationships, which is at the basis of the *economy of communion*, some people glimpse a new key of interpretation which could also enrich the understanding of economic interactions and therefore contribute towards going beyond the individualistic foundation that prevails today in the science of economics.

||

Practice

Chapter 4

Ownership and Business Succession: Considerations from Catholic Social Teaching and the Economy of Communion

Gregory Beabout, St. Louis University

Abstract: Small to medium-sized businesses are a significant part of the economy, and play a very significant role in strengthening local communities. However, few have a clear plan for succession. Business succession is important for owners committed to goods beyond mere profits, and such succession is difficult to manage. The article considers fundamental issues about ownership and owning a business, and draws from Catholic social doctrine to consider ownership as stewardship to promote communion. In response to practical questions about business succession, a series of options are considered with an eye to considering how to sustain community goods beyond profit maximization.

A Case Study

To explain the problem I want to consider in this paper, let me begin with a case study, inspired by the experience of Kevin Lindsey (Lindsey 2017). Lindsey describes the following case.

Background: Kevin Lindsey has a background as an entrepreneur and a financial advisor, having worked at Merrill Lynch, AXA Advisors, BMA, and Berthel Fisher. As an adult, Lindsey became a Catholic. During that process, a parish priest who became familiar with Lindsey's experience and expertise asked him to meet with a group of parishioners.

49

Details of the case: The priest called Lindsey aside and said: "Let me be candid. I'm worried that the parish may not be able to sustain our elementary school. The school has been running a deficit budget, and it continues to worsen every year. I am asking if you would join me at a meeting with about 20 members from the parish. We have several hundred families in the parish, but it's these families that account for most of the financial giving that supports this church. When the parish has a big need—a new roof, significant work on the parking lot, whatever big ticket item that comes up—it's these families that I turn to. About half the families in the parish are steady givers, but these 20 families account for more than three quarters of our budget, and I always know I can turn to them when we are in a pinch. You seem to know a lot about financial advising, especially for people who run businesses. I would like you to join me in a meeting with these parishioners to figure out if there is some sort of financial solution, an endowment or something like that, so we can put the parish school on a more stable foundation. Will you meet with them?"

After agreeing to do so, and then meeting with this group of generous parishioners, Lindsey sat down for a conversation with the pastor. Lindsey suggested that the pastor had misdiagnosed the problem. The issue was not simply a concern about the financial viability of the parish school. Rather, there was a larger crisis looming: the financial viability of the parish. The biggest givers in the parish were virtually all owners of small or medium-sized businesses. Lindsey notes that when businesses are owned within a community, the owners tend to support the local community, and the community is stronger, so it makes sense that these are the cornerstones of the parish. Each business owner had done well for themselves, and for others.

Lindsey observed two further things: all of the parishioners in question were over the age of 60, and, after asking them a few questions, he learned that none of them had a plan in place to pass on company ownership to a local owner who shared their commitment to the community. Lindsey concluded that the financial future of the parish was hanging in the balance. The future of the parish depended on the support of the families with locally owned businesses. In the near future, those businesses would undergo transitions. Would the tie to the parish and the community then be broken?

Issues raised by the case: This case, as described by Lindsey, illustrates a common situation. Two features of this case stand out. First, many parishes and local communities are supported by the generosity of business owners who see it as part of their responsibility to use their gifts and talents as entrepreneurs and owners not only to produce a profit, but also to provide goods and services, to create jobs, and to share profits generously in a manner that strengthens community. A similar vision of business ownership is proposed in the "Economy of Communion" project (EoC), set forth by Chiara Lubich of the Focolare Movement. Lubich's EoC project proposes that business owners become intentional with regard to the purposes of ownership, work, and jobs. In this vision, ownership of a profitable business firm is seen as compatible with communion. As Lubich puts it, profits can be used "to help those in need, to give them something to live on until they find work . . . to develop structures to form 'new people' (as the apostle Paul calls them), that is, people formed and animated by love, suited to what we call the 'culture of giving' . . . [and] for the growth of the firm" (Lubich 1999).

A second important feature of the case worth noting: In the American context, many business owners are aging without any developed business succession plan.

> Roughly 52% of all U.S. businesses are owned by individuals aged 50 to 88. One sub-group of small business, family owned businesses, account for 64% of U.S. GDP, 62% of U.S. employment and 78% of new job creation and face an expected retirement rate of 40% in the next

five years. . . . Less than 30% of [small businesses] surveyed have a succession plan. Only 15% of U.S. family businesses have a succession plan in place. Further, while 70% of family businesses desire to pass ownership to the next generation, only 30% expect to be able to do so. (Lindsey et al. 2018, 2)

For business owners committed to using profits to support non-financial goods of community, questions of business succession are particularly important and more complex than a succession plan where the primary goal is measured solely in financial terms. Given the widespread nature of this problem, my goal in this paper is to turn to Catholic social teaching to consider the question of the transfer of the ownership in small to medium-sized businesses. Business succession matters.

This paper proceeds in four parts. First, having established that issues of succession are important for any small to medium-sized business, I suggest that the question of succession is particularly important for values-based businesses, and perhaps even more difficult to manage than for conventional businesses if the owners wish to see the business continue to realize the non-financial objectives of the firm. Second, I raise several puzzles about ownership, including questions about owning property, owning the means of production, and owning a business. Third, I turn to the social doctrine of the Church in order to draw out principles for thinking about ownership as stewardship. Finally, I consider a series of options that allow business owners to consider more than profit maximization in the succession plan.

Business Succession for Values-Based Businesses

Issues of business succession are important, but especially so for small to medium-sized businesses in which the owners want to see the business continue in order to realize the firm's non-financial objectives. Family businesses almost always operate this way: Part of the goal of the business is to make it possible to sustain a good life for the family; the goal of profitability for the business is connected with but not identical to the goal of promoting a healthy and happy life for the family. Because a healthy and happy life for a family is tied up with a healthy community beyond the family, it is sensible for business owners to recognize the complex relationship between the goal of profit and non-financial goals, such as supporting one's local community, one's church, the employees of the firm, the families of the employees, and other worthwhile purposes which are non-financial in character. Is it possible for business owners to continue those non-financial objectives when it comes time to transfer ownership?

To work toward an answer to this question, I want to consider a company deeply committed to social concerns, fair trade, and ethical entrepreneurship: the British chocolate company Green & Black's. Green & Black's was founded in 1991 by organic food pioneer Craig Sams and journalist Josephine Fairley. The company's name was derived from a wordplay: "Green" refers to the environmental concerns of the founders, and "Black" to the high cocoa solids of the rich, dark chocolate sourced from the Central American nation of Belize. In the early 1990s, Green & Black's developed a relationship with a group of Mayan farmers in Belize; they established an agreement and began purchasing fair trade cocoa. At that time, fair trade was developing as an institutionalized practice for producers of coffee. Fair trade coffee aimed at stabilizing markets, improving the quality and consistency of coffee beans, and establishing fair wage standards for coffee farmers. Green & Black's extended the fair trade concerns from coffee to chocolate. Their chocolate bars were marketed as the world's first organic chocolate, with cocoa beans sourced according to fair trade agreements. In 1994, the Maya Gold chocolate bar was awarded the World-aware Business Award for good business practice, as well as the UK's first Fairtrade Mark. In 1999, entrepreneur William

Kendall bought a sizable portion of the company. That infusion of cash allowed Green & Black's to expand its operations while retaining its emphasis on fair trade.

In 2005, the owners of Green & Black's sold the company to Cadbury's for an undisclosed sum, believed to be around £20 million, the equivalent of $25 million. The terms of the sale included a clause that would maintain fair trade practices. Within a few years, Cadbury was sold to Kraft, which was sold to Mondelez, a multinational American company headquartered in Chicago, previously National Dairy Products. Mondelez is a nonsense word, a name made up to give the sense of a world (*monde*) that is delicious. By 2017, Green & Black's largely dropped its organic and fair trade labels.

The owners reportedly lament selling up. "I regret selling Green & Black's to Cadbury. It was a mistake. A great shame. . . . I wish I'd kept hold of it," Kendall said in an interview (Burn Callander 2015). The sale of Green & Black's has been discussed in the British media, typically focusing on the question of whether Green & Black's current trade agreements should count as fair trade.

I want to point to a different set of questions, that is, questions about fair ownership. In a company committed to interacting in a fair and responsible manner with its various stakeholders, who should benefit from the proceeds of the sale of the company? Should the stakeholders, especially those with whom the company had entered into fair trade agreements, have a say, or participate in the proceeds of the sale? After all, one important part of what made Green & Black's a successful company was its Mayan cocoa; another important part of its success was its fair trade agreement with the farmers who produced and harvested the cocoa. Could we raise questions about fair ownership? Is it fair that the proceeds of the sale apparently went to the owners in Britain, and perhaps not at all to the Mayan farmers in Belize? Would it be better to have a model of ownership in which the benefits of ownership (along with the risks) could be shared with more stakeholders? Is it fair to use a model of ownership in which entrepreneurs and investors benefit from selling a company, while stakeholders and fair trade farmers who provide the key ingredients do not share in the benefits of the sale?

We might ask whether it would be better to be more intentional about fair ownership. After all, returning to the case of Green & Black's, it might seem curious that entrepreneurs who pride themselves on their commitment to fair trade and ethical sourcing sold their company for a tremendous profit (perhaps more than $25 million) apparently without any of the proceeds of the sale going to the cocoa growers who were a key to the company's success. One might ask: Is fair trade enough? Should we be thinking about practicing and institutionalizing fair ownership? What is fair ownership? Which form of ownership is best?

If we turn to business sources or legal sources for answers to these questions, we are likely to get responses that presume that a potential owner is motivated primarily by financial self-interest, or by a framework that presumes an emphasis on equal rights with fair rules. Some of the responses will be rather technical in nature, with answers that vary by political jurisdiction. In the context of the United States, we might ask if a sole-proprietorship is better than a C-corp, S-corp, or LLC. Each of these forms of ownership have various advantages and disadvantages in administrative simplicity, ability to transfer ownership, ability to raise capital, ability to shelter income from various taxes, and ability to shield the owner from liability. However, if we recognize that the questions at hand—What is fair ownership? Which form of ownership is best?—raise both technical and moral issues, we will need to turn to resources beyond business and legal sources for answers.

What should a company do as the owners reach an age when it is prudent to consider a plan that allows the owner to step away from running or owning the company? For companies in which the owners have particular moral commitments, what can be done to insure that the next generation of owners continues the non-financial goals of the company? In some cases, leadership or ownership in the company is transferred to another senior member of the business, or to a family member. In other cases, businesses are sold to other businesses (as in the case of Green & Black's), or to an investor or a private equity firm. The sales agreement may include stipulations that the business would continue to be practiced in a manner that honors the ethical commitments of the original owners (as in the case of Green & Black's), though it is less clear that those commitments will continue to be honored if a company is sold again.

Puzzles about Ownership, Owning the Means of Production, and Owning a Business

To respond to questions about the transfer of business ownership, it may help to pause to raise fundamental issues about ownership and the responsibilities of owning a business by considering a series of puzzles and questions about ownership. A first thing to note when we consider puzzles about ownership is that, at the popular level, there is comparatively little discussion about the ethics of owning property or a business.[1] Of course, one might respond that this is because, in the debate between

---

1.   It is far more common, at the popular level, to engage in debates about the ethics of income or the ethics of trade. With regard to income, there are ongoing disputes about the minimum wage, and about the gap between the income of those who are wealthiest compared with those who are poor or middle class. Within discussions about income, the distinction between ownership and income is rarely drawn or made explicit. Turning to questions about trade, there are many ongoing disputes. Beyond the disputes about tariffs, I note below the way that issues of "fair trade" have emerged into consciousness. In contrast, it is difficult to point to a sustained conversation at the public level about the ethics of ownership. I am not aware of any sustained effort to focus on fair ownership.

capitalism and communism, capitalism won. To which several responses could be made—certain features of the debate seem to persist. In each generation of young people, there seem to be many who are drawn to the view that ownership, especially owning a business, is morally objectionable.

Further, we should note that there are various ways to understand the meaning of ownership. In the next section, I focus on the account of ownership found in Catholic social teaching. For now, I turn to a fundamental question stated in very broad terms: Is it ethical to own property? On the one hand, most of us own some things, such as clothes and personal belongings. Many of us own many other things, too, including computers, automobiles, and perhaps a house, along with items that we have been given, or which we have purchased. On the other hand, we have all heard reasons to call into question whether it is just to own things, especially when we are told of people that own massive amounts of wealth at the same time that there are so many people in the world who have so little, or almost nothing.

The founder of the Economy of Communion movement, Chiara Lubich, faced these sorts of questions during her youth when her father lost his job during Italy's period of fascism because of the socialist ideas that he held. From the socialists who influenced his views, he would have heard the view expressed by Karl Marx: "from each according to his ability, to each according to his needs" (Marx 1875). Some versions of socialism go so far as to claim that ownership is unjust, or that ownership of the means of production by a private individual is unjust.

Or consider the view expressed in the Acts of the Apostles: the fellowship of believers who sold all of their possessions and goods, sharing whatever they had with others, even "sharing their meals with gladness and sincerity of heart" (Acts 2:45–46). Does not this suggest that it is better not to own property, or perhaps that it is wrong or selfish to own property?

When it comes to business ownership, what about the morality of owning massive capital investments, such as those that are required for many kinds of industrial production? Is it wrong for an individual, or a group of individuals, to own the means of production? And what about the ethics of owning a company? Is it wrong for an individual, or a group of individuals, to own a company? Does this imply that the non-owners who work at the company are, in a sense, enslaved by the owners?

Were we to engage in a conversation the aim of which is to respond in detail to these and similar questions, we would need to determine what would count as a better or worse answer to these sorts of questions. We would need to investigate whether there are principles that could be appealed to in order to determine whether a particular action or policy is right or wrong. Further, we would need to determine which moral grammar would be used to engage in this sort of conversation. And in taking up such questions, we would be working toward a more fine-grained way of engaging in shared reflection about the ethics of ownership.

One initial conclusion that can be reached is straightforward: Rather than thinking in sharp dichotomies, as if ownership is either "right" or "wrong," a conversation about fair ownership would require working toward a more graduated and nuanced understanding of what fair ownership is, with distinctions and qualifications that would make possible a more subtle discussion of what makes some forms of ownership better or worse than others in some circumstances.

Catholic Social Teaching on Ownership as Stewardship

Catholic social teaching proposes a distinctive and well-developed account of ownership, articulated especially in a series of modern papal encyclicals. Pope Leo XIII, in *Rerum Novarum*, his 1891 encyclical on the condition of the working class, advanced an argument directed against the socialist's claim that the solution to the social question will come about by abolishing private property. Leo's argument is detailed and subtle; it takes up almost a fifth of the encyclical. The heart of his argument has the form of a natural law argument. What is good for humans is revealed in the nature of human flourishing. Like the other animals, each of which flourishes by living in a manner that makes possible the actualization of one's given powers over the course of one's life, human beings flourish when we live in a manner that actualizes our human capacities. Like the other animals that establish a sense of territory for living and raising one's young, humans flourish by forming families that dwell in a particular space and at a particular time. To provide for the goods of our lives and our families, we have been given the power to plan ahead and to engage in labor. The exercise of one's human powers, "linking the future with the present, and being master of his own acts" (§7) allows the human being to discern an order in the world by which one can guide one's actions. The material goods of the earth are created for "the use and enjoyment of the whole human race" (§8), but two qualifications need to be added. First, in order to transform the earth into productive goods that respond to human desires and needs, humans need to engage in labor. Second, the goods of the earth, which are here for all, do not carry within them a set structure for how we should exercise our intelligence and freedom to divide up those goods in a manner that allows fair distribution. As Pope Leo put it, "no part of it was assigned to any one in particular, and that the limits of private possession have been left to be fixed by man's own industry, and by the laws of individual races" (§8).

To further understand this point, it is worthwhile to reflect upon the wide range of differing structures that humans have used in the exercise of intelligence and freedom to divide up the material goods of the earth in a manner that makes the fruits of the earth available to everyone. Consider the widely different systems of property used in North America. Focusing briefly on those communities in Midwestern parts of the United States, we see in our place names hearkening back to American Indian communities, which practiced a very loose system of property. Many of those people lived semi-nomadic forms of life, even as they practiced some sense of property and belonging. The name of almost every state in the middle part of America, along with countless cities, towns, and villages, comes from the languages of native people, either from the name used by native tribes to designate those people, or from their description or name used to reference that place. So, in that sense, they had a sense of property.

At the same time, we can notice the rather different understanding of property presumed by the early Jesuit missionaries who were among the first European settlers in the middle part of America. As an example, consider Fr. Gravier, the Jesuit missionary who lived with the Kaskaskia people (Thwaites 1900). Like so many of the early Jesuit missionaries who settled along the rivers of the upper Midwest, he brought with him an understanding of property that was shaped by the habits of French village life, especially as this was practiced in Quebec. The communities that he and others developed, typically alongside the communities of native Americans, practiced a system of property with a great affinity to village life in sixteenth-century France: residential life clustered in a village with a church at the center, agricultural crops grown in long lots tended by particular families (typically two plough-lengths wide, so that one pass could be made in each direction), and common fields in which the members of the village had animals put out to pasture in shared land (Ekberg 2000, 6).

Consider briefly a tension faced by Fr. Gravier and other Jesuit missionaries who lived in the area we now call the American Midwest (See Thwaite 1900; Ekberg and Pregaldin 1991). The Kaskaskia people, with whom Fr. Gravier lived, were occasionally attacked by members of other tribes. In retaliation, members of the Kaskaskia people would carry out violent counter-attacks. A significant number of the Kaskaskia people became Christian during the time that Fr. Gravier was working at the mission, and he taught them to reflect on their own actions, including their acts of retaliatory violence. When encouraged to ask, "Who owns this act?," the members of the community were invited to reflect more deeply on the meaning of ownership, responsibility, and stewardship.

Geographers point to the remnants of medieval conceptions of property, imported by French Canadians, in the material culture of the old French villages that dot rivers in the American Midwest. After the War of 1812, when the land in the Midwest more decisively became governed by the laws of the United States, the sense of property and the cultural practices of French village life were rather swiftly replaced by the American system of property, influenced by British law, especially as practiced in Virginia, with its emphasis on clear deeds and individual ownership or unambiguous designations of joint ownership. In some areas, the eye of an attentive cultural geographer still can see in a single place echoes of multiple systems of property: American Indian, medieval French, and US American.

Catholic social teaching does not express a preference for one system of property over another, but it does affirm that it is a feature of human flourishing that a people are called upon to exercise intelligence and freedom to devise a system of ownership that makes it possible for the material goods of the earth to serve the flourishing of all in a manner that promotes the common good.

Forty years after the promulgation of the encyclical *Rerum Novarum*, Pope Pius XI clarified the Church's teaching on property and ownership by pointing to "twin shipwrecks" that should be avoided (1931, §46). One error can be named *individualism*, especially the view that asserts that ownership means "I can do whatever I want with my own property" or that the only limits to the use of property are the rights of other individuals. This type of individualism denies or minimizes "the social and public character of the right of property" by failing to recognize that owning property means being a steward. Stewardship is a responsibility to care for property, treating it as one's own while recognizing that in another sense, it belongs to someone else. So, the flaw of this sort of individualism is the laissez-faire attitude in which one acts without regard for others. The other error can be named *collectivism*, especially the view that asserts that all private ownership is wrong or unjust, or that the means of production should be owned only by the state, and never by a private individual.

Returning to Pope Leo's natural law argument in defense of private property, we can hear the echoes of arguments advanced by Thomas Aquinas. A system of private property is best suited as a way to divide up the material goods of the earth because it promotes better care for material resources, because it promotes more orderly conduct, and because it promotes greater peace (Aquinas 1981, II-II.66.2). At the same time, St. Thomas adds an important qualification: Property ownership comes with the responsibility to insure that one's property is used in a manner that promotes the common good, and in cases of extreme need, the claim of ownership might be overridden by urgent particularities (II-II.66.7).

Thus, *Rerum Novarum* teaches that humans are, in one sense, like the other animals, who work to get food or a place to sleep, making nests or dens, but in another sense, quite different from the other animals, in that we have been gifted with language and a sort of intelligence that allows us to foresee, to some extent, into the future, to plan, and to work together with others on very complex tasks. Accordingly, humans can possess property, not merely for temporary and momentary use, as other living things do, but to have and to hold it in stable and permanent possession. As Pope Leo puts it:

> Private ownership is the natural right of humans, and
> to exercise that right, especially as members of soci-

ety, is not only lawful, but absolutely necessary. "It is lawful," says St. Thomas Aquinas, "to hold private property; and it is also necessary for the carrying on of human existence." But if the question be asked: How must one's possessions be *used*?—the Church replies without hesitation in the words of the same holy Doctor: "One should not consider material possessions as one's own, but as common to all, so as to share them without hesitation when others are in need." (1931, §22)

On the hundredth anniversary of Pope Leo's teaching about owning property in *Rerum Novarum*, Pope John Paul II applied that teaching to the context of 1991. With the collapse of communism in Eastern Europe, he asked whether capitalism is the way forward. In his answer, John Paul II drew an important distinction:

> If by "capitalism" is meant an economic system which recognizes the fundamental and positive role of business, the market, private property and the resulting responsibility for the means of production, as well as free human creativity in the economic sector, then the answer is certainly in the affirmative, even though it would perhaps be more appropriate to speak of a "business economy," "market economy" or simply "free economy." But if by "capitalism" is meant a system in which freedom in the economic sector is not circumscribed within a strong juridical framework which places it at the service of human freedom in its totality, and which sees it as a particular aspect of that freedom, the core of which is ethical and religious, then the reply is certainly negative. (1991, §42)

In other words, the pope is suggesting that it is morally possible to engage in the practice of owning property, including the ownership of capital in a free economy, especially when the market sphere is circumscribed by a polity with a strong juridical framework and a moral cultural sphere that upholds the dignity of every human person.

As we recall the Church's teaching on the economy, it is worth noting how much the central question is the issue of ownership, not income or trade. What is fair ownership? What does it mean to be a good business owner? From the teaching of Pope Leo in *Rerum Novarum* and the other social encyclicals promulgated on its anniversary, a broad answer begins to come into focus. An individualistic attitude toward ownership which says "what's mine is mine" or which sees the responsibilities of ownership only in terms of respecting individual rights is inadequate, as is an attitude that proposes that private owner-ship of property or of the means of production is unjust, as if these are only to be left to the state.

Between these two mistaken views of ownership, there is a more adequate conception that accords with the grammar of stewardship.

> Human beings legitimately exercise a *responsible stew-ardship*. On this earth there is room for everyone: here the entire human family must find the resources to live with dignity, through the help of nature itself—God's gift to his children—and through hard work and cre-ativity. At the same time we must recognize our grave duty to hand the earth on to future generations in such a condition that they too can worthily inhabit it and continue to cultivate it. This means being committed to making joint decisions "after pondering responsibly the road to be taken, decisions aimed at strengthening that *covenant between human beings and the environment*, which should mirror the creative love of God, from whom we come and towards whom we are journeying." (Benedict 2009, §50)

Accordingly, the social doctrine of the Church is a teaching that emphasizes the responsibilities of stewardship. While this has implications for questions of fair income and fair trade, those are not central issues in Catholic social teaching. I have tried to show that the theme of property, and questions about what it means to be a responsible owner of property, is a much more central feature of Catholic social teaching.

In the social teaching of the Catholic encyclicals, ownership is understood in terms of stewardship. Stewardship involves holding something in trust for another. "Historically, stewardship was a means to protect a kingdom while those rightfully in charge were away, or, more often, to govern for the sake of an underage king" (Block 1993, xx). As Peter Block has put it, the task of the steward is to "choose service over self-interest" and to "preside over the orderly distribution of power" (1993, xx). In order to do this, Block points to the importance of systematically moving decision-making and resources "closer to the bottom and edges of the organization" (1993, 18). Understood this way, stewardship is "the willingness to be accountable to the well-being of the organization by operating in service, rather than in control, of those around us" (1993, xx).

Ownership (understood as stewardship) is thus a responsibility that involves recognizing that, in owning something, one has the responsibility to exercise one's intelligence and freedom as a wise steward. As Pope Leo put it, "the earth, even though apportioned among private owners, ceases not thereby to minister to the needs of all" (§8).

Succession Plans for Wise Stewards

What options are available to business owners in their succession plan, especially for those who desire to consider more than profit maximization? For owners who want to do more than cash out, what are the strengths and weaknesses of various options for business succession?

For a variety of reasons, many owners of small and medium-sized businesses tend to avoid the question of succession. Yet business owners who practice stewardship in a way that promotes non-financial objectives of healthy community have the responsibility to consider whether and how the business will be sustained when it comes time to transfer ownership, and whether the business succession plan will include a way to sustain a commitment to non-financial goals, including supporting the community. The particularities of each such business make it so that it is impossible to treat this topic in an abstract, one-size-fits-all manner. Instead, it is worthwhile to consider a range of options, along with the strengths and weaknesses of each.

Since many small and medium-sized businesses began as family businesses, a common consideration is to pass on the business to the next generation in the family. However, in practice, most family businesses do not pass on to the next generation, and this for a variety of reasons. Many families do not have children with the interest or skill level to continue the firm. The roles in a family, where each child is loved unconditionally and equally with a recognition of personal gifts and talents, may be different from what is required in choosing a leader for the company, as it may be that one child is better suited than others for the role of owning and running the company. Further, the founder's goals, vision, passion, engagement, and years of experience may differ quite significantly from that of the next generation. Thus, family succession may be suitable in some instances, but not others.

Perhaps the most common path for a small business, when the owner decides to retire or discontinue running the business, is simply to go out of business and liquidate the company's assets. Any real estate, equipment, or inventory is thus converted to cash. If the proceeds generated from liquidating assets is significant, these (finite, one-time resources) can be used, in part or in whole, to advance the non-financial goals of the owner. Much is lost when a business closes; many assets, both tangible and intangible, quickly evaporate, including the steady stream of cash flow, jobs, customer relationships, and brand recognition.

In some cases, a successful small or medium-sized business may have an opportunity to sell, whether to an individual, to another business, or to a private equity firm. Each has advantages and disadvantages. Selling to an individual may make sense in some cases, though the new owner may do things with the business that the founder finds surprising or objectionable. Selling to another firm may yield significant proceeds, though this typically involves stepping away from the firm and giving up influence.

Some successful small companies may be suitable candidates for sale to a private equity firm. Assets for such investments have reached record levels, and there is a large amount of capital available and raised each year for the acquisition of businesses (Lindsey et al. 2018, 3). As in the example of the sale of Green & Black's, some of these transactions may seem quite attractive to business owners; these also may include agreements to honor ethical commitments of the firm's original owners. However, it is also the case that the sale of a company typically changes a company's culture. Features of the sale may incentivize an over-emphasis on short-term efficiencies, and the new owners may feel reduced ties to the local community following an acquisition.

What can be done when the controlling owners value non-financial and community-related outcomes? Is it possible to find a stewardship-based exit strategy? Is it possible to balance the financial aspects of the sale of the business with agreements that strengthen an ongoing sense of concern for the well-being of other stakeholders? In the case of Green & Black's, the sales agreement included stipulations that the business would continue to be practiced in a manner that honored the ethical commitments of the original owners, though those commitments seem *not* to have been honored when the company was resold. In some cases, it may be sensible for a business owner to work with a private equity firm like the one founded by Kevin Lindsey: Social Impact Sustainable Private Equity. This sort of private equity firm connects investors and business owners preparing to sell where all the parties are committed to sustaining community ties. Such transactions may require a range of commitments and virtues. Part of what is needed is the patience to find investors interested in supporting the next generation of business owners as they acquire and build stable businesses that are long-term members of a local community. The goal of these sorts of private equity firms is to provide financial vehicles that allow the transfer of ownership of companies "for investors who appreciate how enduringly profitable small to mid-sized businesses are the bedrock of local communities" (rerumnovarumcapital.com). Their philosophy is based on the belief that "if more businesses are owned within a community and support a community, the community is stronger."

The question of transferring ownership of a business is complicated in part because there are multiple forms of ownership practiced by small and medium-sized businesses. Many small firms begin as a sole proprietorship. However, as a firm grows and develops, and especially as a firm reaches a point where the original owner is ready to sell the firm, it may be appropriate to consider which form of ownership is best for this firm, if it is to go forward under new ownership. This may involve raising questions such as those previously mentioned: Is a sole-proprietorship better than a partnership, a merger, a C-corp, S-corp, or LLC?

In addition, business succession may give rise to other questions: Should the company consider an employee ownership model? Are there enough employees in the firm who have a sufficiently stable relationship with the company that it would be appropriate for them to consider cooperative ownership? Are there ways to transfer ownership from a sole proprietor to an employee-owned business cooperative in which the employees become the new owners?

Employee-owned business cooperatives typically retain local ownership, with a structure where management decisions are accountable to their employee members and communities. The cooperative model helps promote a balance between people and profit. There are many models of these sorts of successful community-owned businesses, and many indications that such firms can be sustainable and resilient while strengthening local economies and communities.

In order for a company to convert through a sale to become an employee-owned cooperative, there are many questions in addition to determining the financial vehicle appropriate for the sale. Is the business owner willing to consider this alternative? Who are the potential member owners? Will the current owner stay on as a member? Is the business viable and sustainable? How would the sale transaction be financed? What would be the details of such a sale? What plans would need to be put in place for ongoing education and training in the responsibilities of cooperative ownership? Is there a support system in place to help the potential new cooperative owners learn from existing co-ops and networks? In order to answer these questions, it is worthwhile to explore the subculture of worker-owned cooperatives and the resources in place to help companies transition to adopt an employee-owned cooperative model.

As a company is sold, there are also questions about management and culture after the sale. Does the upper management have adequate financial literacy, governance experience, and management experience to sustain the transition? Will management operate in a manner that is transparent and supportive of the goals of the firm? A firm has many day-to-day decisions that must be made: organizing, scheduling, problem-solving, etc., along with other larger strategic decisions that involve planning and leading. How will those roles be carried out during and after the transition to the new ownership? Who will get to participate in making those decisions? Will there be transparency? If so, how much will be made open, and to whom? Will the costs and profits associated with running the business be shared with the employees? If so, will this include employee pay? Who will be involved in making personnel decisions to hire and fire members of the firm?

For many small and medium-sized businesses, the cooperative model of employee ownership may be unsuitable, as most employees have neither the skills nor the motivation to be owners. Many employees do not desire the commitment, risks, or responsibilities of ownership, and they may lack the stomach to make the sorts of decisions that business owners have to make, involving hundreds of thousands, or perhaps millions, of dollars. Further, the employees may not share the commitment of the owners to worthwhile non-financial goals.

Another viable alternative is for the owner of a small business to transfer ownership through something like mentorship. In some instances, an employee within a small firm may be well-suited to take over ownership; a period of mentorship may therefore be needed to help with the transition, and this may include financial agreements about the financial transition of ownership. In other cases, a person outside the business may enter into an agreement involving a non-standard buyout along with a period of learning relevant details about the business. There is no simple formula for successful relationships of mentoring, as there are particularities that vary with each person and relationship; certainly some relationships can be fraught with difficulties, and some individuals are not well suited for learning from others—most of us get along better with some people than with others. Further, there is no single plan for the best way to arrange the financial transfer of ownership, and such a plan may go awry in various ways. Still, in some cases, a mentoring relationship may be part of the financial transfer of company ownership from founder to successor.

Different firms obviously need to be attentive to the particularities of each circumstance. Reviewing these options for transferring ownership is intended to bring into focus some of the issues involved in engaging in thoughtful reflection about the responsibilities of ownership.

Conclusion

The important role that small and medium-sized businesses play in supporting communities is frequently unnoticed. The Economy of Communion project proposed by Chiara Lubich includes an invitation for members of the Focolare Movement to bring their spirituality into the practice of business organizations, including those with a calling as founders and sustainers of for-profit businesses. Embedded within this invitation are two opportunities. First is the occasion to acknowledge the important role played by such business owners in promoting and sustaining healthy communities. Second is the opportunity to recognize the difficult questions for such owners when it comes time to consider business succession. Starting and owning a business is sometimes described as exciting, daring, exhilarating, and purposeful. Owners of small and mid-sized businesses frequently take on personal responsibility for the activities of the business while developing an eye for the health of the community in which the business is situated. Such owners sometimes become quite generous and committed to the flourishing of the community. When it comes time for such a business owner to make a decision to scale down, scale back, or sell the business, it is necessary to consider how to make wise decisions that serve the common good. A consideration of the responsibilities of ownership informed by Catholic social teaching and awareness of the advantages and disadvantages of various business succession plans is crucial for ownership as a wise steward.[2]

---

2.   I am grateful to the editors for very helpful suggestions.

Bibliography

Aquinas, St. Thomas. 1981. *Summa Theologiae*. Notre Dame: Ave Maria.

Beabout, Greg. 2013. *The Character of the Manager: From Office Executive to Wise Steward*. New York: Palgrave MacMillan.

Block, Peter. 1993. *Stewardship*. San Francisco: Berrett-Koehler.

Burn Callander, Rebecca. 2015. "I Wish I'd Never Sold Green & Blacks to Cadbury." *The Telegraph*. https://www.telegraph. co.uk/finance/newsbysector/retailandconsumer/11951398/I-wish-Id-never-sold-Green-and-Blacks-to-Cadbury.html.

Benedict XVI. 2009. *Caritas in Veritate*. http://www.vatican.va/ content/benedict-xvi/en/encyclicals/documents/hf_ben-xvi_ enc_20090629_caritas-in-veritate.html.

Ekberg, Carl, J. 2000. *French Roots in the Illinois Country: The Mississippi Frontier in Colonial Times*. Urbana, IL: University of Illinois Press.

Ekberg, Carl and Anton Pregaldin. 1991. "Marie Rouensa and the Foundations of French Illinois." *Illinois Historical Journal* 84, no. 3:146–160.

John Paul II. 1991. *Centesimus Annus*. https://www.vatican.va/ content/john-paul-ii/en/encyclicals/documents/hf_jp-ii_ enc_01051991_centesimus-annus.html.

Leo XIII. 1891. *Rerum Novarum*. http://w2.vatican.va/content/leo-xiii/en/encyclicals/documents/hf_l-xiii_enc_15051891_rerum-novarum.html.

Lindsey, Kevin. 2017. "The Church, Private Equity, and the Catholic Entrepreneur: Why the Church Needs Good Capital Institutions for a New Catholic Business Ecology for the Common Good." Paper presented at the Common Good Conference, the Tenth International Conference on Catholic Social Theory and Business Education (June 22), University of St. Thomas.

Lindsey, Kevin, Nathan Mauck, and Ben Olsen. 2018. "The Coming Wave of Small Business Succession and the Role of

Stakeholder Synergy Theory." https://papers.ssrn.com/sol3/papers.cfm?abstract_id=2925608.

Lubich, Chiara. 1999. "For an Economy Based On Communion." *Nuova Umanità: Rivista Bimenstrale di Cultura* 21, 121: 7–18. https://eocnorthamerica.files.wordpress.com/2015/11/chi_19990129_en.pdf. See also this volume, *Finding Faith in Business: An Economy of Communion Vision*, edited by Andrew Gustafson and Celeste Harvey. Hyde Park, NY: New City Press.

Marx, Karl. 1875. *Critique of the Gotha Programme*, Part I. https://www.marxists.org/archive/marx/works/1875/gotha/index.htm.

Pius XI. 1931. *Quadragesimo Anno*. http://w2.vatican.va/content/pius-xi/en/encyclicals/documents/hf_p-xi_enc_19310515_quadragesimo-anno.html.

Rerum Novarum Capital. 2020. Website at http://rerumnovarumcapital.com.

Thwaites, Reuben G., ed. 1900. *The Jesuit Relations and Allied Documents: Travels and Explorations of the Jesuit Missionaries in New France 1610-1791*, vol. 65. Cleveland, OH: The Burrows Brothers Company. Available online at http://moses.creighton.edu/kripke/jesuitrelations/relations_65.html.

Chapter 5

Simplicity of Lifestyle as a Goal of Business: Practicing the Economy of Communion as a Challenge to Consumer Society

David Cloutier, The Catholic University of America

Abstract: This paper illuminates why following genuine principles of one's Christianity is so challenging in the contemporary economy, and then turns to a specific aspect of the challenge: the importance of *simplicity of lifestyle* and the rejection of luxury and consumerism in all spheres of our lives, including our business practices, an idea often overlooked in thinking about the consistency of lifestyle. Finally, it will suggest two somewhat daring ways in which that simplicity might be manifested by EoC businesses. These suggestions are meant to be challenging, but I will close by noting that both actually address really important problems in our current economic situation. Therefore, they are potentially effective business strategies, and not only utopian moral imperatives.

Introduction

In her 1999 address on the Economy of Communion, Chiara Lubich identified several key "characteristics" of the Economy of Communion (EoC). Her first principle is very important: "The actors within the Economy of Communion businesses seek to live out, in the particular way that their productive organization requires, the *same lifestyle* that they live in the other areas of their life" (Lubich 2002, 18).

In the rest of her address, she notes a number of aspects of this "same lifestyle": the importance of setting aside profits, organizational relations of "openness and trust" even with business competitors, a "culture of giving," an "attention to the least," and a "respect for the environment." This is not meant to be an exhaustive list. The more important point is the umbrella under which all these particular claims gather: a rejection of the "compartmentalization" of different spheres of life and the divided self characteristic of modern society, and especially modern business culture (see MacIntyre 1984; Alford and Naughton 2001, 7–21). "Greed is good" is not a principle widely applied and admired in family relations! By seeking to live according to the same values and principles in all spheres of life, the Economy of Communion business represents a powerful example of the core call of Pope Benedict's *Caritas in Veritate*: the insistence that principles of what he called "gratuitousness" cannot simply occur "outside" or "after" economic activity, but must be present within it (2009, §36). He analyzes the market failures of the 2008–2009 Great Recession in terms of a loss of basic trust and fraternity; key to the crisis was the construction of complex investment instruments that obscured and encouraged the increasingly irresponsible lending in the mortgage market. At the time, it looked like everyone was getting great deals, but in fact there were layers of deception that later resulted in much human suffering. What looked for a time to be "success" in purely economic logic could not ultimately be sustained, because that economic logic was not built on its necessary social foundation of genuine human and Christian values.

My first task in the paper will be to illuminate why following genuine principles of one's Christianity is so challenging in the contemporary economy, and then I will turn to a specific aspect of the challenge: the importance of *simplicity of lifestyle* and the rejection of luxury and consumerism in all spheres of our lives, including our business practices. This idea is often overlooked in thinking about the consistency of lifestyle, but it should not be, both because it is an important element of Catholic social teaching (CST) and because of genuine economic reasons for why such simplicity is a necessary component of more abstract goals such as justice, solidarity, and sustainability. Finally, I will suggest two somewhat daring ways in which that simplicity might be manifest by EoC businesses. These suggestions are meant to be challenging, but I will close by noting that both actually address really important problems in our current economic situation. Therefore, they are potentially effective business strategies, and not only utopian moral imperatives.

Zamagni on Business and Social Aims

Let me start by addressing the broad challenge of consistency of lifestyle. The Italian economist Stefano Zamagni's work has been very important for the EoC and for CST. Zamagni's overall work develops a vision of what he calls "civil economy," a genuinely alternative way of thinking about how an economy works. The key hallmark of the notion of "civil economy" is the re-connection of business activity and public, social aims. As it has developed, modern economics tends to assume what Pope Benedict has called "the market-plus-state binary," in which the "market" represents private individuals and groups pursuing their own self-interested ends, and the "state" represents the pursuit of public, social ends. Put simply, business is for pursuing private goods, while government is for pursuing common goods. Zamagni's work, as I will outline in a moment, seeks to show that this division of work is rooted in problematic historical processes and is not ultimately sustainable; the civil economy is a model where this compartmentalization is overcome, such that businesses become vehicles for pursuing genuinely social ends. In an article on the EoC, he points out the importance of EoC businesses as a testimony against this market-state binary "since [EoC] demonstrates, through facts, that it is possible to use the market as a means to manage to reach goals which are by their nature public" (Zamagni 2002, 134). In an EoC business, "the market can become an instrument which can reinforce social ties" (134), rather than undermine them, such that they must be repaired by actions of the state. For example, he notes that EoC businesses act to distribute wealth more fairly in the first place (instead of just *re*-distributing it) and to regenerate the social values such as trust on which the market depends (instead of just depending on things like churches, schools, and families to teach those values sufficiently such that they will hold up under market pressure).

Zamagni's notion of a civil economy in which businesses pursue and reinforce common, public ends actually makes better sense of the needs of economic reality than do the alternatives. For example, it is widely accepted that markets ultimately depend on social trust, a fact underscored by Partha Dasgupta's *Economics: A Very Short Introduction*, which begins its analysis of wealth creation and markets not by talking about supply and demand, about technological innovation, or even about the motive power of self-interest. Instead, he begins with a chapter on trust—trust that makes possible much wider economic relationships, which then make possible larger-scale enterprises, division of labor, and everything else that actually contributes to more economic production (Dasgupta 2007, 30–63). This notion that the market cannot stand alone is even found in Adam Smith himself (Kennedy 2009).

However, for all that common sense, the position is not dominant in our ordinary thinking about the economy. Why not? In a more recent article, Zamagni seeks to excavate the division between private markets and public government historically. He points out that the markets of medieval and Renaissance Italy, for example, generated much wealth, but were quite unlike modern markets. He notes that—for all their flaws—these markets existed within an institutional and moral ethos of control and civic solidarity. Nevertheless, they were real markets. He further notes that the three basic mechanisms of market economics—the division of labor, the development of innovative organization and new technology, and the freedom of enterprise—are present in both the older civil and the newer capitalist contexts. So what was the difference? Zamagani suggests the differences were not the market mechanisms, but rather *the ends pursued by agents*; thus the *same* mechanisms ended up performing *different* functions. So, for example, he notes that in a civil economy context, the division of labor can serve as an inclusive principle that enables the community to find useful work for everyone, given different gifts and abilities; by contrast, in a capitalist economy, the division "is used to discriminate between categories of workers for the purpose of increasing the productivity of the system" (2017, 183). It may well be that, in both instances, one result is that people are able to get jobs despite low skill levels, but in the latter instance, that is not the goal—and therefore, of course, the tendency will be to use up and dispose of such workers, rather than sustain them as productive contributors to the common good.

This insight about the ends intended by agents may seem a modest one—and we may think about ways in which our organizations, EoC or not, continue to practice everyday habits that look more like civil inclusion than capitalist disposability. The dilemma for contemporary versions of inclusion comes at the moment we can all imagine: when business realities force owners and managers to make a hard choice about such workers. Why is that scenario of the hard choice—and the much more likely outcome of that choice—so depressingly familiar in our context?

Here Zamagni offers some remarkable insight. For him, the root problem lies in what he terms the "pessimistic interpretation of human nature" (2017, 185). This is often represented by dark figures in political philosophy like Machiavelli and Hobbes, who insist that any politics must reckon with the realities of human nature as nasty and self-seeking. But more seemingly optimistic figures, like Locke and Adam Smith, also shared in this sense that an effective economy and politics depended upon a recognition that individual human beings were not simply occasionally flawed, but were fundamentally self-interested. Thinkers like Locke and Smith moderated this picture, often by appealing to a separate internal sphere such as Smith's moral sentiments (very telling!), but they agreed that economic and political life needed to be based on a recognition of realistic self-interest. The definitive account of this transition is a fairly short and readable classic by Albert Hirschman called *The Passions and the Interests*, which explains that the new goal was more or less to curb more violent passions in favor of somewhat more benign interests—especially the interest in acquiring new and interesting things (1977). The way to social peace came to be the pursuit of fancy luxuries which, as Hume (1953, 134–137) above all noted, spurred the lower classes to work, and according to Smith (1976, 181–185), more positively, made the folly of rich people trickle down to others through their spending. It seemed preferable to more violent competitions.

I should stress here that ultimately, even the gentler version of this "pessimistic account of human nature" is not compatible with the EoC vision. To the contrary—the EoC vision clearly expects a lot from people. So we should be troubled when Zamagni goes on to explain exactly how this version of human nature has become invisibly entrenched in the way we think about society. This "pessimistic account" is not just an idea in intellectual history; it is manifest by conceptual and institutional assumptions. How so?

The original pessimistic account of human nature leads to the twofold error at the heart of our current divided system: that the market sphere "coincides with the sphere of selfishness" and the state sphere "coincides with the sphere of solidarity and the pursuit of collective interests" (Zamagni 2017, 185). This sets up an inevitable and unresolvable "clash of concepts" between those who view the market as a "necessary evil" that must be closely monitored by the state and those who (not wrongly) view the state as also potentially corrupt, and so see "the market as an ideal place to resolve also the political problem" by applying market logic "to all spheres of social life" (2017, 186). This clash essentially dominates our public discourse, but beyond that, seems almost a fact of nature to many people. The only question is what side you are on. But Zamagni notes how both sides agree on a "cultural outcome that is antithetical to the civil economy": that whatever we think of market logic, what it means is "the impersonality of exchange relations" and "the exclusive self-interest of participants" (2017, 187). The only debate is whether the sphere of the state can manifest the opposite ideals of solidarity, or whether an appropriate pessimism should also extend to the self-interested ambition of those who run the state. Zamagni trenchantly concludes, "a society in which the principle of fraternity evaporates has no future" (2017, 188).

I have outlined Zamagni's compelling argument for two reasons. One is that Chiara Lubich's original principle—a unity of lifestyle in all spheres of life—faces this complicated and difficult overall landscape. The barriers to the problem are not simply a matter of changing individual intentions (although this must be done). It is at least as much a matter of getting people to think differently about how they understand society and economic activity in ways that do not and—if Zamagni is right—*cannot* find an easy fit in the society as it is. But my second reason for citing it is how Zamagni's account makes clear the deep root of the problem, and therefore the place we must target: the underlying pessimistic account of human nature. That's the big root that we must get leverage on. Where do we turn for such leverage?

Economics and the Pessimistic View of Human Nature

I think the obvious place to start is the place where people learn this pessimistic lesson about human nature most directly, quickly, and pervasively: the idea that as consumers, we have insatiable desires that we are right to satisfy (so long as we do not do anything illegal). As I alluded to earlier, the real engine of capitalist success is not the few Gordon Gekkos, but the very many eager consumers who seem never to cease their seeking for more and better goods and services from whomever can provide them. Luxury, long understood in both Greco-Roman and Judeo-Christian thought as a vice that undermined both individual flourishing and social solidarity, was reimagined by early economic thinkers such as Bernard Mandeville as a public virtue that actually led to industriousness and social prosperity (Cloutier 2015). Eventually this led to our current presumption that frenzied spending is necessary for all of us to keep the economy strong. This is an everyday (false) lesson in pessimism about human nature: We have unlimited wants, and they just keep growing. Thus, I think it is the place where we need to un-learn this lesson. We need to start thinking and acting like we expect people of human virtue to live simple lives. And we need to do so in ways that link this concern to how businesses make crucial decisions.

Admittedly, some people may be surprised to consider a life of luxury as contrary to Christian faith. But we should recognize that this criticism of luxury is everywhere in our ancient traditions. The great prophets of the Old Testament rail against "those who lie on beds of ivory / and lounge upon their couches" (Amos 6:4); Jesus consistently calls for the renouncing of concern for possessions and warns the rich; Plato views the enticements of luxury as the first step in the downfall of his virtuous republic; and Cicero typifies Roman disdain for "private luxury" (Cloutier 2015, 26–31). But we need not simply look to the ancients; this resistance to what gets renamed "consumerism" is an established and crucial aspect of Catholic social teaching in recent centuries. John Paul II, in his 1991 encyclical *Centesimus Annus*, notes that "in singling out new needs and new means to meet them, one must be guided by a comprehensive picture of [the human person] which . . . subordinates his material and instinctive dimensions to his interior and spiritual ones" (§36). The economic system itself cannot identify these "artificial new needs which hinder the formation of a mature personality," and so larger cultural norms must communicate that "what is wrong is a style of life which is presumed to be better when it is directed towards 'having' rather than 'being'" (§36). This criticism echoes his earlier critique of "super-development" involving "an excessive availability of every kind of material goods" which "easily makes people slaves of 'possession' and of immediate gratification, with no other horizon than the multiplication or continual replacement of the things already owned with others still better" (1987, §28). The "sad effects" of such super-development are not only a "crass materialism" but "a radical dissatisfaction" in which "the more one possesses the more one wants, while deeper aspirations remain unsatisfied and perhaps even stifled" (1987, §28). Moreover, in addressing the environmental crisis, Pope Francis adds to this witness by highlighting the importance of the virtue *sobrietas*, a "conviction that less is more" that enables us "to be serenely present to each reality, however small it may be," instead of being a person "dipping here and there, always on the look-out for what they do not have." He sums up: "Even living on little, they can live a lot" (2015, §222–223).

Some commentators on the Economy of Communion have also commented on the necessity of the intentional choosing of simpler lifestyles. Luca Crivelli distinguished two forms of poverty—one is unchosen, and the poverty that we usually fight to overcome, but the other, chosen poverty, is something that should be sought. He writes that this second type of poverty ... is the poverty which is born from the awareness that all that I am has been given to me; likewise, all that I have must, in turn, be given. This is the foundation of the dynamics of reciprocity. This poverty prompts us to free ourselves of goods as absolute possessions in order to make them gifts, and thus to be free to love, ... the goods themselves become bridges, occasions of community, paths of reciprocity. (Crivelli 2020, 22)

Thus, Crivelli notes, "The economy of communion aims at defeating indigence (the poverty that is not chosen but suffered) by inviting everyone to freely choose a moderate and poor style of life" (2020, 22).

Pope Francis has reminded EoC leaders forcefully about their obligation to work to overcome the first sort of poverty within a capitalism whose "principal ethical dilemma . . . is the creation of discarded people, then trying to hide them or make sure they are no longer seen. A serious form of poverty in a civilization is when *it is no longer able to see its poor*, who are first discarded and then hidden" (2017). Francis calls on the EoC not simply to find the poor, but to prevent the discarding of anyone in the first place. But importantly, the failure of people to then move toward Crivelli's chosen form of poverty is the often-unspoken root of the whole economic problem faced in advanced economies. It is not merely a matter of private temperance; it is a bug in the whole economic program. Even as far back as Paul VI's *Populorum Progressio*, CST offers an account of integral human development that assumes the great struggle for impoverished nations is to overcome material poverty. But this is not to say that they simply need to become like the developed nations. Paul VI sets out a hierarchy of "less human" conditions that strikingly begins with both "the lack of material necessities" and the "moral deficiencies of those who are mutilated by selfishness." As he progresses toward "more human" conditions, he highlights both "the passage from misery toward the possession of necessities," but also "the turning toward the spirit of poverty" (1967, §21). The problem here is, very often, rich Christians concerned with social justice who focus on the problems of others (their basic material deprivation) but do not recognize their own problems along this scale (the lack of a movement toward the spirit of poverty). And we do not notice this issue precisely because of the splits Zamagni identifies—we tend to think instead that problems like inequality or environmental sustainability can be best solved by the state.

Let me take a little time to explain this. It is no secret that the full turn to what economists call the principle of scarcity happens only, as Charles Clark pointed out, as industrial production became widespread; technology was actually making it possible to overcome genuine scarcity for the first time in human history (2006, 43–44). It is not an accident that the main heterodox economist at that time, Thorstein Veblen, first theorized the *consumer* basis of *advanced* capitalist society, and explained at length how the *artificial* scarcity manufactured by business owners and salesmen would only be fixed, in his view, if we put the engineers in charge. It is also telling that John Maynard Keynes is sometimes wrongly taken to be an apostle of the economic importance of increasing consumption. But Keynes recommends stimulating demand only as a temporary way of combatting economic slumps. In the long term, however, he assumed quite forthrightly that an economic abundance of the future would depend on three things: an end to war, a control of population, and the limiting of personal wants. One recent commentator notes acerbically that the last—limiting personal wants—seems to be the furthest from being realized (Minsky 1975, 155).

Why, if even these economists recognized this problem, does it so often go unnoticed? I think we labor under a certain illusion—the illusion that Mandeville himself created in his *The Fable of the Bees*—that a society devoted to lots of consumption is an economically successful society. People are industrious and produce. And this ends up benefitting everyone, for lots of reasons. Mandeville terms this "private vice, public benefit"—to us, it looks like consumer confidence makes for a big Christmas, which makes for jobs, which makes for a better economy. It's like an equation: free markets + mass consumption = a better economy.

But in fact, there are reasons to think that, even if the environmental challenges of such consumption somehow went away, we would encounter inherent *economic* problems. Chief among these reasons is the extended case made by Robert Gordon, in his magnum opus *The Rise and Fall of American Growth*. In this book, Gordon argues (and extensively documents) that the American economy benefitted from a series of what he calls "one-time-only" transitions between 1870 and 1970. These transitions all resulted in dramatic economic growth by increasing the productivity of the economy exponentially. Gordon points to a whole range of innovations—from water systems and electricity to agricultural mechanization and enormously improved transportation—all of which represented quantum leaps in productivity. This growth can be most easily represented by recognizing that America needed 40% or so of its population working in agriculture to feed the nation around the turn of the twentieth century, but needs only 1% today—to be a large exporter and to produce so much food that it is cheap and wasted too easily. It is crucial to recognize that increased consumption only helps the economy if it is *linked* to such efficiency gains. If we *cannot* feed everyone, market competition to buy and sell more goods for less cost can drive innovations in production that make goods cheaper and less labor-intensive. Eventually, these innovations—not simply the fact that people are consuming more—are what grow the economy. Put another way, the increased demand from consumers is only a means to economic growth if it spurs innovations in productivity.[1] Simply buying more and more stuff does not by itself overcome scarcity.

Thus, this kind of increasingly consumption-driven economy only produces its benefits for the whole population *if* it feeds into the productivity-growth cycle. What Gordon argues is that, in various ways, we have now reaped all the gains that these innovations produced, and that further innovations—however fancy they might be—are unlikely to produce the kinds of massive gains inherent in going from a society without washing machines and running water to one that has these goods and services cheaply. Rather than thinking about economic growth as a steady, abstract force, he instead insists that such growth depends on productivity improvements. But aren't these always happening? Yes, he says, but his "central thesis is that some inventions are more important than others" (Gordon 2016, 2). The gains in what he calls the "special century" are due to certain leaps in basic food, shelter, transportation, and health care that really revolutionized daily life—in a way that even something like Uber does not "revolutionize" transportation productivity. He writes:

> The speed of transportation was increased from that of the "hoof and sail" to the Boeing 707. The temperature of a room was wildly variable in the 19th century but by now is a uniform 70 degrees year round. The transition from rural to urban in the US could only happen once. Only once could electricity be invented and create rapid transit, machine tools, consumer appliances, and the entire electricity-dependent set of entertainment devices from the radio to the TV to

---

1. As Keynes and others saw, in such an economy, there is a need for moderate redistribution in periods of economic recession to keep up effective demand.

the internet and its multiple spin-offs such as the iPod,
iPhone, and iPad. (Gordon, 2012)

The slowdown in growth in advanced economies after 1970
cannot, he says, be somehow turned around with "more markets" producing much more efficiencies and innovations—
there will be innovations, but they simply cannot conceivably
match the leaps that these earlier innovations made, simply
because the exponential gains of the past era are limited by
certain constraints of reality (e.g., we cannot make a day longer
than 24 hours). Thus, dealing with problems like inequality
will require a different strategy, an approach that cannot be
the one used under the growth conditions of the past.

The Context of Economic Systems

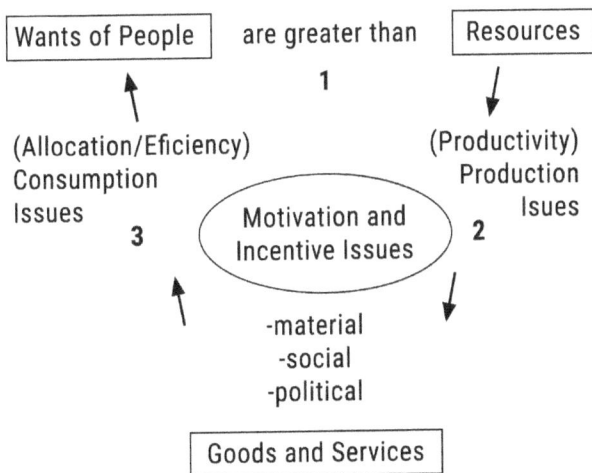

Wants of People	are greater than	Resources

↑ 1 ↓

(Allocation/Eficiency)   (Productivity)
Consumption   Production
Issues   Isues

Motivation and Incentive Issues

3   2

↑
-material
-social
-political

Goods and Services

We can see this vividly if we look at a diagram from Christian economist James Halteman. Halteman's diagram depicts three aspects of how an economy must deal with scarcity (1995, 16). Essentially, a working economy tries to shrink the gaps. Side #2 in the triangle involves improvement in production processes. A good economy improves the efficiency of turning resources into goods and services. Farmers buy equipment that allows higher yields per acre and more acres to be farmed by a single person, or a company develops equipment that it sells to water utilities for processing more water in less time with less energy and fewer workers. Side #3, Halteman says, involves consumption, but what he means is what economists call allocative efficiency—that is, the mechanisms for getting the farmer's food or the clean water to the people who actually need them. Insofar as the price system and Walmart/Amazon (i.e., efficient distribution mechanisms) are improved, goods and services end up going most easily to people who actually need them. The price system, as Econ 101 teaches, is supposed to balance supply and demand in the most efficient way, so that people compare various prices in trade-offs for what they really want, and companies respond by raising or lowering prices. But Halteman concludes (as most economists do), "If the allocation side of the triangle is putting products to their best use and if the production side is using the best resource mix to produce the right goods, then the economy is doing its job" (1995, 18). He leaves out side #1—or rather, he says that in a steady-state economy, the shrinking of side #1 by shrinking people's wants is the only way to go about addressing the economic problem of scarcity, of unmet genuine needs. But now, let's combine Gordon and Halteman: If in fact we have limited possibilities for improvements on sides #2 and #3, maybe the time has come again to solve problems by addressing side #1, instead of suggesting that its gap (between what we have and what we want) should always expand!

This digression into economics could be continued, but I merely wanted to highlight this takeaway point: There are strong *economic* reasons to believe that a key way our developed economy improves for all is by shrinking the side #1 gap—that is, by identifying criteria for "enough," so that goods and services become more available to others who may lack basics. The support for this theory is strengthened if we recall Zamagni's point that the root problem with our current economy is the pessimistic view of human nature, which suggests that every individual is insatiable and therefore rationally selfish. The root problem is we think side #1 in Halteman's diagram is a hopeless project because people are ever-increasing in their wants. I think as Christians we all recognize personally that this is not a lifestyle compatible with Christianity. But we then compartmentalize this insight, assuming it is merely a personal project of spiritual growth. However, I want to push Lubich's original point as a question for EoC businesses: How can that insight about avoiding luxury and embracing simplicity in personal lifestyle be consistent with our way of doing business?

Economy of Communion Simplicity: Compensation Structures and Marketing Practices

I think there are many ways one could imagine doing this—in part, my paper is an invitation to apply these lessons creatively in different EoC settings. But I want to identify two in particular: one, how compensation structures are designed, and two, how products are marketed. Both involve interesting challenges for thinking differently about business—and in somewhat risky ways, but also in ways that could genuinely be beacons of light for a civil economy way of thinking and acting. And both ultimately hinge on taking seriously the need for simpler lifestyles.

First, compensation structures. It is well known that Catholic teaching insists on a basic living wage for workers (an ideal that, I would mention, can only be met if we are willing to define "basic"!), but also allows for differentials in compensation based on rewarding specialized skills and extra contributions (Alford and Naughton 2001, 130–149).[2] A just wage is always a living wage, but it is also a wage that makes some differential judgments about contribution and skill.

The question I want to raise is about other factors often key to compensation. For example, the definition above says nothing about the justice of rewarding seniority, nor does it talk about the degree of differentiation that is fair. Yet these factors often play a large role in wage differentials. Moreover, compensation structures may also unjustly reward what Pope Francis calls "the meritocracy invoked by the elder son [in the Prodigal Son parable] and by many who deny mercy in the name of merit." The pope continues: "An entrepreneur of communion is called to do everything possible so that even those who do wrong and leave home can hope for work and for dignified earnings, and not wind up eating with the swine" (Pope Francis 2017).

I can speak most easily to the (somewhat unusual) business I am in. In academia, seniority among faculty often plays a very large role in wage differentiation, and there is also considerable angst about the differential in wages between faculty and administration, sometimes because it is not clear that administrators contribute significantly more to the enterprise than faculty. Resolving these problems is not an exact science, to be sure. However, a road I have not seen taken is to ask a new set of questions about needs. In my own situation in Washington, DC, the presumptions of the seniority system have created some real challenges. On the one hand, junior faculty just out of grad school, especially ones with young families, are faced with an exorbitantly priced housing market that is driven by the large population of white-collar professionals in the region

---

2. For a detailed explanation and application of these magisterially-established criteria, see Alford & Naughton, *Managing*, 130–149.

who make (to put it mildly) considerably more than our assistant professors. But on the other hand, I have senior colleagues who are full professors, who bought houses decades ago when the DC market was actually pretty reasonable, and who have paid them off, and whose kids are grown and on their way. Yet these senior colleagues make considerably more right now than do my junior colleagues.

You can probably see what I'm getting at—and why it is pretty challenging! I am not suggesting that anyone should be pushed to live on the margins (although some of the junior faculty I know pretty much qualify!). I am genuinely asking whether a more fair—or at least a more communion-oriented—compensation scheme would ask *some* questions about needs, and make *some* adjustments to compensation based on these needs, rather than simply following the typical norms that govern compensation arrangements in the ordinary economy.

What does this have to do with simpler lifestyles? Well, such a proposal requires everyone at an organization to ask hard questions about what they really need. Of course, there are many other related questions: Are there other areas of expense that could be targeted to give junior faculty a raise? Could the organization do something unique to address the specific cost crisis (in housing) that could be dealt with separately from compensation structures? But unless the enterprise is truly awash in money, it would seem reasonable to suggest that compensation structures could also be questioned, insofar as the ever-rising pay for seniority implies the inevitable selfishness of the agents and their ever-increasing wants. Of course, many senior employees may in fact use their higher salaries in non-self-interested ways—the point is that by not even asking this question about what is needed, and instead merely presuming that more senior employees will want higher compensation, we may unwittingly reinforce the pessimistic account of human nature of inevitable self-interest.

Secondly, in thinking about consistency of simplicity of lifestyle, EoC businesses can think creatively about marketing. John Gallagher and Jeanne Buckeye have already commented on the importance of thinking about promotion efforts in EoC businesses. Ideally, they suggest that advertising should perform the admirable task of communicating to consumers that are "hungry for information" about a company and its product, while also being "on guard" against "depend[ing] heavily on psychology to turn wants into needs or . . . promot[ing] consumerism" (Gallagher and Buckeye 2014, 51). This description is a helpful place to start thinking about how a business can market with simplicity of lifestyle as a moral value. I recently wrote an essay in which I fleshed out the business responsibilities for producing what the Magisterium calls "goods that are truly good"—and in it, I suggested that one of the key areas of interest is the tendency of our society to market "futile goods"—goods that may not be in themselves bad, but which in their marketing suggest that somehow the consuming of this good is genuinely a path toward happiness (Cloutier 2018). But at issue in the marketing is not simply whether a particular good is futile, but whether the promises made in the advertising make the consumer believe in a certain (false) vision of happiness. The promises go far beyond, as one author puts it, the functional. In marketing literature, there is almost no neutral marketing in terms of implying a vision of happiness that is associated with the product or service. As marketing theorist Allan Kimmel puts it, "Choices of goods and services . . . are intimately linked to consumer lifestyles: the distinctive or characteristic ways of living adopted by consumer segments or communities" (Kimmel 2015, 101). All marketing implies something about lifestyles, whether it is the reckless adventure that Taco Bell or Mountain Dew associate constantly with their "extreme" food or the care for farmers and land that brands like Whole Foods and Chipotle tie to their products. We are often preoccupied by the question of whether marketers are lying, but perhaps we overlook the further question: What's the value or dis-value of the lifestyle that is being sold?

It is obvious, I think, that in terms of lifestyle, marketing almost always aims aspirationally. That is to say, it presents a lifestyle higher than the one people are actually living. The people at the restaurant are more carefree than we are, the SUV inevitably ends up parked on an incredibly scenic mountain vista or outside a swanky restaurant, the kitchen in which the dish soap is used looks better than our kitchen. How often, by contrast, do we see marketing for a product where well-off people come off as fools or where a store (rather than suggesting endless selection) advertises how well-selected its simple products are? How about a realtor or a housing developer that, instead of emphasizing everything luxury, says "What we're about is getting you a solid, safe, simple house at the best price"?

Conclusion

As these examples may display, I probably would not have made a good marketing executive! But the point here is to recognize that marketing matters morally. Living a consistent lifestyle is not simply a matter of making products that are actually good for people, but marketing them in a way that pays attention to the lifestyle assumptions embedded in the messaging. The typical aspirational messaging, whether directly or indirectly, reinforces the idea that consumers should cultivate ever-higher lifestyle standards. While risky, I do not think it is far-fetched to imagine marketing that emphatically connects a good or service with a simpler, rather than a more luxurious, life. Indeed, we very much need that counter-message out there, and there are probably ways to do it that would in fact appeal to a portion of many people's value systems. In writing on this, Catholic business ethicist Jim Wishloff notes that marketing should "do even more today" to "encourage people to simplify their lives" and "help people find a place for contemplation and prayer" (2016, 129).

These two suggestions for EoC businesses are certainly not meant as exhaustive; there may be many other ways to approach the underlying project of integrating simplicity of life into the workplace, rather than simply viewing it as a private personal commitment.[3] In this essay, I have pointed out the reasons to pursue this project extending beyond Chiara Lubich's original call for EoC businesses to overcome "split lifestyles." Such an account can be important to challenge inadequate pessimistic accounts of human nature as inherently and inevitably self-interested, as well as to address real economic challenges of inequality faced especially in developed economies. In doing so, EoC businesses can continue to function as important beacons of light and hope for an economy that serves the real ends of human life and the unity of the human race.

Bibliography

Alford, Helen and Michael Naughton. 2001. *Managing As If Faith Mattered: Christian Social Principles in the Modern Organization.* Notre Dame: University of Notre Dame Press.

Benedict XVI, Pope. 2009. *Caritas in Veritate.* http://www.vatican.va/content/benedict-xvi/en/encyclicals/documents/hf_ben-xvi_enc_20090629_caritas-in-veritate.html.

---

3. Further explorations might attend to Richard Reeves' analysis of the tendencies of the aspirations of upper-middle class families to crowd out others in the society (see *Dream Hoarders: How the American Upper Middle Class is Leaving Everyone Else in the Dust, Why that is a Problem, and What to Do About It* [Washington, DC: Brookings, 2017]) and Craig Gay's theological critique of how consumer societies encourage a "romanticist" view of self-creation through ever-more-complex consumption habits (see "Sensualists Without Heart: Contemporary Consumerism in Light of the Modern Project," in *The Consuming Passion,* ed. Rodney Clapp [Downers Grove, IL: InterVaristy Press, 1998], 19–39).

Clark, Charles M.A. 2006. "Wealth as Abundance and Scarcity." In *Rediscovering Abundance*, edited by Helen Alford et al., 28–56. Notre Dame: University of Notre Dame Press.

Cloutier, David. 2015. *The Vice of Luxury: Economic Excess in a Consumer Age.* Washington, DC: Georgetown University Press.

_____. 2018. "Delivering a Truly Better Life: How Can Consumers and Firms Seek Good Goods?" presented at the 2018 True Wealth of Nations conference at the Institute for Advanced Catholic Studies at the University of Southern California. Subsequently published in 2021 as "How Consumers and Firms Can Seek Good Goods." In *Business Ethics and Catholic Social Thought*, edited by Daniel K. Finn. Washington, DC: Georgetown University Press.

Crivelli, Luca. 2020. "Economy of Communion, Poverty and a Humanized Economy." In *Business, Faith and the Economy of Communion,* edited Andrew Gustafson and Celeste Harvey. Special Volume of *Journal of Religion and Society*, supp. 22: 20–26. See also this volume, *Finding Faith in Business: An Economy of Communion Vision*, edited by Andrew Gustafson and Celeste Harvey. Hyde Park, NY: New City Press.

Dasgupta, Partha. 2007. *Economics: A Very Short Introduction.* New York: Oxford UP.

Dicastery for Promoting Integral Human Development. 2018. *Vocation of the Business Leader: A Reflection.* St. Paul, MN: University Of St. Thomas Press. https://www.stthomas. edu/media/catholicstudies/center/ryan/publications/ publicationpdfs/vocationofthebusinessleaderpdf/ FinalTextTheVocationoftheBusinessLeader.pdf.

Francis I, Pope. 2015. *Laudato Si'.* http://www.vatican.va/content/ francesco/en/encyclicals/documents/papa-francesco_20150524_ enciclica-laudato-si.html.

_____. 2017. *Address of His Holiness Pope Francis to Participants in the Meeting "Economy of Communion", Sponsored by the Focolare Movement.* https://w2.vatican.va/content/francesco/en/ speeches/2017/february/documents/papa-francesco_20170204_ focolari.html.

Gallagher, John and Jeanne Buckeye. 2014. *Structures of Grace: The Business Practices of the Economy of Communion*. Hyde Park, NY: New City Press.

Gay, Craig. 1998. "Sensualists Without Heart: Contemporary Consumerism in Light of the Modern Project." In *The Consuming Passion*, edited by Rodney Clapp, 19–39. Downers Grove, IL: InterVarsity Press.

Gordon, Robert J. 2012. "Is US Growth Over?" September 11, 2012. https://voxeu.org/article/us-economic-growth-over.

Gordon, Robert J. 2016. *The Rise and Fall of American Growth*. Princeton: Princeton University Press.

Halteman, James. 1995. *The Clashing Worlds of Economics and Faith*. Scottsdale, PA: Herald Press.

Hirschman, Albert. 1977. *The Passions and the Interests: Political Arguments for Capitalism Before Its Triumph*. Princeton: Princeton University Press.

Hume, David. 1953. "Of Commerce." In *Political Essays*, edited by Charles W. Hendel, 130–141. Indianapolis: Bobbs-Merrill.

John Paul, Pope. 1987. *Sollicitudo Rei Socialis*. http://www.vatican.va/content/john-paul-ii/en/encyclicals/documents/hf_jp-ii_enc_30121987_sollicitudo-rei-socialis.html.

_____. 1991. *Centesimus Annus*. http://www.vatican.va/content/john-paul-ii/en/encyclicals/documents/hf_jp-ii_enc_01051991_centesimus-annus.html.

Kennedy, Gavin. 2009. "Amartya Sen's Two Brilliant Essays on the Relevance of Adam Smith Today." http://adamsmithslostlegacy.blogspot.com/2009/03/amarya-sens-two-brilliant-essays-on.html.

Kimmel, Allan. 2015. *People and Products: Consumer Behavior and Product Design*. New York: Routledge.

Lubich, Chiara. 2002. "The Experience of the Economy of Communion: A Proposal of Economic Action from the Spirituality of Unity." In *The Economy of Communion: Toward a Multi-Dimensional*

Economic Culture, edited by Luigino Bruni, 14–20. Hyde Park, NY: New City Press.

MacIntyre, Alasdair. 1984. *After Virtue*. Notre Dame: University of Notre Dame Press.

Mandeville, Bernard. 1714. *The Fable of The Bees: or, Private Vices, Publick Benefits* (orig. 1714). https://oll.libertyfund.org/titles/mandeville-the-fable-of-the-bees-or-private-vices-publick-benefits-vol-1#chapter_66840.

Minsky, Hyman. 1975. *Keynes*. New York: Columbia UP.

Paul VI, Pope. 1967. *Populorum Progressio*. https://www.google.com/search?q=Populorum+Progressio%2C+no.+21.&rlz=1C-1GCEA_enUS819US850&oq=Populorum+Progressio%2C+-no.+21.&aqs=chrome..69i57j0l2.1341j0j4&sourceid=-chrome&ie=UTF-8.

Pielke, Roger Jr. 2012. "Gordon vs. Gordon on Growth." October 14, 2012. http://rogerpielkejr.blogspot.com/2012/10/gordon-vs-gordon-on-growth.html.

Reeves, Richard. 2017. *Dream Hoarders: How the American Upper Middle Class is Leaving Everyone Else in the Dust, Why that is a Problem, and What to Do About It*. Washington, DC: Brookings.

Smith, Adam. 1976. *The Theory of Moral Sentiments*. Oxford: Clarendon Press.

Wishloff, Jim. 2016. "Freedom as the Call to Being: Restoring the Foundations of Ethical Enterprise." In *Free Markets with Solidarity and Sustainability*, edited by Martin Schlag & Juan A. Mercado, 113–134. Washington, DC: CUA Press.

Zamagni, Stefano. 2002. "On the Foundation and Meaning of the Economy of Communion Experience." In *The Economy of Communion: Towards A Multi-Dimensional Economic Culture*, edited by Luigino Bruni. Translated by Lorna Gold, 130–140. Hyde Park, NY: New City Press.

_____. 2017. "Traces of Civil Economy in Early Modern French Economic Thought." *International Studies in Catholic Education* 9, no. 2: 176–191.

Chapter 6

Economy of Communion:
A Different Attitude to Work

Angus Sibley, Paris, France

Abstract: Conventional economic theory and practice see work as a disutility: something that we dislike and prefer to avoid. So we eliminate work wherever possible, replacing human workers with machinery or electronics, thus enabling us to produce and consume more, with less input of work. But we in the richer countries are now producing and consuming too much, overstraining the earth's resources. The theory of disutility is radically wrong, because we need, and God intends us, to work; "where there is no work there is no dignity!" (Pope Francis). Elimination of human work also reflects the belief that the primary duty of a business is to maximize profits; this is a basic error, implying that owners of a business are entitled to manage it solely for their own benefit, without regard for the common good. Economy of Communion firms endeavor to put into practice a more humane and civilized conception of work.

Work as Disutility: a Too-Common Error

Our views on work, as they have developed during the latter decades of the last century, leave a great deal to be desired. Orthodox economics generally assumes that work is something we would always rather not do: a disutility, in economists' jargon. In this jargon, the word utility means what we consider desirable and satisfying, what makes us happy, what we all are believed to aim for.

Thus David Spencer, professor of economics and political economy at Leeds University Business School, has noted, with disapproval, that "in the language of economics, work is a 'disutility' that all of us would prefer to do without" but to "reduce work's importance to a feeling of pain is to miss the fundamental role of work in the fulfilment of our needs both as consumers and producers" (Spencer 2013). He has hard words for those who "see workers as incorrigible 'shirkers.'" The belief that work has no value to us apart from the money it earns, or the results it produces, leads naturally to the view that work should be eliminated wherever technology (or, for that matter, shirking) makes that possible. In this school of thought, there is no place for the notion that work can and should be in itself a source of enjoyment and satisfaction. Nor is there recognition of the fact that there is a real human need to perform work, quite apart from the need for its remuneration. As Pope Francis observes, "it is hard to have dignity without work" (2013).

In case you think that Spencer exaggerates, I point out that the well-known Austrian economist Ludwig von Mises (1881–1979) explicitly endorsed the theory of shirkers. He claimed that obligatory health insurance is "an institution which tends to encourage disease by weakening or completely destroying the will to be well and able to work" (1951, 477). He also condemned all assistance for the unemployed, arguing that "what the unemployed miss is not work but the remuneration of work" (1951, 485), implying that unemployed workers will always prefer to remain idle if they can claim benefits. These offensive diatribes would not matter if Mises were just an obscure and deservedly forgotten foreign economist. Unfortunately, he has a significant following in America. The Mises Institute in Auburn, Alabama, is a research institute

which regards him almost as a demi-god; with more than 350
faculty members, it publishes a stream of books and periodi-
cals, organises seminars, and runs a gigantic website.

An Exaggerated Pursuit of Efficiency

Negative views of work underpin the massive emphasis, in
economic theory and practice, on enhancing labor productivity: that is, producing what we need or desire with less
input of human labor. Or, indeed, producing more with the
same, or even less, input of work. This is seen as "more efficient," and therefore better. The famous American journalist
Henry Hazlitt (1894–1993), an admirer of Mises', gave us an
egregious example of this way of thinking when he ridiculed
the "mirage of full employment," asserting that "it would be
far better . . . to have maximum production with part of the
population supported in idleness by undisguised relief, than
to provide 'full employment' by so many forms of disguised
make-work that production is disorganized" (Hazlitt 2008,
56). In other words, industrial efficiency should take precedence over human welfare. Such a notion stands in sharp
contrast with the EoC principle of "the priority of human
labor over capital," reflecting Pope John Paul II's words (1981,
§12). Or, indeed, those of Abraham Lincoln: "Labor is the
superior of capital, and deserves much the higher consideration" (Lincoln 1861).

The Economy of Communion (EoC) philosophy embraces
the view that a business should not insist on employing people
solely on the basis of their contribution to profits, but should
be willing sometimes to employ workers who, in particular
situations, do not guarantee economic returns, for example, to
help people with disabilities to earn their living. This reflects
the EoC principle that "love can occupy a central position in
economic life," meaning love not in its romantic sense but as
agape, that is, "a feeling of brotherhood and goodwill towards

other people, a deep concern for the other as a person" (Bruni and Zamagni 2004, 91). Needless to say, in conditions of intense competition it may be impossible for a business to follow that precept. Here we have a strong argument for willingness, by both lawmakers and entrepreneurs, to accept certain restraints on competition, as I shall discuss below. We should note also that EoC principles imply a decisive rejection of the attitude of the all-too-dominant libertarian economist Friedrich von Hayek, who argued that we should "gain from not treating one another as neighbors" (Hayek 1992, 13).

Our current obsession with efficiency leads to major problems. One is that, if we persist in enhancing labor productivity, then we have ever-rising unemployment, unless we continually increase our production, and hence our consumption. Therefore, in order to avoid intolerable levels of unemployment, we are all obsessed with achieving and maintaining conventional economic growth. But we in the richer countries are already producing too much; we are using up the earth's resources in an unsustainable manner. Orthodox economic strategy is running into the buffers of limited planetary resources. Hazlitt's enthusiasm for "maximum production" is clearly obsolete.

On July 29, 2019, the Global Footprint Network announced that "earth overshoot day" had arrived. This meant that, between the beginning of the year and that date, human consumption of renewable natural resources had reached the level of what can be regenerated in one full year. Thus, for the rest of that year we were in "overshoot." Only five years prior, in 2014, overshoot day was reached 21 days later, on August 19. Clearly, the problem of overconsumption of resources is rapidly growing worse.

Yet we cannot tackle this issue simply by drastically cutting back our consumption, and thus our production. That would lead straight to massive unemployment. The basic problem is that, globally speaking, our highly efficient industries are now producing too much, but employing too few of us (International Labor Organization 2019, 1–2).[1] If we were to cut our production and consumption to sustainable levels, without other major changes in our habits, levels of unemployment would be horrific. This is the dilemma we have brought upon ourselves by treating work as a disutility and eliminating it as far as possible.

What Kind of Productivity?

We have concentrated too heavily on labor productivity and given too little attention to other kinds of productivity. The fishing industry provides a vivid example of this error. It is estimated that the global catch of marine fish, about 80 million tons per annum (FAO 2018, 8),[2] is divided more or less equally between traditional small-scale fishing, commonly defined as using boats of no more than 15 meters, and large-scale "industrial" fishing (Jacquet and Pauly 2008, 832–33). The latter employs about half a million people worldwide, while small-scale fishing employs more than 12 million for a similar total catch (Jacquet and Pauly 2008, 833). Thus, industrial fisheries show far higher labor productivity than traditional—a spectacular example of the economies of scale favored by conventional economic theory.

But the industrial sector consumes four times as much fuel as the small-scale sector; so industrial fishing has much worse fuel productivity, while also, of course, producing much higher carbon emissions. Moreover, industrial fishing discards substantial quantities of unwanted dead fish, while small-scale fishers discard very little. So the industrial sector performs

---

1. The ILO's report shows a worldwide unemployment total of 170 million (5.0% of total workforce) and highlights the "poor quality" of many jobs: "overall, 2 billion people were in informal employment in 2016, accounting for 61% of the world's workforce" (2).
2. This figure excludes farmed fishing (aquaculture).

worse in terms of resource productivity—it consumes more of the natural resource (live fish) for a similar output of saleable fish. It can also be very damaging to marine ecology. Having our fish caught by as few fishers as possible has proved to be bad for employment, bad for the environment, and wasteful of natural resources.

We see that our obsession with conventional efficiency has led us badly astray. A move back toward more traditional methods, in agriculture and other sectors as well as in fishing, could yield more employment opportunities, less pollution, less waste of resources, and less damage to our environment. It is encouraging to note that, in many countries, there are significant trends toward reinstating local small-scale production. An American example is the rapid growth of craft breweries, which now number well over 7,000, as compared with fewer than 550 in 1994 (Brewers Association 2018). Craft brewing, whose market share is now estimated at more than 13 percent, continues to grow, even though total beer production in America has been declining in recent years.

It may be objected that traditional, small-scale production methods generally imply more expensive products. But at present we use many of our products very wastefully. According to a well-known scientific estimate, "30–50% of all food produced never reaches a human stomach" (Institute of Mechanical Engineers 2013); in developed countries, this wastage occurs largely in shops, restaurants, canteens, and homes. We buy more than we eat. Eliminating much of this waste could compensate for higher costs per unit of production. And higher prices would, of course, discourage waste.

The Degradation of Work

As the Czech economist Tomas Sedlacek has observed, "in our constant desire to have always more, we have sacrificed the agreeable aspects of work" (Sedlacek 2011, 217). High-productivity industry has long been a source of tedious and un-satisfying work. In effect, there has been tacit agreement to a kind of trade-off: workers should willingly endure the dismal grind of the assembly line, because this enables them to enjoy an abundance of consumer goods in their leisure time. Here again we see a denial of the idea that work should be not only useful, but also agreeable and good for us. It is an example of the dichotomies often found in the conventional economic world, such as the idea that, while one is expected to be gen-erous and considerate to others in private life, in business life one is expected to be ruthless, even rapacious. Chiara Lubich expressly rejected this "separation of spheres": "Those involved in the business enterprises of the economy of communion seek to follow . . . the same style of behaviour that they live out in all ambits of life" (Lubich 1999).

According to leading English economist John Kay, emer-itus professor at Oxford University and London School of Economics, in recent times many businesspeople have come to "accept that business values are different from those of other activities; they describe the nature and purpose of busi-ness in terms that would seem grotesque if applied to other spheres of life" (Kay 1998, 25). Kay ridiculed the widespread, but deplorably narrow, view that business managers have no responsibility to society "other than to make as much money for their stockholders as possible" (Friedman 2002, 133), as the Chicago economist Milton Friedman notoriously put it. Outside the business world, it is normal to recognize a diversity of responsibilities that need to be kept in balance. As a parent, for example, one has responsibilities to one's children, but also to one's spouse, to one's employer or one's clients, perhaps to one's church, labor union, political party or other organization, not to mention one's duty to respect the environment and generally to behave as a good citizen. The idea that, in business management, one can forget diverse responsibilities and focus exclusively on the bottom line leads to grave problems; in particular, to human resources policies that treat employees as disposable commodities, unworthy of respect or consideration.

The French telephone company France Télécom (now called Orange) became notorious in 2009 and subsequent years for its efforts to enhance profitability and to adapt to a fiercely competitive business environment by way of drastic cuts in its staff. The company resorted to intensive harassment of workers with intent to make them resign voluntarily. A consultant's report based on a questionnaire submitted to all employees stated that "the general sentiment was very bad, particularly concerning working conditions, health, and stress" (Calignon 2009). Between 2008 and 2011, the Observatoire du Stress, a watchdog organization set up by two leading labor unions, recorded among France Télécom employees more than 60 suicides and almost 40 attempted suicides, while many other workers suffered serious depression and other psychological symptoms (franceinfo).

Profit and Its Functions

Friedman's theory of absolute priority for shareholder value is theologically objectionable. It implies that stockholders are entitled to expect management to exploit their business exclusively for its proprietors' maximum private benefit. This runs counter to the doctrine, common to both Christianity and Judaism, that all earthly property basically belongs to God, and that we hold it as tenants or stewards, not as absolute owners. Accordingly, our claims to property are limited by the duty to use it in ways that are consistent with the common good. The Catholic Church teaches that "man should regard the external things that he legitimately possesses not merely as his own but as common, in the sense that they should be able to benefit not only himself but also others" (Paul VI 1965, §69).

Businesses run on EoC principles do indeed aim for profitability, but not as an end in itself. Profits are used for the development of the business, for education in EoC principles and practice, and to help those who suffer poverty and exclusion. Profits should be adequate rather than maximum.

The Case against Excessive Competition

Another EoC principle is fair behavior toward competitors, as opposed to the ruthless competition recommended by free-market economists. These theorists want unrestrained competition to force firms to crack down on costs, so as to provide consumer goods and services at the lowest possible prices, so that we can all consume as much as possible. This is the behavior that has led us to our present situation, where consumption of resources has expanded till it is extravagant and unsustainable, while fierce competition often leads to niggardly treatment of workers.

In fact, unrestrained competition is at variance with the aim of maximizing profits. Logically, businesses that seek to make as much profit as possible should agree among themselves not to compete too fiercely, so as to keep their prices high. But that is considered a mortal sin by free-market economists. It is prohibited by law in many countries today, with severe penalties for those who are caught attempting to behave less than fully competitively. Here we have an internal contradiction in the theory and practice of orthodox economics.

Too much competition has left us with too few competitors. In the absence of restraint on price-cutting, the bigger producers, thanks to their economies of scale, are able to undercut the smaller producers' prices, and often to drive them out of business. Thus we have the excessive concentration that is evident today in many business sectors, contributing to our problems of exorbitant inequalities and of undue corporate political influence.

Restraint of Competition

We have not always been so obsessive about maximizing competition. As recently as 1970 Sir Antony Hornby, senior partner in the London stockbroking house Cazenove & Co., gave a speech on his retirement in which he said: "One must be generous as well as competitive. One cannot profit at other people's expense. One's friends and even competitors must be allowed to profit as well" (quoted in Chancellor). That was in the days when, in the City of London, many restraints on competition were tolerated. Hornby's remarks would be widely ridiculed today.

But the idea that competition should be restrained has a long history. In the Jewish world, the extent to which competition may be permitted to damage livelihoods has been debated since ancient times, and it is debated still. The Talmud records (Bava Bathra 21b) the argument of Rabbi Huna (c. 216–296 AD): If a man has set up a mill in an alley, and another arrives later and sets up a similar mill next door, "the first one may prevent him from doing so if he wishes, as he can say to him: You are disrupting my livelihood by taking my customers." Elsewhere (Makkoth 24a) it is said that the phrase "he that does no evil to his neighbour" (Psalm 15:3) may be taken to mean "he who does not infringe upon another's trade" (Talmud).

In the thirteenth century, the Spanish rabbi Adret Solomon ben Abraham (known as The Rashba) ruled that "while one may open a rival business, one may not actively pursue people who are known to be regular customers of the first proprietor" (Jachter 2000). In our own times, a leading Jerusalem rabbi, Moshe Sternbuch, has ruled that one may open a new restaurant next to an existing one, but must not set prices so low as to drive the older house out of business (Pfeffer 2015).

These rulings are based primarily upon the prohibition in the Torah of *hasagat gevul* (or *hasagas gevul*), a phrase whose original meaning was encroachment upon one's neighbor's land by moving the boundary stones. Thus we read "cursed be he who removes his neighbor's landmark" (Deuteronomy 27:17).[3] This prohibition is deemed to extend to unfair or predatory competition that may damage or destroy the livelihood of others; the phrase *hasagat gevul* has indeed become a synonym for unfair competition. Such behavior is viewed as a form of theft. Thus it is argued that, although the Bible does not explicitly discuss commercial competition, the EoC principle of fair treatment of competitors is, in fact, implied by the Law of Moses.

The idea that elimination of a person's livelihood is a kind of theft may appear bizarre from the standpoint of present-day economic ideology. It is not theft, it is simply "creative destruction"! And is it not said that "bankruptcy is a sign that the free market is working"? Same goes for loss of employment. But perhaps we need to take that seemingly bizarre idea rather more seriously. The legal obligation, in many countries, to provide special cash payments on severance or redundancy recognizes, up to a point, that termination of employment is an injury that requires compensation. In America, there are no statutory rights to such payments, though some contracts of employment—usually those agreed between employers and unions—do impose compensation requirements.

Transmuting Needs into Benefits

The EoC philosophy embraces the idea that "the poor offer us a gift of their needs," a concept that seems strange at first sight. Need is, after all, a negative condition, a lack of something. How can anyone offer us a negative gift? This concept is generally understood to mean that the existence of poverty

---

3.   See also Deuteronomy 19:14, Proverbs 22:28, Hosea 5:10.

provides opportunities for those who are better-off to behave compassionately and generously by helping the poor.

Pope Leo XIII, in his encyclical *Graves de Communi Re* of 1901, wrote that "No one is so rich that he does not need another's help; no one is so poor as not to be useful in some way to his fellow man; and the disposition to ask assistance from others with confidence and to grant it with kindness is part of our very nature" (§16). Thus we may say that giving a helping hand to those in need is an expression of the better part of our nature, a kind of self-fulfilment for those who practice charity, and thus a "gift" for us helpers as well as for those we help.

We should be careful, however, to avoid the error of thinking that it is a good thing, or even the will of God, that some people are very poor, since these people give others an opportunity to gain merit, or to achieve self-fulfillment, by assisting them. That is an argument for not attempting to reform our society and economy, for confining ourselves to soothing the wounds of those who are damaged by our deeply flawed systems. We need to tackle the flaws.

It has been said, rather unkindly, that some rich people "use the poor as the vehicle of their own salvation." One hears occasionally the argument that, if we were to succeed in eliminating serious poverty, we might become callous and insensitive, because then no one would need our compassion and help. But this argument is feeble. Quite apart from poverty, there are plenty of other reasons for people to need help. There are illnesses and disabilities, disappointments of all kinds, problems in our work, our personal relationships, the care of our children, the difficulties of old age and bereavement. . . . Everyone needs the help of others, and there is nothing wrong with that. Total self-reliance is neither possible nor desirable.

We read that "there will be no poor among you . . . if only you will obey the voice of the LORD your God, being careful to do all this commandment which I command you this day" (Deuteronomy 15:4–5). This endorses the view that severe poverty is a result of human misbehavior, and not, as some would have it, of divine intention. We should strive to make our societies function in such a way that, ideally, nobody falls into a state of destitution. According to Pope Benedict, "the pursuit of justice must be a fundamental norm of the state. . . . The aim of a just social order is to guarantee to each person . . . his share of the community's goods" (2005, §26).

For another understanding of the paradox of the negative gift, it may help to recall the old saying "necessity is the mother of invention." Many a valuable invention has been devised to meet a specific need. Long ago, our ancestors invented the wheel in response to the need to shift heavy loads. Today, the development of wind turbines and photovoltaic panels helps us meet our need for greener energy. Thus a negative state of need can be transmuted into a positive innovation that benefits everyone.

Today, poverty is very often a consequence of unemployment, or of low-quality employment: jobs that are ephemeral, unstable, underpaid, in degrading conditions, or seriously disagreeable and unsatisfying. As Pope John Paul II observed, "the 'poor' appear . . . because a low value is put on work" (1981, §8). There are many people who have a real and pressing need for better-quality jobs. This necessity challenges us to invent, or reinvent, or develop more humane and civilized forms of employment. By taking up this challenge, we may hope to find better ways of organizing our economy, leading us to a fairer and happier society, a benefit or gift for us all.

The Need for Opportunities to Work

We should never forget that work is intended by God to be in itself a source of satisfaction, and even enjoyment, not simply a pain to be suffered in exchange for its results. St. Thomas wrote that the work of Adam in the Garden of Eden, before his disobedience and fall, "would not have been laborious, but joyful, being the exercise of his natural powers" (Aquinas 1981, I.102.3). One seems to hear a distant echo of that fine sentence in Marx, who claimed that, in his socialist utopia, "labor becomes attractive work, the individual's self-fulfilment, which in no way means that it becomes mere fun, mere amusement" (Marx 1973, 611). Marx's very positive view of work no doubt helps to explain his enduring appeal to many people, despite the serious flaws in his arguments.

The ideal, toward which we must strive, is that everyone should have opportunities to work, and to enjoy their work itself, as well as the rewards it earns. This means that we must discard the notion that it is always desirable to cut back the need for human work, replacing it with machinery or electronics.

There exist practical and successful examples of better-quality employment, not only in small or medium-sized private companies, but also in large businesses. The British retail stores group John Lewis Partnership is wholly owned by a trust whose beneficiaries are the group's 85,000 employees, known as partners or members. This firm has a constitution that makes clear its goals: The Partnership's ultimate purpose is the happiness of all its members. Here is a striking contrast with businesses that claim that their primary purpose is to please their customers, or that follow Milton Friedman's advice by prioritizing maximum profits for their stockholders. But if you think that John Lewis must be a shaky outfit with discontented customers and weak finances reflecting inadequate profits, you are mistaken. The firm, whose constitution dates from 1929, has a long record of steady growth, excellent customer service, and financial soundness.

The MIT Sloan School of Management professor Zeynep Ton has published The Good Jobs Strategy, a fascinating study of employment practices in retail businesses. She argues that "model retailers err on the side of overstaffing, and cut waste everywhere they can find it except when it comes to labor" (2014, 15 and 154). This notion flies in the face of much current thinking and practice, which aims to prune payroll costs to the bone for the sake of competitiveness. But it accords with the Catholic and EoC view that labor must not be regarded as a commodity like oil or copper or paper, of which we should not consume more than is strictly necessary.

Ton argues that "understaffing costs are higher than overstaffing costs" (2014, 161). She sharply criticizes retailers that strive to shrink their costs by employing too few people, neglecting to train them in good working practice, and demotivating them by treating them meanly. Stores managed on these lines, she says, turn out to be badly run, wasteful of stock and unattractive to customers: "more and more customers complain about understaffed stores" (158). She cites several examples of retail groups that avoid these errors, including Costco in America (quoted on NASDAQ), and Mercadona in Spain (a family-owned concern). Both these companies "explicitly put customers and employees ahead of their shareholders" (198); yet both have long records of successful, profitable trading.

A More Civilized Understanding of Work

The Jewish philosopher Michael Walzer writes that "work itself is one of the things that men and women need, and that the community must help provide whenever they are unable to provide it for themselves and for one another" (1993, 92). Professor Spencer highlights "the necessity to create and widen opportunities for people to experience their work as fulfilling, rather than as just a disutility" (2013, 485.). Pope Benedict XVI eloquently describes work as it should be:

> Work that expresses the essential dignity of every man and woman . . . effectively associating workers, both men and women, with the development of their

community ... work that permits workers to organize themselves freely, and to make their voices heard; work that leaves enough room for rediscovering one's roots at a personal, familial and spiritual level; work that guarantees those who have retired a decent standard of living. (2009, §63)

EoC businesses strive to put these ideas into practice. There are around 800 of these firms worldwide. Many have demonstrated that it is possible to run a viable and successful business without following the inhumane, worker-unfriendly habits that too often flow from reliance on economic doctrines that were prevalent in the nineteenth century, were largely suspended in the mid-twentieth, but unhappily have become fashionable again since the 1970s.

Ever since Adam Smith, economic orthodoxy has, more often than not, been biased against us workers and in favour of us consumers. Smith called for the abolition of craftsmen's guilds, to prevent workers from "organizing themselves freely," as Pope Benedict put it. Smith argued that this would cut the profits of the master-craftsmen, and the wages of their workmen; thus "the public would be a gainer, the products of all artificers coming in this way much cheaper to market" (1776, I.2.2). In other words, squeeze us workers to indulge us consumers, to enable us to consume more. But today, we consumers are consuming too much, overstretching the earth's resources. So this strategy no longer makes any sense, if it ever did.

We face an urgent need to turn the page on much of our conventional economic thinking. The Economy of Communion movement is helping to show us the way.

Bibliography

Aquinas, St Thomas. 1981. *Summa Theologiae*. Notre Dame, IN: Ave Maria Press.

Benedict XVI, Pope. 2005. *Deus Caritas Est.* https://w2.vatican.
va/content/benedict-xvi/en/encyclicals/documents/hf_ben-
xvi_enc_20051225_deus-caritas-est.html.

_____. 2009. *Caritas in Veritate.* https://www.vatican.va/
content/benedict-xvi/en/encyclicals/documents/hf_ben-
xvi_enc_20090629_caritas-in-veritate.html.

Brewers' Association. 2018. Brewers Association Website. (www.
brewersassociation.org).

Bruni, Luigino and Stefano Zamagni. 2004. "The Economy of
Communion: Inspirations and Achievements." *Revue Finance
et Bien Commun* 20: 91–97.

Calignon, Guillaume de. 2009. "L'enquête de Technologia accable la
direction de France Télécom." *Les Echos* (December 15). https://
www.lesechos.fr/2009/12/lenquete-de-technologia-accable-la-
direction-de-france-telecom-470307.

Chancellor, Edward. 2001. "City Slackers." *Prospect Magazine*
(July 20). https://www.prospectmagazine.co.uk/culture/56305/
city-slackers.

Food and Agriculture Organization of the United Nations. 2018.
The State of World Fisheries and Aquaculture. http://www.fao.
org/state-of-fisheries-aquaculture.

Franceinfo. 2019. "Suicides à France Télécom: l'article à lire."
Franceinfo. https://www.francetvinfo.fr/economie/emploi/
carriere/vie-professionnelle/sante-au-travail/suicides-a-france-
telecom-l-article-a-lire-pour-comprendre-pourquoi-orange-
se-retrouve-devant-la-justice_3423431.html.

Francis, Pope. 2013. *Address to Workers in Cagliari.* http://w2.vatican.
va/content/francesco/en/speeches/2013/september/documents/
papa-francesco_20130922_lavoratori-cagliari.html.

Friedman, Milton. 2002. *Capitalism and Freedom* [1962]. Chicago:
University of Chicago Press.

Hayek, Fredeich von. 1992. *The Fatal Conceit.* London: Routledge.

Hazlitt, Henry. 2008. *Economics in One Lesson* [1946]. Auburn, AL: The Ludwig von Mises Institute.

The International Labor Organization. 2019. "World Employment Social Outlook: Trends 2019." https://www.ilo.org/global/research/global-reports/weso/2019/WCMS_670542/lang--en/index.htm.

Institute of Mechanical Engineers. 2013. *Global Food: Waste Not, Want Not.* https://www.imeche.org/policy-and-press/reports/detail/global-food-waste-not-want-not.

Jachter, Chaim Rabbi. 2000. "Hasagat Gevul: Economic Competition in Jewish Law." JLaw.com. http://jlaw.com/Articles/hasagatgevul.html.

Jacquet, Jennifer and Daniel Pauly. 2008. "Funding Priorities: Big Barriers to Small-Scale Fisheries." *Conservation Biology* 22, no. 4: 832–35.

John Paul II, Pope. 1981. *Laborem exercens.* https://www.vatican.va/content/john-paul-ii/en/encyclicals/documents/hf_jp-ii_enc_14091981_laborem-exercens.html.

_____. 1991. *Centesimus Annus.* http://www.vatican.va/content/john-paul-ii/en/encyclicals/documents/hf_jp-ii_enc_01051991_centesimus-annus.html.

Kay, John. 1998. "Good Business." *Prospect Magazine.* 20 March. https://www.prospectmagazine.co.uk/magazine/goodbusiness.

Kynaston, David. 2001. *The City of London.* Vol 4: A Club No More,1945–2000. London: Chatto & Windus.

Leo XIII, Pope. 1901. *Graves de Communi Re.* https://w2.vatican.va/content/leo-xiii/en/encyclicals/documents/hf_l-xiii_enc_18011901_graves-de-communi-re.html.

Lincoln, Abraham. 1861. First Annual Message, December 2, 1861. The American Presidency Project. Santa Barbara, CA: UC Santa Barbara. https://www.presidency.ucsb.edu/documents/first-annual-message-9.

Lubich, Chiara. 1999. "For an Economy based on Communion," *Nuova Umanità: Rivista Bimenstrale di Cultura* 21, 121: 7–18. https://eocnorthamerica.files.wordpress.com/2015/11/chi_19990129_en.pdf. See also this volume, *Finding Faith in Business: An Economy of Communion Vision,* edited by Andrew Gustafson and Celeste Harvey. Hyde Park, NY: New City Press.

Marx, Karl. 1973. *Grundrisse* (1858). Translated by Martin Nicolaus. London: Penguin.

Mises, Ludwig von. 1951. *Socialism* [1922]. (*Die Gemeinwirtschaft,* 1922). Translated by J. Kahane. New Haven: Yale University Press.

Paul VI, Pope. 1965. *Gaudium et Spes.* http://www.vatican.va/archive/hist_councils/ii_vatican_council/documents/vat-ii_const_19651207_gaudium-et-spes_en.html.

Pfeffer, Yehoshua Rabbi. 2015. "Opening Shop? Laws of Hasagas Gevul" Kollel 8/31/2015 http://dinonline.org/2015/08/31/opening-shop-laws-of-hasagas-gevul.

Sedlacek, Tomas. 2011. *The Economy of Good and Evil* (*Ekonomie dobra a zla,* 2009). Translated by Douglas Arellanes. Oxford: Oxford University Press.

Smith, Adam. 1776. *The Wealth of Nations.* London: Methuen & Co.

Spencer, David. 2013. "To Reduce Work's Importance to a Feeling of Pain Is to Miss the Fundamental Role of Work in the Fulfilment of Our Needs Both as Consumers and Producers." London School of Economics and Political Science Blog. August 1, 2013. https://blogs.lse.ac.uk/politicsandpolicy/the-disutility-of-work/.

Talmud. www.sefaria.org.

Ton, Zeynep. 2014. *The Good Jobs Strategy.* Seattle: Lake Union.

Walzer, Michael. 1993. *Spheres of Justice.* Oxford: Blackwell.

Chapter 7

The Economy of Communion:
Catholic Social Thought Put to Work

Andrew Gustafson, Creighton University

Abstract: This more biographical essay will attempt to bring together theory about Economy of Communion (EoC) practices with the real-life experiences the author has had as an EoC entrepreneur. While Gustafson rehabs and then rents out properties in midtown Omaha, he is motivated by the vision of EoC in his business practices. Here he explains how the EoC vision impacts who he employs, how he treats them, who he rents to, his typical rental practices, and finally how he himself has been impacted spiritually through his business activities, trying (imperfectly) to live out gratuity and reciprocity in his day-to-day practices. Ultimately, he has come to see his work as lived-out theology—practicing redemption by rehabilitating rundown properties, and providing grace and mercy and living out his faith through his business activities.

As a professor of business ethics and society at a Jesuit university, I do the typical things a professor does—I teach classes, read and write articles, and participate in various committees and service work. All of this is normal. But I am also an entrepreneur with rental properties and thereby responsible for around 95 toilets, most of them located in midtown Omaha. More importantly, we try to run our business according to Economy of Communion values. This includes having our business activities focused on the benefit of people rather than mere profit, seeing our business as a means to help others (whether the poor, our workers, our clients, or our neighborhood), and finally, seeing business as a means of communion—bringing unity through relationships created and built by our business activities. This vision and these values have led me to make intentional efforts to befriend and employ homeless or otherwise less fortunate people in our neighborhood, to rent to people whom other landlords might not rent to (such as convicts or those with poor credit), to aid and extend grace to tenants in difficult situations in unusual ways, and to be mindful of our community and the common good as we make business decisions.

Since I am both an EoC entrepreneur and a professor of business ethics and society, I have a unique opportunity to reflect upon the experiences of trying to live out Economy of Communion principles as an entrepreneur and to reflect on how Catholic Social Teaching can apply in very concrete ways in business practice. Through my practical lived experience and academic research I have found that the vision of the EoC and principles of Catholic Social Thought have helped give direction to a way of living and doing business which integrates my faith and business practices. This intersection of theory and praxis will be the focus of this essay.

The Entrepreneurial Project: Communion Properties

I started buying old houses and fixing them up in my hometown in 1999 when I was in grad school. When I came to Creighton University (in Omaha, Nebraska) in 2005, I bought one, then two, then more properties in my neighborhood just a few blocks west of Creighton. I loved working with my hands, I loved the challenge of completing projects, and I really loved the renovating work involved—bringing dilapidated houses or buildings which most saw as hopeless back from the brink of being torn down by the city, and turning them into beautiful, very livable homes for people again.

But this initial desire to restore old houses and buildings developed and was enriched with time. I am not a theologian, but I started to view this renovation work as lived practical theology—a very small imitation of God's redemptive work in the world: God reaches out and gives grace and acts in faith to restore people seen as hopeless by the rest of the world. Many of the buildings I bought were seen as hopeless causes, perhaps better to be torn down than restored. At first, I considered primarily the buildings we were renovating as redemptive works, but as I worked in our neighborhood, I began to get to know a variety of characters, many of them homeless or near homeless, and many of them with addictions of one sort or another. And as I began to get to know them, and they helped me, and I helped them, I found that their friendship was a blessing to me in ways I would not have expected. I also found that I really enjoyed interacting with tenants and getting to know them and help them, sometimes through difficult times such as a job layoff or other financial strain.

As we have acquired more properties, people have often asked me why we don't outsource the management so I don't have to "hassle" with tenants. I always find this question strange precisely because I enjoy interacting with tenants, and that is one of the things I especially like about this sort of business. I like solving their problems, extending mercy or grace to them when they have a difficulty, and making sure they are generally happy with where they live. Of course it is not always pleasant, and it frequently gets messy when you are involved in your tenants' or workers' personal problems, and of course, at times I fail to act as I ideally should. But despite these things, what I have found to be especially rewarding about being an entrepreneur, doing real estate rehab and rental business, is the redemptive/restorative nature of our building renovations and the human interaction with my workers, tenants, and others I encounter through business dealings.

My Introduction to EoC

Although I started doing home renovations and rentals in 1999, it wasn't until 2015 that I first heard of the Economy of Communion, and I attended my first Economy of Communion Conference in the summer of that year. I felt like I had found a group of people who thought about business as I did, and they seemed to think the same about me. The EoC spirit embodied in the people of EoC were what attracted me. As Linda Sprecht has pointed out, "The EoC developed from a charism, not from economic or business theory. Unlike many business or economic models that are founded in theory and must be tested in the 'real world,' the inspiration for the EoC project emerged from a lived spirituality, and was immediately brought to life in the 'real world'..." (Sprecht 2008, 7). As Crivelli points out, EoC goes beyond mere efficiency to think of business in terms of giving, solidarity, reciprocity, gratuity, and even spirituality (Crivelli 2020). I saw that the spirituality and concern for others was at the heart of this more humane business practice.

What also attracted me to the EoC was the model of doing good through business itself—rather than just making money and then doing good through charity given out of the excess of profits. There is surplus benefit created by any successful business—typically in the form of profit. The question is, how do you use it? The traditional model of generous businesses is to make a profit, and then donate that surplus. But it is also possible to run your business so as not to have as much remaining surplus by running your business with more intentional grace, for the benefit of others. For example, we charge lower rates (20–50% less) on apartments and houses here in Omaha than the average Omaha rate (and so we have many tenants who have been in the same place for 5+ years).[1] What this means in our case is that on a monthly basis we take in about $20,000 less than we would if we charged the median rent rate for Omaha. Now of course that means we run on much tighter margins, because we pay the same taxes, insurance rates, and utility costs as any normal landlord. Additionally, we also take more financial risk by renting to tenants who may not meet typical credit or income requirements, and we frequently provide grace and stability/security when people fall behind, allowing them to catch up over time (one tenant has lost her jobs three times, and each time, we have let her stay, giving her an opportunity to catch up again). And in over twenty years, while I have chosen to not renew leases on occasion, I have never evicted someone through legal action. When tenants fall severely behind, and have had to move out, I have not ever pursued a former tenant for the money owed (in one case a tenant owed over $7,000 in backrent). We have tenants who leave us with significant debts—we have had four people in the last year who vacated owing us over $3,000—and we do not go to court to try to retrieve that money. These decisions are about surplus—not after-the-fact decisions about how to "spend our profit" but rather decisions made to limit our profits. We make less, risk more, extend more grace, and typically take on the burden of financial and other messes that tenants leave us with, by choice of how we operate our business. We do this because we find it to be a meaningful way of helping people. The tenants we have offered grace to are not

---

1. The average rent for apartments in Omaha for January 2023 was $1,101 (rentcafe.com) and specifically $674 for a studio, $915 for a one bedroom, $1,151 for 2 bedroom and $1,337 for 3 bedrooms (apartments.com/omaha-ne). We rent studios for $375–550, 1 bedrooms for $550–600, and 2 bedrooms for $600–750 (many of those also include utilities). The average price for home rentals is $1,352 (Zillow.com) and most of our houses rent for $800–1000 for a 2 or 3 bedroom home.

(generally speaking) looking to take advantage of others. They have been in difficult situations, with few options, and had no one else to fall back on. They have been people in need of help. These are choices we make about how to run our business in a way which helps others, rather than attempting to make as much money as possible, and then giving some away through charity. Our more flexible and humane approach to running things allows us to frequently be a support to our tenants in ways which are quite unusual.

As Pope Francis has said, "Capitalism knows philanthropy, not communion" (Francis 2017). This communion is especially *communion with the poor.* EoC sees business as a means to help the poor, to be with the poor, and to bring the poor into the circle of communion, not simply to give them money or resources. At the core of EoC business practice is a faith-inspired intention to make the world better for those in need through helping them to enter the market and participate with dignity, and entering into communion with others in this way. This free-market, private-enterprise approach of responding to poverty was very attractive to me, because it seemed sustainable. In this way, EoC businesses share at least one similar point with Prahalad's bottom of the pyramid thesis (Prahalad 2004)—and as films like *Poverty, Inc.* help to show—that the poor can be helped (frequently more so) by market participation, rather than simply charity.

Perhaps what the EoC also has helped me to see is that there are many forms of poverty—some much more important than economic poverty. Poverty of sociality—of friends, of a safety net, of community—is a poverty which leaves one feeling alone and without any support, emotionally or otherwise. The guys I have met who were squatting or living in their truck and drinking all the time were not only without money, they were without community, without a place in society, without work to give them something to do, and so without a purpose. The jobs I frequently give to the guys (painting, digging dirt, tearing out walls, etc.) are not especially meaningful work, but it is work which gives them a sense of achievement and frequently they greet me with "Did you see what I got done?" because they take pride in their work. I began to see that the poverty of community, purpose, and sense of achievement are often at least as significant as financial poverty.

It Is Personal and Humane:
EoC in Contrast to Traditional Market Thinking

We are all familiar with the phrase, "It's simply a business decision, it's nothing personal" or quotes like Theodore Levitt's (1958), that "the business of business is profits." The Economy of Communion has a much different vision of business practices and activities. Business is personal. Despite the common idea that professional business is impersonal, business is in fact fundamentally human interaction revolving around meeting personal human needs and wants—and not merely the abstract market demands of "consumer" or "customer." Bears and squirrels do not conduct business. It's a human affair, and it is with, by, and for humans. Modern economics has sometimes pretended that business activities are somehow a sphere of their own, distinct and set apart from the rest of our human activities. As Bruni has pointed out, "theorizing a distinct economic sphere governed by principles essentially different from those of the social sphere is an element typical of modernity" (Bruni 2012, 27). In this dualistic view of business and society, the market interactions in the business sphere are not normal human relations. They are simply business relations (thus, "the business of business is business," etc.). To be "professional" typically means to not mix one's personal interests or human social concerns with the business transactions in which one is involved (i.e., "it's just business, it's nothing personal"). We see this for example in Milton Friedman's famous admonishment to managers not to let their own personal interests influence their business decisions, which should always be aimed at profit for the owners of the company, since they are acting as agent of the company (Friedman 1970).

Business is no place to make friends, according to this modern economic view. Again, Bruni has pointed out that in Adam Smith's view, "friendship (or fraternity, in the language of the Enlightenment) cannot be a characteristic of *normal* market relations" (Bruni 2012, 27). Business is conceived to be focused on efficiency, hard, cold, and calculating, without passion or personal interests (which may be construed as inefficient biases), and certainly business should not be a place for gift, but for calculated, self-interested exchange. In contrast to this view, EoC emphasizes the central place of gift in a humane orientation to business activity (Grevin & Bruni 2018).

But we sometimes lose sight of what a peculiarly modern view this is: "In fact, only in the eighteenth century was the economic sphere conceived and presented as the ideal place for instrumental, self-interested and measurable relations, and the market as the essentially self-regulating interweaving of those relationships" (Bruni 2012, 27). Economy of Communion apparently violates the modern conception of economics, insofar as it is rooted in a form of other-concern which cannot be reduced to self-interest.

In *The Wound and the Blessing: Economics, Relationships, and Happiness*, Luigino Bruni observes that business frequently does all it can to eliminate the potential wounds of human interaction in business by depersonalizing market transactions and keeping people at an arm's distance. But he argues that without the wound there cannot be a blessing: "If it is true that there is no blessing without wound, then there is no good life or happiness—no *Eudaimonia*—without a risky and potentially tragic encounter with the other" (2012, 63). We see the truth of this in many of our human relationships—with our family, spouse, close friends—and I see it as well in my relationships with tenants as well as my "employees."

Two fundamental Economy of Communion principles are *gratuity* and *reciprocity*—and these deserve some explanation. First, gratuity: normally business transactions are based on justice and fairness—one thing is exchanged for something else, agreed upon in advance. There is in such a transaction a logic of reciprocation—but a reciprocation of what is owed, and of what is (justly) due. But the logic of gratuity and gift is different. It is a logic of superabundance, where people act for and on behalf of the other out of love, and gratuity goes above and beyond what is due. Now, when we do go above and beyond out of care for the other through business actions, this does "create an obligation that is based on the special ties that bind us to one another" (Zamagni 2014, 53). Reciprocity sees the relational aspects of the persons involved as central to business decision-making. Business exchanges are rooted in personal relationships which cannot be disassociated from those exchanges. Reciprocity overtly denies the impartial and anonymous impersonal nature of business. From such a reciprocal view of business, the saying "it's nothing personal, it is just a business decision" makes no sense whatsoever. Speaking of this impersonal business environment of the typical modern economic view, Bruni says:

> The market has been thought out and defined by modernity as the typically ideal place for non-gratuitousness; this is why the relational crises and the malaise that pervades many economic environments today can be considered a result of the "famine of gratuitousness" that is afflicting our development model. (Bruni 2012, 45)

Economy of Communion is a movement to overcome this famine of gratuitousness. This happens in multiple ways, but certainly it happens when your model for doing business is oriented around humane relationships rather than contractual or transactional relationships. When we are in relationship with each other as humans, as "brothers and sisters" even, the professional shield of impersonal relating and the dualistic notion of acting in the business realm rather than the social-political realm is called into question: How can I treat another person as merely a customer, as merely an employee, or as merely a supervisor? And since many of us do this frequently and seem to be adept at it, perhaps the real question then is, how can we live such a bifurcated, schizophrenic life, maintaining a sphere of economic life distinct and impervious to the socio-political life of my truly human self?

Adam Smith was right to see the freeing and equalizing power of the markets. "When we enter the market we no longer depend hierarchically on each other—the beggar on the rich, or the farmer on the landlord—and in the interaction of the market we meet on equal footing, where, thanks to the contract, we are freed from dependence on the benevolence of others" (Bruni 2012, 29). In the market, we are all on equal footing, and it is up to us to better our position through our activity in the market. And as Albert Hirschman demonstrates in his excellent book *The Passions and the Interests*, capitalism was originally advocated for in the belief that "it would activate some benign human proclivities at the expense of some malignant ones" (Hirschman 1977, 66). In other words, people's desire for wealth and prosperity would distract them from more malignant intentions toward others (wars, etc.). Amartya Sen explains this in a simple example. In a situation where you are about to be attacked by a group of thugs who want to do you harm, suppose you throw a bunch of money in the air and run for it—and the thugs are distracted, wanting to grab money more than wanting to harm you (Sen 1977, x). Such is capitalism—it keeps us busy with the pursuit of wealth so that we don't spend our energies on more insidious, harmful efforts. But today, the original "benign" proclivity to make money—often called greed—has become the main point of criticism from capitalism's critics. The pursuit of money can lead to all sorts of evils, including oppression, self-concern over all else, and a materialism which loses sense of the transcendent. When market values trump all, anything can be commodified, so that nothing is sacred or sacrosanct. All is for sale—even social standing and political power.

In this sort of market-dominated world, there is no more gift, no more gratuity, and certainly not reciprocity, because the market is an attempt to efficiently use one's resources to achieve what one wants—and the more you can get without giving for it, the better (in fact, this is a kind of efficiency). It is an economy of getting, not giving, and more humane notions of grace and reciprocity dissipate. In such a stark game, if one does not put one's resources toward the goal of getting more than others, you will lose. As Frank Knight, a founder of the Chicago School of Economics put it, "In the long run, all producers are forced to use the most efficient methods, or give place to others who do" (Knight 1976, 191). This is why, in business transactions, we may do something to another which we would never do to them as a friend, as a relative, or even as a stranger on the street necessarily. But in the business situation, "it's just business, it's nothing personal," and so it is allowed, for the sake of efficiency, for the sake of profit, which is the ultimate justification.

Catholic Social Thought

While the Economy of Communion has given me resources to consider and develop alternative ways of thinking about my business activities, I have also found the principles of Catholic Social Teaching (CST) to be very insightful and instructive in helping me integrate my faith with my business practices. I think it speaks to the wide applicability of EoC and CST principles that they are so very useful to me as a Protestant. Catholic Social Teaching is the catch-all phrase for some recurring themes which are raised in various Church writings (papal encyclicals, letters of bishops' committees, etc.). There is no set

official list of such principles, but some of the most common
ones below have given me helpful guidance in thinking about
how I practice business with an EoC mindset, and help develop
some of the EoC themes further.

1. Human Dignity: All humans have dignity simply because
they are created in God's image. This is the starting point or
foundation for most of the other principles: Everyone has unconditional worth and value, which is independent of anything
they do or achieve. This affects how I interact with the people
who work for me, as well as the way I treat those who live in our
buildings. I frequently tell people that we operate relationally,
not transactionally. I am not simply interacting with them
in order to get rent (tenants) or to get work done (workers). I
tend to be concerned about their whole person and the issues
they are dealing with, whether that is family issues, job issues,
personal situations, or other things not typically brought up
in "professional" business transactions.

2. Association/Participation: Each individual has value, but
we are meant for community through family, social relationships, and participation in creation. Work has an important
role in this:

> Work is more than a way to make a living; it is a form
> of continuing participation in God's creation. If the
> dignity of work is to be protected, then the basic rights
> of workers must be respected—the right to productive
> work, to decent and fair wages, to organize and join
> unions, to private property, and to economic initiative.
> (USCCB 1998)

3. Preferential Option for the Poor and Vulnerable: Given
that everyone has dignity, and all should be in community, we
should have a special concern to make sure that the poor are
brought into community—thus the Biblical command to take

special care of "the orphan, the widow, and the stranger." Some of the guys who have worked for me have been homeless—living in their cars or squatting, sometimes for years—prior to us meeting. I've typically provided them a place to stay and I work with them. Others who work for us are not homeless, but they are financially vulnerable in various ways, and we have provided work and wages, as well as friendship, to help make their lives better. Being in this business also allows us to extend grace to tenants who are living on the edge and who face a financial pitfall such as an unexpected car repair or the loss of a job.

4. Solidarity: Loving your neighbor as yourself is a command rooted in a view that we are our brother's and sister's keeper, since we are all children of God. This may mean I give up my own interests for the sake of others—particularly those quite "other" than me. Vera Araùjo writes: "EoC isn't a matter of being generous, of giving charity; it isn't philanthropy or merely a way of providing assistance. It has to do with acknowledging and living the dimension of giving and giving of oneself as essential to one's own existence" (2002, 23). Luca Crivelli describes EoC culture as "above all a culture of 'self-giving' and of unconditional giving" (21). When we do this for a purpose beyond ourselves, we act with solidarity.

5. Stewardship/Social Mortgage/Universal Destination of Goods: CST considers all that we have is on loan from God, ultimately. We are responsible to be stewards of what God has given to us. Any encyclical which speaks to economics brings up the importance of private property: It is essential so that all people (including the poor) may give some inheritance to their children (Leo XIII 1891, §13). But if we have enough wealth for ourselves, we are also called to share it with others. We are called to be good and generous stewards of our wealth, and of the world itself. We are to share it, not to only get more and more and hoard it. As Pope Francis told the EoC gathering in Rome, "May the 'no' to an economy that kills become a 'yes' to an economy that lets live, because it shares, includes the poor, uses profits to create communion" (Pope Francis 2017).

6. Subsidiarity: People should be empowered to make decisions which are rightfully theirs. Being able to freely act and choose is an essential part of our dignity as human beings, and we should not take away the rightful voice of others by micromanaging in decisions which could and should be made by others. Subsidiarity is an organizing principle which directs matters to be handled by the relevant parties, rather than by others who should not be making the decision (Naughton et al. 2015). So I let my workers make decisions about many day-to-day work situations. I let my tenants modify their apartment, most usually by painting, but even sometimes by selecting new light fixtures or countertops.

7. The Common Good: This is typically defined as "the sum total of social conditions which allow people, either as groups or as individuals, to reach their fulfillment more fully and more easily" (Catechism 1906). The common good is almost a meta-principle—providing an overall view of that toward which our actions should be aiming. Flourishing—as individuals and as a society—comes as a result of acting in accordance with God's desires for creation. One of my favorite things as a landlord is when a tenant lets me know that they are going to move out and buy their own home. Many have told us that we helped make that possible quicker because of our very reasonable rents. This gives me a lot of joy.

This is a challenging list of principles to follow. But the truth of it is that when we act with these principles in mind, our work and our lives will flourish, because we are acting as we were created to, in the world with others. And these principles are part of a whole cloth—it is difficult to isolate one out from the others. So in my business, as I interact with my workers and my tenants, I try to treat them with dignity, provide them freedoms and opportunities they may not have otherwise, engage them in ways which provide social connection, help the poor (especially in the case of my workers), and act in solidarity with them (on projects, in work, etc.). I use my assets with steward-ship in mind, considering the good of others and not just my own. These principles are congruent with the values of the EoC. More of this may become clear through a few examples.

Being an EoC Entrepreneur Is...

a. Relational instead of Transactional

As I mentioned before, once people discover that I have 34 properties, and that I essentially manage all of them myself, they often ask me why I don't outsource the management to someone else. The answer, quite simply, is because I generally like the relationships which come about through managing the properties. When someone texts me about an issue, I help solve that problem for them. When I meet prospective tenants and rent them one of our places, I am bringing new neighbors into our own neighborhood. I don't see them so much as tenants and rent-payers as neighbors and prospective friends—and I tell them that we run our business relationally. This has diffi-culties of its own, of course. When you start to become a friend and not just an impersonal professional landlord or "the boss," things get more messy, but this is part of the wound which can lead to blessing (or blessing which can lead to a wound), in the words of Luigino Bruni.

Doing things relationally, rather than in a transactional way, makes a very real difference. Once during a seminar on ethics I was doing with a group of doctors, someone asked me if I ever used the law to evict anyone. I told them I never had. Most landlord-tenant relationships are primarily transactional or contractual—meaning that the basis of your relationship is primarily for one to promise to give the other something in exchange for money. If my approach to tenants is primarily relational in a sense of seeing them as a person, rather than merely transactional or contractual, then my relationship is not so oriented around our lease or contract—although of course we do have leases. But this is what I mean, and what I said to the doctors: If I come home one day and my wife is not happy and says to me, "I've been talking to our lawyer, and he says you have a marital obligation to be doing more dishes," I would be concerned. Of course, I would realize I should probably wash more dishes, but the most concerning thing would be that my wife is resorting to legal counsel to resolve a problem in our relationship. In the same way, on the rare occasion that a tenant has been upset about something and started to bring up that "they were talking about this issue with a lawyer" (which is usually not true, but nonetheless), I immediately either try to heal the relationship, or if that seems impossible, I start to look for an exit strategy which can be to their benefit because, at this point, the relationship must be pretty far gone. If they are seeing our relationship as legal, contractual, or transactional, then we no longer have the kind of human relationship I want to have with my tenants. If a problem arises (and they do) I almost always use sugar instead of a stick to help the tenant ease out of our relationship. One of the first such situations was a guy who did a lot of meth who lived in a building I purchased early on. I knew he needed to move out because he was very aggressive and loud with his music, and no one would want to live in the apartment building with him there. So I went to discuss the possibility of his moving out. He gave me two options: a. try to evict him, or b. give him $600. He said that if I chose eviction, the process would take 2–3 months, he would fight it all the way, and when the police came to drag him out kicking and screaming he would make sure every single window in the building was broken. I quickly agreed to the second option, we set a date, and on that date I gave him $600, and he moved out. That's when I realized sugar was much better than threats or making it a legal matter. I don't run my business in a professional manner—if by professional one means that I run it with policies and rules and treat human beings primarily as a means to profit. But of course, sometimes this means that I end up forgoing what is owed to me.

b. Working with Me versus Working for Me

One of the blessings of doing rehab and rental in midtown Omaha has been the great people I have gotten to know as I engaged with many in our neighborhood who were in difficult financial situations. I hadn't been in the Gifford Park neighborhood for very long before I started to meet some of the local characters. I purchased two properties next to each other—a classic fourplex apartment building next to a big old Victorian house which had been cut up into three apartments and was under repair orders by the city. A 50-something-year-old Puerto Rican man who called himself "Vernie"[2] asked if I would let him keep living in his Chevy pickup behind the house until I got it fixed up and rented. Since it was November in Nebraska (with temperatures frequently below freezing) I said, "Why don't you live in the house and help me fix it up?" and he agreed. And so for 12 years Vernie worked on projects of mine. He had been a mason much of his life prior to meeting me, and he had a lot of skills. But alcohol was a habit with him, and at times we used to be concerned how much longer he would live. Sometimes he would quit drinking for months at a time and really enjoy life. Shortly after meeting Vernie, I met Al, a smart guy who also drank and did everything a little too fast—more than once, he painted himself into the corner of a basement (literally)—but he always had an interesting

---

2. Not his real name. The names of other friends in this paragraph have also been changed, to preserve their privacy.

story and a great sense of humor. He was bright and funny and knew he should have made more of himself. George, a member of the Omaha tribe, was homeless when I met him. He was big, gentle, had an easy laugh, and liked to paint houses on tall ladders. Another long-time worker, Mark, likes country music and NPR and Old Milwaukee beer, has a strong work ethic, and is expert at meticulously cleaning up apartments or other messes for me.

These guys would come over to the porch at my house and talk and have coffee, and I'd come up with projects for each of them to do. When you employ semi-homeless alcoholics for projects, you are bound to be let down frequently, and of course I have been. But it was far more like a little family than a business. These guys didn't have jobs because they would have been fired by most employers. But frequently the words of Pope Francis come to mind, that we should not deny mercy in the name of merit and that "No son, no man, not even the most rebellious, deserves acorns" (Francis 2017). I often feel that I was half employer and half social worker with these guys. As Vernie used to say, "you help me, and I help you." Vernie would frequently tell me that I was like a big brother to him—despite the fact that he was 17 years older than me. I made sure the guys had a place to stay, ways to get around, and of course I paid them for their work. But what became more important to them over time was simply respect and our friendship—that I respected them as human beings and appreciated not only their work, but who they were as people.

Vernie, Al, and George have all passed away now. The guys who have worked for me did a lot for me, but they also became good friends, and it feels more like they worked with me than just for me. This is also something Bruni mentions:

> But even more normal capitalistic enterprises could not grow and endure if, in certain contexts and moments of the organizational dynamic, the staff in the

workgroups, offices or university departments did not experience friendships that lead them beyond the stipulations of the contract—for example, to forgive or to thank. (Bruni 2012, 51)

Just as I approach my tenants on a relational basis, I have definitely considered my workers to be first of all relationships, and then hired labor. In situations where there was especially dirty or nasty cleanup to be done, I typically took those projects on myself. I didn't feel right asking the guys to do that kind of work (cleaning up cat feces in a cat hoarder's house, removing toilets in abandoned buildings which had continued to be used long after the plumbing had been shut off, etc., etc.). Who was I to ask them to do such degrading work? And them seeing me take on those less dignified tasks helped them realize my respect for them as persons.

c. Subsidiarity in Practice

Michael Naughton et al. describe subsidiarity in the following way:

> The word "subsidiarity" comes from the Latin *subsidium*, that is, "to assist and strengthen" the other. Within organizations, subsidiarity serves as a moral principle that directs leaders to place decision-making at the most appropriate level of an organization so as to utilize the gifts of employees for their own good, the good of the organization, and the good of the organization's clients or customers. (2015, 1–2)

Along with respecting my workers, I have tried to empower them to make decisions (subsidiarity). Every person I have encountered has different gifts, and an important part of managing them was to discover what they could and couldn't do. Some of them liked to paint on tall ladders, others could do masonry, and still others were great at demo and cleanup.

One woman who helps us out a lot has been an artist and sign-painter most of her life, but she discovered how to sand and stain floors. She has become our floor magician, bringing the wood floors in our buildings back to their original beauty. I also have a responsibility not to ask someone to do something they really are not equipped to do, and also not to ask them to do work which would produce unsatisfactory results for tenants. I haven't always gotten that balance right, and it's more difficult when you have the worker pool that I typically use. But as much as possible, I try to treat them in an egalitarian way—as equals—and to expect good things and solutions from them. I have a charge account at the local hardware store, and I would frequently send my guys to the store to get things, with authorization to charge things to my account. I trusted them, and they were faithful to that trust. This trust has many positive benefits, as I have also seen the attitudes of those who work for me change over time. I think they hadn't had many people offer them grace or kindness before, so they tended to be quite self-protective. But once they experience generosity and kindness, they seem to be more able to act with kindness and generosity toward others. This demonstrates the connection EoC sees between gratuity and reciprocity. To be generous, we need enough for ourselves and some overflow, and once my workers have experienced the security enabled by generosity and kindness to them, I see that they then frequently enjoy being able to provide kindness to others. This is also the theme found in the *Vocation of a Business Leader* document based on *Caritas in Veritate*, which says "The first act of the Christian business leader . . . is to receive what God has done for him or her" (§70) because only then will they be able to give generously. Again, Luca Crivelli puts it very well when describing the EoC vision. In responding to poverty of the poor, we respond by giving up our wealth, something he calls a "second type of poverty," which is:

. . . one that is freely chosen and which truly renders a person blessed. This is the poverty which is born from the awareness that all that I am has been given to me; likewise, all that I have must, in turn, be given. This is the foundation of the dynamics of reciprocity. This poverty prompts us to free ourselves of goods as absolute possessions in order to make them gifts, and thus to be free to love, the only thing that is truly important. In this way the goods themselves become bridges, occasions of community, paths of reciprocity. (2020, 22)

Others have spoken of this, but for me the EoC has challenged me to run our rental and rehab business not so much with an attitude of how much wealth can we obtain, but rather, what can we do with the resources that this enterprise generates, and how can we help people—workers, tenants, and others—through these opportunities and resources God has given to us? Making decisions which lead to more communion but don't always lead to the most efficient bottom line may not make sense to many, but the EoC sees the practice of business as a means to enhance spirituality as we build community and practice reciprocity. This is why Pope Francis said in his talk to the EoC:

By introducing into the economy the good seed of communion, you have begun a profound change in the way of seeing and living business. Business is not only capable of destroying communion among people, but can edify it; it can promote it. With your life you demonstrate that economy and communion become more beautiful when they are beside each other. Certainly the economy is more beautiful, but communion is also more beautiful, because the spiritual communion of hearts is even fuller when it becomes the communion of goods, of talents, of profits. (2017)

When one finds a way to live out the EoC vision through one's work, work is no longer just a job, nor even a career, but rather a vocation with a sense of calling and purpose which integrates one's personal values with business actions in such a way that business itself is not merely informed by faith, but becomes an expression of it and a means of spiritual development.

Conclusion

Although I found the Economy of Communion group and discovered Catholic Social Thought more than a decade after I had started my business, I have found them to be rich sources of thought and direction for me as I live out my faith in my business. I now see my business activities essentially as spiritual activities, and the relationships I have with others through the business as essentially human relationships, which happen to have a financial component. Pope Francis is absolutely correct when he says that "economy and communion become more beautiful when they are beside each other" (2017).

By approaching one's business activities with an EoC mindset, business itself becomes a spiritual activity, fostering spiritual enrichment in you and others as you see those interactions as a means for communion.

Bibliography

Araùjo, Vera. 2002. "Personal and Societal Prerequisites of the Economy of Communion." *The Economy of Communion: Toward a Multi-Dimensional Economic Culture*, edited by Luigino Bruni. Translated by Lorna Gold. Hyde Park: New City Press, 21–30.

Bruni, Luigino, ed. 2002. *The Economy of Communion: Toward a Multi-Dimensional Economic Culture*. Translated by Lorna Gold. Hyde Park, NY: New City Press.

Bruni Luigino. 2012. *The Wound and the Blessing.* Hyde Park, NY: New City Press.

Catechism of the Catholic Church. 1906. "The Common Good." https://www.vatican.va/archive/ENG0015/__P6K.HTM#-22N.

Crivelli, Luca. 2020. "Economy of Communion, Poverty and a Humanized Economy." In *Business, Faith and the Economy of Communion,* edited Andrew Gustafson and Celeste Harvey. Special Volume of *Journal of Religion and Society,* supp. 22: 20–26. See also this volume, *Finding Faith in Business: An Economy of Communion Vision,* edited by Andrew Gustafson and Celeste Harvey. Hyde Park, NY: New City Press.

Francis, Pope. 2017. *Address of His Holiness Pope Francis to Participants in the Meeting 'Economy of Communion', Sponsored by the Focolare Movement.* https://w2.vatican.va/content/francesco/en/speeches/2017/february/documents/papa-francesco_20170204_focolari.html.

Friedman, Milton. 1970. "The Social Responsibility of Business is to Increase Its Profits." *New York Times Magazine* (September 13). https://www.nytimes.com/1970/09/13/archives/a-friedman-doctrine-the-social-responsibility-of-business-is-to.html.

Grevin, Anouk and Luigino Bruni. 2018. *L'economie Silencieuse.* Hyde Park, NY: New City Press.

Hirschman, Albert. 1977. *The Passions and the Interests: Political Arguments for Capitalism Before Its Triumph.* Princeton: Princeton University Press.

Knight, Frank. 1976. *Ethics of Competition.* Chicago: University of Chicago Press.

Leo XIII, Pope. 1891. *Rerum Novarum.* http://w2.vatican.va/content/leo-xiii/en/encyclicals/documents/hf_l-xiii_enc_15051891_rerum-novarum.html.

Levitt, Theodore. 1958. "The Dangers of Social Responsibility." *Harvard Business Review* 36: 41–50.

Naughton, Michael J., Jeanne Buckeye, Kenneth Goodpaster, and T. Dean Maines. 2015. *Respect in Action: Applying Subsidiarity in Business*. St. Paul, MN: University of St. Thomas.

Prahalad, C.K. 2004. *The Fortune at the Bottom of the Pyramid*. Philadelphia, PA: Wharton School Publishing.

Poverty, Inc. 2016. Directed and Produced by Michael Matheson Miller.

Sen, Amartya. 1977. "Foreword." In Albert Hirschman, *The Passions and the Interests: Political Arguments for Capitalism Before Its Triumph*. Princeton: Princeton University Press.

Specht, Linda B. 2008. "The Economy of Communion in Freedom Project: A Resource for Catholic Business Education." (conference paper for 2008 *Business Education at Catholic Universities: The Role of Mission-Driven Business Schools*). https://www.stthomas.edu/media/catholicstudies/center/ryan/leadershipdevelopment/documents/SpechtFinalPaper.pdf.

United States Conference of Catholic Bishops (USCCB). 1998. *Sharing Catholic Social Teaching: Challenges and Directions*. http://www.usccb.org/beliefs-and-teachings/what-we-believe/catholic-social-teaching/sharing-catholic-social-teaching-challenges-and-directions.cfm.

Zamagni, Stefano. 2014. "The Economy of Communion Project as a Challenge to Standard Economic Theory." *Revista Portuguesa de Filosofia* 70, 1: 44–60.

III

Theory

Chapter 8

Economy of Communion, Poverty, and a Humanized Economy

Luca Crivelli, University of Applied Sciences
and Arts of Southern Switzerland

Abstract: This contribution makes more explicit the link existing between the Economy of Communion and the objectives of the Office of the United Nations High Commissioner of Human Rights, in particular with regard to the human rights approach to poverty reduction.

The Spiritual Humus of the Economy of Communion

Let me start my talk by reminding that the Economy of Communion (EoC) is not an economic model that has emerged from a discussion held by some economists around a conference table or a project drawn up by experts in sustainable development. The EoC is an experience based on a "spiritual humus," which gives the EoC its identity and meaning. While maintaining a continuous and fruitful dialogue with various expressions of the so-called "social economy," the EoC follows its own trajectory. The culture from which the EoC has emerged is well described by Vera Araùjo, a sociologist who has accompanied this project from its very beginnings. She writes: "EoC isn't a matter of being generous, of giving charity; it isn't philanthropy or merely a way of providing assistance. It has to do with acknowledging and living the dimension of giving and giving of oneself as essential to one's own existence" (2000, 36; author's translation).

This culture of giving, therefore, is above all a culture of "self-giving" and of unconditional giving. It requires a mentality that leads people to develop certain ways of behavior not so much for the benefits they will bring but because they have value in themselves, because we experienced their goodness and truth in our lives.

In April 2001, Chiara Lubich explained that "giving" and "unconditional giving" in the EoC are synonymous with "loving": "Love your employees, even your competitors, your clients and suppliers too, love everyone. The life-style of the company has to change, everything has to be evangelical, otherwise it isn't Economy of Communion" (37–38; author's translation).

By speaking explicitly of love, the EoC goes against the mainstream with respect to the ordinary way of understanding economics in theory and in practice.

The conviction that love as communion must characterize the life of the company lies at the heart of this project. And this conviction, that love must have a central place in the world of business, is a nonconformist and revolutionary proposition. Apart from a few luminous exceptions, the mainstream of economics has not only used terms that are less challenging to describe unselfish conduct (like altruism, philanthropy, donation), but, above all, it has been skeptical of behavior motivated by love for others and has dismissed it as inefficient. Economics has focused on the sphere of human life in which love can be avoided and considers that the more the market is able to cut down on love, the more efficient it will be. There is also a second cause of conflict between love and economics: Love requires the gift to be free and unconditional, which is a scandal for economics, which believes a price must be attributed to everything.

Unconditional giving isn't present in EoC companies only in the form of devolving a part of the profit, but it is manifest in many other actions as well, that change in a very deep way the operating of these businesses. Love means the ability to create options even when a correct carrying out of one's own role would not seem to allow them. Love does not only give or do something for others, it also knows how to love its neighbor, to stand by him or her, to put itself in its neighbor's place without being intrusive. When a solution to the problems does not emerge in the short run, love requires one to be concerned by sharing the difficulties of the employees, providing support in seeking an alternative solution, and in certain cases, in offering help which goes beyond the company's expected role. This "something more" of unconditional giving in relationships is the secret behind the companies of the EoC.

There is plenty of room for action and choices, which no contract could ever regulate. In those situations, the decision to love or not to love comes into play, and the company's values matter greatly.

A Different Attitude Toward Poverty

The EoC project shares the fundamental values and the objectives of the United Nations Millennium Declaration, in particular those regarding development and eradication of extreme poverty, but fulfills them in a peculiar way. Central to the ethos of solidarity underpinning the Focolare is the idea of building relationships based on communion, emphasizing the importance of overcoming material inequalities principally through radical sharing. The EoC recognizes that there are two different kinds of poverty. On the one hand there is a poverty which people suffer, almost always brought about and fomented by the injustices of human beings and by the "sinful structures": This is indigence, misery, the lack of the most basic needs so as to live a life worthy of human beings; it is poverty which must be opposed with great commitment and on all levels (personal and institutional), because it attacks the dignity of the human person and cannot make anyone happy and fully human.

In the last years, as EoC we tried to support some initiatives promoted under the leadership of the United Nations with the objective of fighting against this form of poverty. For instance we were part of the United Nations Expert Group Meeting in Copenhagen on Social Responsibility of the Private Sector and gave our modest contribution to other U.N. initiatives in the area of development financing.

On the other hand, there is a second type of poverty, one that is freely chosen and which truly renders a person blessed. This is the poverty which is born from the awareness that all that I am has been given to me; likewise, all that I have must, in turn, be given. This is the foundation of the dynamics of reciprocity. This poverty prompts us to free ourselves of goods as absolute possessions in order to make them gifts, and thus to be free to love, the only thing that is truly important.

In this way the goods themselves become bridges, occasions of community, paths of reciprocity. Consequently, while the first indigent poverty is suffered (by persons or events), this second poverty can only be chosen. Therefore, in addition to the measures which directly address the first type of poverty, the Economy of Communion fights against misery and indigence also by proposing to all a "chosen poverty" in accordance with the evangelical meaning of poverty. A chosen poverty which is the precondition for understanding the logic of communion and for experiencing the greater freedom and profound happiness that constitutes the typical characteristic of communion.

In one word, the proposal, the humanism of the economy of communion, aims at defeating indigence (the poverty that is not chosen but suffered), by inviting everyone to freely choose a moderate and poor style of life. Being convinced that every interaction both on the inside and on the outside of the company can be transformed into personal face-to-face encounters, the EoC logically alters also the attitude toward the poor.

Poor people are understood and considered as crucial stakeholders, and they actively contribute to spreading this concept of communion to other persons who live in similar circumstances of poverty.

In fact the Economy of Communion is much more than a simple process of redistribution of goods and resources. It is a new process of production that—through sharing goods and activities of a company—generates an immaterial yet touchable output: the experience of communion. A new understanding of poverty emerges therefore from the manifold experiences of the Economy of Communion with the poor: We could even use the term of a new "culture of poverty," where everybody involved would experience a climate of substantial equality between those who give and those who receive, as everybody gives and receives at the same time. On the one hand, the poor people assisted by the Economy of Communion find themselves on an equal level of human dignity. Many people who were supported by the EoC started sharing spontaneously and voluntarily what they have received.

So it does not come as a big surprise to find former persons in need among today's entrepreneurs of the Economy of Communion. On the other hand, through the choice of the second type of poverty, the entrepreneur himself becomes poor: not indigent, but the one who out of love uses his talents in order to generate resources to be put in communion, even by taking economic risks.

Humanizing the Market Economy

Therefore, the EoC can also be seen as an attempt to humanize the market economy. The vision of the market (understood in the broad sense of the term) and of a business entity that emerges from the EoC is substantially positive but not blind to the damage and harm that a wild market could cause. (To make that clear it is enough to remind ourselves that the founding intuition of the EoC emerged precisely in Brazil where the market miserably failed to solve the problem of extreme poverty.)

The EoC recalls all economic activity to its original vocation, which is a peaceful encounter between free persons. That is why the EoC does not radically condemn private entrepreneurship and the free market, but admonishes us to see them too as places where true well-being, happiness, and authentic encounters between people can be brought about. At the same time the EoC is also a radical criticism against today's common understanding of market economy and its ways of thinking. The EoC tries to propose a multi-dimensional view of entrepreneurial activity, where efficiency has its place but is not the only factor that counts. Apart from efficiency, the businesses adhering to the EoC add other, just as essential, dimensions to their business models such as giving, solidarity, reciprocity, beauty, gratuity, and—why not—spirituality and the sense of communion. Moreover, the EoC challenges market economics in at least three additional ways.

When Chiara Lubich launched the Economy of Communion in 1991, she did not suggest the creation of foundations, of charity or social assistance organizations—as one might naturally expect. Instead, from the very beginning, she spoke of companies as an unusual instrument for resolving a problem of solidarity. The fact is that communion penetrates these seemingly normal economic organizations and installs itself therein. With the creation of production areas which have been built beside the settlements of the Focolare Movement in recent years, something new is occurring. The construction of these areas gets the entire community involved in a kind of popular shareholding. It enables the raising of capital necessary to start up new companies, especially in developing countries where it can be very difficult and costly to access capital markets ("We are poor, but many" was the slogan of the EoC from the beginning). These areas are becoming an original and important form of production. They are not classical business groups (holdings) nor are they a simple industrial district (meaning areas characterized by the almost exclusive presence of one industry which leads to the development of many small companies), even if the social culture that accompanies them plays an important role as it does in traditional industrial districts. The development of these zones represents a new stage for the EoC, a coming-out of the project into public life and a qualitative leap on the institutional-organizational level.

Secondly, the Economy of Communion shows that it is possible to overcome the dichotomy between the production of wealth and the distribution of it. This is an old dichotomy. Many think that in business one can behave in the following way: No ethical norm must be binding at the moment of production, since the only objective is to maximize economic results and therefore efficiency. Once the maximum size of the cake has been obtained (even if it means that a certain behavior violates fundamental norms and infringes upon fundamental human rights), that is when one can remember the existence of others and their needs and can therefore be generous at the time of distribution. This is the conception that dominates in today's economy, even among Christians at times. Many think that the important thing is to make a lot of money and then to try to distribute it in an equal way according to some law of redistribution. Unfortunately this is a perverse logic because it tends to dichotomize the person. It makes people schizophrenic. The same person cannot ignore others to obtain better economic results or more profit and then go on to handle the distribution of that wealth. And that is because he will never be able to do justice for the evil produced at the moment of generating that wealth, even if he works toward a more equal distribution. The EoC represents an example of going against the trend, demonstrating that it is possible to remain in the market successfully without following this dichotomizing logic.

The third contribution to the humanizing of economy is the following: The Economy of Communion shows that economic transactions are inseparable from human relationships. For this reason, exchange—even that which takes place in the market—cannot be anonymous or impersonal. The principle language used by economists today is the language of incentives. Economic science tells us it is necessary to offer an economic incentive in order to direct the choices of the individual toward desired behavior. However, using systems of incentives always hides a relationship of power. Certainly power is better expressed in the form of an incentive than in direct coercion. Nevertheless there is a third path which provides an alternative to both, incentives and coercion, in directing individuals in a certain direction as opposed to another. The alternative is persuasion. Perhaps this is the ultimate secret of the Economy of Communion model: Those who are involved act without a scheme of incentive—which is always expensive and can produce undesired side effects, by crowding out intrinsic motivation; they act because they are deeply persuaded. And this persuasion is derived from the precise adhesion to the very strong cultural matrix which is the one Chiara Lubich so vigorously upholds.

Solidarity in a Spirit of Brotherhood

In seeking a new relationship between market and society, the Economy of Communion sees companies as a social good and as a collective resource, and it transcends the idea of the market as a place where relationships are only self-serving. In envisioning and living business in this way while remaining fully inserted in the market, the experience of the EoC joins together the market and civil society, efficiency and solidarity, economy and communion. And this is not trivial. If the market economy wants to function and to have a future which is sustainable and human, it must allow for the development of behavior founded on these other principles.

Most human communities are sustained by the interaction of three fundamental principles: exchange, redistribution of wealth, and donation. In the course of history there have been villages without exchange but there have never been villages that have survived without some form of donation. In our view, market economy, which is centered around the principle of contract, has a tremendous need to incorporate the principle of unconditional giving. But how can we justify the extension of unconditional giving from the private sphere—which no one contests—to the economic sphere, to markets? With the French Revolution modernity has launched its civil and cultural program: freedom, equality, and brotherhood. Liberty has given rise to and is fully expressed in market exchange. Equality has given rise to the experiences of the welfare state founded on the redistribution of wealth. Brotherhood has been recognized as an important element for a peaceful cohabitation of people. For instance, we can find explicit mention of brotherhood in article 1 of the Universal Declaration of Human Rights. However, the spirit of brotherhood has still a long way to go in order to enter, with equal rights, into the framework of modern society.

Unconditional giving could become a regulating principle of economics and of society if acting toward one another in a spirit of brotherhood is recognized as a founding principle, of which communion is the most immediate concrete expression.

A New Approach to Scientific Work

The fact that an ever-growing number of scholars, economists, entrepreneurs, and cultural leaders show attention to and interest in the EoC seems to be a sign that there may be some universal elements in this concept that started as the experience of a small group of people. In other words, while the EoC in strict terms is a concrete project with a history and a well-defined scope, some principles stick out that are universally applicable in order to create the category of communion in economics.

A detailed presentation of the first elements of economic theory emerging from the studies on the EoC goes surely beyond the objectives of this round table. However, I would like to quickly highlight one aspect. In the EoC we encounter a different type of economic actors, who can inspire also economic theory. They are quite different from the individual economic actors (the so-called *homo economicus*) that dominate most economic theories and can provide undesired legitimacy for the behavior of many people in business. Nevertheless, the EoC does not question the centrality or autonomy of the subject that chooses and decides in an autonomous way. What it does, is to complicate the image of the human being, proposing a new anthropology. It does not substitute the individual subject with the community or with the group. Rather, it substitutes the subject—defined without reference to its relational dimension—with a relational-subject which has been called *person* by a typically Christian tradition coming out of twentieth-century philosophy. The EoC challenge to economic theory is to go from the methodological individualism—which explains collective phenomena as a result of individuals' actions and choices—to a methodological personalism in which the person, seen intrinsically and ontologically as being in relation to others, is at the center of the theory.

The theory that emerges from the experience of the EoC tells us in various ways that relationships with other people can also be considered as goods (that is: good things that satisfy us and meet our needs) and that poverty is not only defined by the lack of resources but just as much by the lack of genuine relationships. If business and market interactions become a qualifying moment for civil life, we can hope to brake the massive growth, all over the world, of relational poverty in addition to material poverty.

Bibliography

Araùjo, Vera. 2000. "Quale visione dell'uomo e della società?" In *L'economia di comunione: Verso un agire economicoa misura di persona*. Milan: Vita e Pensiero

Lubich, Chiara. 2001. *L'economia di comunione: Storia e profezia*. Rome: Città Nuova.

Chapter 9

Pope Francis and the Economy of Communion

Jesús Morán, Focolare Movement
International Headquarters, Rocca di Papa, Italy

Amelia J. Uelmen, Georgetown University Law Center

Abstract: As leader of the global Catholic Church, Pope Francis, like his predecessors, has offered critical reflection on what it might take to help move the world toward greater attentiveness to economic justice and sustainable development. One of the obstacles that stands in the way of broader reception of this message is the tendency to interpret his proposals through a divisive ideological lens. This essay considers how Pope Francis's proposals might best be understood through the lens of reconciliation, and most specifically, of the paradigm of the unity of opposites. It then explores how the Economy of Communion project exemplifies promising dimensions of the unity of opposites in action.

Introduction

Concerns about severe levels of social inequality and environmentally unsustainable lifestyles have exploded into protest movements throughout the globe. In the words of the teenage activist Greta Thunberg: "Humanity is now standing at a crossroads. We must now decide which path we want to take" (Stubley 2019). What might it take for humanity to decide for the path toward sustainable living? Who might be the leaders and partners who can help the peoples of the world to envision both the necessity and the goodness of this path, and to gather the social and cultural resources they need for the journey?

One person with tremendous global convening power for this venture is Pope Francis. And one reason that Pope Francis holds such convening power is that the institution he leads, the global Catholic Church, has a long history of standing with humanity at the crossroads of crises. The saint whose name he took, Francis of Assisi, also confronted a world marked by severe social inequality, desperately in search of a vision that could help humanity choose a different path. In response, Francis of Assisi put everything on the line. Son of a wealthy merchant, he "stripped himself of all worldliness in order to choose God as the compass of his life, becoming poor with the poor, a brother to all" (Francis 2019).

Saint Francis's form of protest was not limited to a critique of the inequality and corruption of his day, but also "gave rise to a vision of economics" that still speaks to us today. As the Pope explains, it is a vision "that can give hope to our future and benefit not only the poorest of the poor, but our entire human family. A vision that is also necessary for the fate of the entire planet, our common home . . ." (2019).

Building on the legacy of Francis of Assisi, Pope Francis is using his global convening power to invite the next generation of economists, entrepreneurs, and thought leaders to explore together "a different kind of economy: one that brings life not death, one that is inclusive and not exclusive, humane and not dehumanizing, one that cares for the environment and does not despoil it." Like Greta Thunberg, the pope acknowledges that it is not easy to get this message across. "Sadly," the pope notes, until now "few have heard the appeal to acknowledge the gravity of the problems and, even more, to set in place a new economic model, the fruit of a culture of communion based on fraternity and equality" (2019). So he too banks on the next generation's capacity to generate a captivating vision and commitment.

An important step in this journey will be the March 2020 *Economy of Francesco* event in Assisi.[1] As the pope explains, it will be an occasion to come together to "enter into a 'covenant' to change today's economy and to give a soul to the economy of tomorrow." The aim of the meeting is, together with the next generation, to "appeal to some of our best economists and entrepreneurs who are already working on the global level to create an economy consistent with these ideals" (Francis 2019).

While it may be true that relatively few have heard the appeal to develop new economic models, there are notable exceptions in the life of the church and civil society. One widely recognized project is the Economy of Communion (EoC), an initiative of the Focolare Movement, and one of the organizing entities for the March 2020 gathering. The project originated in 1991, when Focolare founder Chiara Lubich reflected with the community in São Paolo, Brazil, on how to respond to acute social problems such as poverty and unemployment. Inspired in part by a reading of Pope John Paul's encyclical *Centesimus Annus*, the idea emerged to establish businesses that after an appropriate investment in the sustainability of the business, commit a part of their profits to direct aid for those in need and another part toward nurturing a "culture of giving" (Bruni & Uelmen 2006, 645–651).

As the Economy of Communion has developed over the years, it now includes not only businesses but also an international incubator network, projects focused specifically on sustainability and social integration, systems to welcome and integrate migrants, and professional training centers. Pro-

---

1. The Economy of Francesco event 2020 was postponed (due to covid) and took place instead in September of 2022 (see: https://www.humandevel-opment.va/en/eventi/2022/economy-of-francesco-the-pope-will-be-in-assisi.html).

phetic Economy dimensions of the work also aim to network various initiatives throughout the globe and to encourage academics in their efforts to develop scholarship and theories to sustain new economic, business, and cultural models (EoC Website 2019; EoC Report 2018; Sophia University Institute Website). According to the most recent EoC report, in 2018 more than 1.5 million Euros were collected and distributed to fund various developmental and educational projects. A part of the funds were also allocated to respond to the urgent necessities (health, housing, education, and food) of people with material needs throughout the world.

How has this project been received by Catholic leadership? In his 2009 encyclical, *Caritas in Veritate*, Pope Benedict noted the need for expanded categories to describe the relationship between business and ethics and current modes of production: "It would appear that the traditionally valid distinction between profit-based companies and non-profit organizations can no longer do full justice to reality, or offer practical direction for the future" (§46). Pope Benedict used the term "economy of communion" to describe an aspect of the emerging "intermediate area":

> In recent decades a broad intermediate area has emerged between the two types of enterprise. It is made up of traditional companies which nonetheless subscribe to social aid agreements in support of underdeveloped countries, charitable foundations associated with individual companies, groups of companies oriented towards social welfare, and the diversified world of the so-called "civil economy" and the "economy of communion." (§46)

Resisting the terminology of a "third way" or a "third sector," he then described these projects in terms of their human and social goals:

This is not merely a matter of a "third sector", but of a broad new composite reality embracing the private and public spheres, one which does not exclude profit, but instead considers it a means for achieving human and social ends. Whether such companies distribute dividends or not, whether their juridical structure corresponds to one or other of the established forms, becomes secondary in relation to their willingness to view profit as a means of achieving the goal of a more humane market and society. (§46)

Many scholars opine that that with the term "economy of communion" Pope Benedict was referring at least in part to Focolare-inspired enterprises (Allen 2009; Christiansen 2015, 201; Duncan 2017, 162; McCann 2012, 57; Guitián 2010, 288; Lucas 2018, 126).

Pope Francis has also been explicit in his reflections on the project's meaning and potential. On the occasion of the twenty-fifth anniversary of the project he delivered a lengthy address to an audience of Economy of Communion business owners, scholars, and other participants in the project (Francis 2017), which will be discussed at length *infra*.

At the outset, it is important to acknowledge that formidable obstacles stand in the way of broader reception of the challenge launched by Pope Francis to develop new economic models. Perhaps the most difficult lies in currently intense levels of social, political, and ecclesial polarization, which also foster the tendency to interpret his proposals through a divisive ideological lens. To open out the complexity in this challenge, we first consider how the current reflections and proposals of Pope Francis might best be understood through the lens of reconciliation, and most specifically, of the paradigm of the unity of opposites. We then turn to the twenty-five-year history of the Economy of Communion to explore how the project exemplifies promising dimensions of the unity of opposites in action.

The Mind of Pope Francis: The Unity of Opposites

In his *Brief Essay on the Time of Pope Francis*, French Benedictine monk Ghislain Lafont highlights how the strong resistance that Pope Francis has encountered over the course of his papacy marks the prophetic character of his pontificate. He writes: "Prophecy, in fact, never seems to be in direct continuity with the past and so initially arouses resistance and misunderstanding" (Lafont 2017, cover).

Right from the start of his pontificate it was evident that Pope Francis offered a complete novelty, even for those who had hoped for substantial changes. After an initial phase of disorientation, commentators and observers from disparate positions delved into heated debates that were also expressed in the form of publicly visible articles, interviews, and essays. What is at times missing in some of these debates is a sincere and serious effort to try to grasp with any depth who Jorge Mario Bergoglio was before becoming pope. As a result, some arguments lack important interpretive keys that could lead to a greater understanding of the ministry of Pope Francis.

We believe that it is impossible to understand with depth the key themes of his papacy and what his words, gestures, speeches, and magisterial documents represent for humanity without some exposure to his intellectual biography. While his personal history and pastoral actions are important, even more crucial are elements of cultural, intellectual, and spiritual formation, including times of difficulty and darkness, that forged his identity and also prepared him for his service as pope.

Into this gap steps the thorough and thoughtful work of Massimo Borghesi, author of Bergoglio's intellectual biography, *The Mind of Pope Francis* (2018). A core theme of this work is understanding the pivotal conceptual role that the "unity of opposites" plays in Bergoglio's intellectual framework. Borghesi writes:

Bergoglio's entire system of thought is one of reconcili-ation—not an irenic, optimistic, naively progressivist thinking, but rather a dramatic thinking, marked by a tension, that, having matured during the course of his Ignatian studies in the 1960s, finds its first formula-tion in the 1970s in the tragic context of an Argentina divided by a right-wing military and left-wing revolu-tionaries. It is a contrast that marks both the church and the Society of Jesus. (xxiv)

This, according to Borghesi, is the "golden thread of Bergo-glio's thought," and "his original, conceptual core." "Bergo-glio fought for a synthesis of the oppositions that lacerated the historical reality," proposing "an antinomian unity, an agonic solution achieved by way of the contrast" (xxiv). The character and quality of this reconciliation reaches beyond an interior or spiritual act, and the action it calls for extends beyond a personal or even collective level. Instead, it is a form of thought, a paradigm, to aim for synthesis that integrates two poles in tension. For example, Bergoglio finds in the work of Romano Guardini a further confirmation of a "synthet-ic," "integral" model, "capable of explaining and embracing the principal personal/social/political contrasts that tend to crystalize into dialectical contradictions that fuel dangerous conflicts" (Borghesi 2018, 105).

In an interview with Italian Jesuit journalist Antonio Spadaro, Pope Francis further explained how Guardini shaped his thought:

Opposition opens a path, a way forward. Speaking generally, I have to say that I love oppositions. Roma-no Guardini helped me with his book *Der Gegensatz*, which was important to me. He spoke of a polar op-position in which the two opposites are not annulled. One pole does not destroy the other. There is no con-tradiction and no identity. For him, opposition is resolved at a higher level. In such a solution, however, the polar tension remains. The tension remains, it is not cancelled out. The limits are overcome, not negated. Oppositions are helpful. Human life is structured in an oppositional form. The tensions are not necessarily resolved and ironed out; they are not like contradictions. (Borghesi 2018, 105)

How does this form of thought manifest in the work of Pope Francis? Borghesi writes:

The distinction between opposition (Gegensatz) and contradiction (Widerspruch) is crucial, because it allows us to think of the Catholic *communio* not as a flat, uniform unity, but as a dynamic, polyform reality, which for that reason does not fear to lose its unity. Ecclesial unity isn't to be understood as a monolithic block in which unity comes down from on high, in a fixed and direct manner. It is not afraid of accommodating different poles and reconciling them in the Spirit who unites everything, as in a musical symphony. This *communio* is realized in a *dialogical* form, in the patient development of interconnections that does not pretend to negate the accents, the variety of approaches that remain. (106)

In the vision of Pope Francis, what might it mean for mercy and truth to meet in this historical moment? As Borghesi explains: "Mercy is not being placed 'against' the truth, but as a manifestation of the truth" (259). In seeking out a wounded humanity, "[t]he 'glory' of God shines in the 'Samaritan' church, that is, in the form of *mercy*. In the contemporary world, which no longer knows the gratuitousness of true love, divided as it is between inaffectivity and *eros*, mercy unites beauty and goodness in the communication of truth" (258–59).

Similarly, the work of Austen Ivereigh challenges those who read the work of Pope Francis through the lens of a polarizing "rupture" from his predecessors Popes Benedict and John Paul II. Ivereigh writes:

> Francis's radicalism is not to be confused with a progressive teaching or ideology. It is radical because it is missionary, and mystical. Francis is instinctively and viscerally opposed to "parties" in the Church: he roots the papacy in the traditional Catholicism of God's holy faithful people, above all the poor. He will not compromise on the hot-button issues that divide the church from the secular West—a gap liberals would like to close by modernizing doctrine. Yet he is also, just as obviously, not a pope for the Catholic right: he will not use the papacy to right political and cultural battle he believes should be fought at the diocesan level, but to attract and teach. (Ivereigh 2014, xxi)

Anyone with their finger on the pulse of current discourse surrounding polarizing political, social, and ecclesial questions knows that the work of generating a synthesis is neither easy nor simple. Even if we aim to see the world and social problems from a perspective of unity, or from a systemic perspective, we are still left with a host of questions regarding how to *interpret* that perspective and *apply* it to concrete situations.

What models of thought might help to us to move from polarizing rupture to more multi-faceted modes of interpretation? In *Evangelii*, Pope Francis contrasts a spherical model with a more dynamic polyhedron.

> Here our model is not the sphere, which is no greater than its parts, where every point is equidistant from the centre, and there are no differences between them. Instead, it is the polyhedron, which reflects the convergence of all its parts, each of which preserves its distinctiveness. Pastoral and political activity alike seek to gather in this polyhedron the best of each. There is a place for the poor and their culture, their

aspirations and their potential. Even people who can be considered dubious on account of their errors have something to offer which must not be overlooked. It is the convergence of peoples who, within the universal order, maintain their own individuality; it is the sum total of persons within a society which pursues the common good, which truly has a place for everyone. (2013, 236)

As Borghesi notes, "polyhedral differentiation" captures well the ideas of "*unity in difference*, the single reality with many facets" (118). "Only the polyhedron maintains the supremacy of the whole without eliminating the polarity with the parts that make it up" (118–19).

Similarly, for German theologian Christoph Theobald, the metaphors of the sphere and the polyhedron in *Evangelii* shed light on keys to interpret the Second Vatican Council. As he explains, only an approach "that is sensitive to the confluence of all the partial elements in particular situation, insures that the elements preserve their originality while at the same time they are permeated by the whole, which is the fullness and richness of the gospel." For Theobald, this is "the key to the evangelical hermeneutics of Pope Francis . . . as well as to his conception of the church as God's people" (Theobald 2016, 53).

In this model, guidance does not emanate from the center of a sphere according to equidistant and uniform relationships, because such a model risks losing not only its own uniqueness but also the particular gift or talent that could be put at the service of the whole. The polyhedron preserves the originality of particular gifts and talents because the central point of reference is not located at a point equidistant from all the others. Instead, the center is present, in a certain sense, everywhere and nowhere. The relationship is less a function of dogmatic direction, and more a service that animates, unifies, and broadens to more universal horizons. As Theobald notes, these are the complex relationships that can make "the *entirety* of the Gospel visible in its inexhaustible depth thanks to the *multiplicity of its modes of expression*" (2016, 74).

The Economy of Communion: the Unity of Opposites in Action

When we consider the origins of the Economy of Communion, it is interesting to note the parallels between Bergoglio's intellectual formation and one of the insights at the heart of Focolare founder Chiara Lubich's thought. As the Focolare interdisciplinary study center was developing in the late 1990s, Lubich explained that the doctrine which was emerging would be like a new synthesis: "because the ideal of unity brings about the unity of opposites." Initial steps within the study center itself included work to reconcile tensions between differing currents and schools within theology. As Lubich challenged, the project is "to bring about a synthesis and not a compromise" (Lubich 2006, 160; Voce 2012, 21).

Thus is it not surprising that Pope Francis, in his own commentary on the Focolare's economic project, would highlight the oxymoronic challenge that the project's name embodies:

> Economy and communion. These are two words that contemporary culture keeps separate and often considers opposites. Two words that you have instead joined, accepting the invitation that Chiara Lubich offered you 25 years ago in Brazil, when, in the face of the scandal of inequality in the city of São Paulo, she asked entrepreneurs to become agents of communion.... With your life you demonstrate that economy and communion become more beautiful when they are beside each other. (Francis 2017)

One could explore numerous dimensions of how the *practices* of the Economy of Communion exemplify the unity of opposites in action. Generally, what does it mean to run a business with a responsible attention to profit as a sign of its health and potential for growth, and at the same time remain profoundly attentive to the intervention of God in the material life of the business and all of its various relationships?

In their study of Economy of Communion businesses in North America, Gallagher & Buckeye reflect on the distinctiveness they found in these practices: "EoC companies are indeed different. And that difference is centered on a conviction of the business as a set of relationships, or more accurately, a *community*, and the conviction that the purpose of economic activity—the production and distribution of goods and services—is to bring people together, to create *community*" (2014, 188–89).

Can these projects even survive on the market? As Gallagher & Buckeye report, the priority placed on creating community takes many forms: "We find EoC companies walking away from business opportunities, scrupulously following regulations, cheerfully (sometimes reluctantly) refunding payments, participating in the civic process while avoiding attempts at undue influence, making restitution where appropriate, and looking to reconcile with detractors" (186). Reflecting on competitive behavior in EoC business, they note:

> ... clearly the guiding principles for these companies is their view of their business as a set of relationships, and this has a significant effect on the approaches to competition.... It's fair to describe these companies as more customer focused that competitor focused. This appears to carry over in their approaches to pricing. Most of these companies take a purely "cost-based" approach to pricing that is not in any apparent way geared or pegged to competitors. (183)

Over the course of its twenty-five year history, scholars of the Economy of Communion have probed many of these layers (Argiolas 2017; Gallagher & Buckeye 2014; Gallagher 2014; Gomez 2015; Frémeaux & Michelson 2017).

What happens when the characteristics of the Economy of Communion are mapped onto the tensions inherent in the social and economic development? The next sections explore some of the contrasts that tend to permeate development work, to consider whether the nexus between core insights of Pope Francis and the experience of the Economy of Communion might help to illuminate a path toward reconciliation of opposites.

1. The Protagonists of Development: El Pueblo Fiel and the EoC

Who are the protagonists of social and economic development? Whose voices and perspectives should be taken into consideration when working to develop viable models for economic development? Many aspire to foster a broader sense of participation and ownership at all levels of their projects, and even recognize that this is often the key to long term success. But often even those with the best intentions for leveraging the kind of financial resources that seem to promise immediate positive impact for the poor struggle with the unintended consequences of destroying the potential for local markets to thrive. For example, as the documentary *Poverty, Inc.* recounts, projects to distribute free shoes in developing countries can severely damage the business prospects for local shoe manufacturers. Similarly, large scale efforts on the part of non-profit organizations to supply developing countries with free solar panels severely impeded the hopes for a promising local solar panel business that had just been getting traction.

Reflecting on this tension, what comes into relief is the *popular* origins of the Economy of Communion. The idea did not emerge from the mind of an academic, at a conference, or in the office of a Washington think-tank. It emerged in response to a vital community-based contact with the poor, who themselves were an integral part of Focolare communities in Brazil. The first creative sparks for the businesses, and the first "shareholders" for the businesses, emerged from people who were poor, who responded, for example, even by selling chickens and other livestock in order to participate (Masters & Uelmen 2011, 152; Bruni & Uelmen 2006, 656; cf. Gold 2010, 81–102).

The images that circulate in local EoC conferences often refer to the growth of what is small but vital. For example, the EoC is like a tiny seed that has taken root in a concrete wall: Sooner or later it will grow, take over, and bring the wall down, because it is alive. As repeatedly stressed by Giuseppe Maria Zanghì, one of Chiara Lubich's closest collaborators for the elaboration of the Focolare's cultural projects, this "incarnational" dimension is essential:

> Without the incarnation of thought, there is no over-coming of the abyss that separates reality from reality: each remains closed in its solitude. Now, if incarnation of thought means the entry of the spirit of man into the profound being of reality through the often con-tradictory becoming of them, Incarnation of the Word means the entry of God in the flesh and in the history of man: of the man with his sins, his miseries, his limits, his denials, his unfinished dreams. (Zanghì 2015, 17)

With these tensions in mind, it is interesting to consider the Economy of Communion in light of Pope Francis's reflections on *el pueblo fiel*, the faithful people. As Borghesi explains, *el pueblo fiel* "is distinctly separate from both the *populist ideologies* and the Marxist system, which is fixed to the 'abstract' categories of the bourgeoisie and the proletariat." Instead, "The concept of the believing people refers for him to the *historical* ways that faith animates life, reality, culture. It points to the *how* of the incarnation. It is not a question of academic sociology but of the historical, lived terrain that nourishes the faith of the church." In sum: "*Popular spirituality is culture, an organic web that links together all aspects of existence*" (53).

The Latin American Bishops Conference reflection following the meeting in Puebla in 1979 affirmed not only the wisdom,
but also the *synthesis* that emerges from concrete experience:

> The Catholic wisdom of the common people is capable
> of fashioning a vital synthesis. It creatively combines
> the divine and the human, Christ and Mary, spirit
> and body, communion and institution, person and
> community, faith and homeland, intelligence and
> emotion. This wisdom is a Christian humanism that
> radically affirms the dignity of every person as a child
> of God, establishes a basic fraternity, teaches people
> how to encounter nature and understand work, and
> provides reasons for joy and humor even in the midst
> of a very hard life. (Borghesi 2018, 53; quoting *Puebla*)

All of these elements come together in the 2007 document
which followed the Latin American Bishops Conference meeting in Aparecida, Brazil, and on which Bergoglio had a very
strong influence. As Borghesi notes: "The *pueblo fiel*, the poor,
the witnesses, the ecclesial communities, become 'theological places,' places where the face of Christ manifests itself
today. It is the face of the humiliated Christ, the Samaritan,
the crucified one, the one who surprises and attracts by his
mercy, his embrace, his singular humanity. Aparecida valued
everything" (300).

When applied to the work of social and economic development, the concept and reality of *el pueblo fiel* helps us to
appreciate with depth the insights that emerge from popular
and grassroots origins. It also illuminates the *value* of the fact
that many of the people who are involved with the project are
unsophisticated little people. Just as Jesus received from the
little boy five small barley loaves and two small fish as raw
material for a miracle (John 6:9), the message of Aparecida
helps us to value everyone's contribution to development work.

There would be numerous ways to illustrate how the Economy of Communion project emerged and continues to develop

within the dynamic creativity of *el pueblo fiel*. As noted above, the initial businesses emerged from the active contribution of people with few material resources making small contributions to purchase "shares" for initial capital for the start-ups.

The life of *el pueblo fiel* is also evident in the stories that the entrepreneurs share about how they see the "providential" intervention of God in the midst of their effort to run their businesses according to Economy of Communion principles. As Gallagher & Buckeye recount, the owner of a violin craft shop had set aside time to call a list of customers who were behind in their payments, but got sidetracked because of his effort to help an immigrant employee with the application process to buy a house, which ended up taking the whole day. "Unnoticed at first, but confirmed later, was the fact that while everyone's attention was focused on helping the employee, a full payment from every delinquent customer arrived in that day's mail" (2014, 143).

Another business recounted the unexpectedly positive results of how it handled employee terminations in the wake of the 2008 economic downturn. "The terminated employees did recognize the significant effort that the company made with the severances . . . and there were many scenes where they were consoling the remaining employees who were in tears" (2014, 170). Happily, with a month, every employee had found a new job, even in the midst of the economic crisis. As economic conditions improved, the company also realized that even the terminated employees were providing positive references for the company with customers and with new prospective employees. The owner explained:

> This crisis ended up being a moment of truth. It truly cemented our team and its belief in our corporate values. In times of hardship, we were able to stick to our core principles and not throw them away in the name of economic imperatives. . . . Our employees

have seen firsthand that doing the right thing not only makes one a better person and brings a lot of serenity and peace but can also pay off in the long term too. They experience some of the fruits of providence in their lives. (2014, 170–71)

In answering the question of who is, or who should be, the protagonist of development projects, the experience of EoC entrepreneurs points in an interesting direction. As Gallagher & Buckeye summarize:

> EoC leadership reflects a *pragmatic generosity* fueled by a dependence on providence. There is an acute awareness that they shouldn't give away so much that they ruin the business, become the needy, or are forced into borrowing money, yet there are several owners who gladly give away everything they can over and above identified, concrete needs. This conviction about providence, in fact, might be the bedrock of their culture. (2014, 153)

According to Gallagher & Buckeye, for the EoC businesses that they studied, the protagonist of development is the loving intervention of the divine.

> The EoC explicitly, consciously, intentionally, and deliberately acts in a way that suggests that providential intervention is imminent. This is really an active expression of a profound sense of hope. It is not a distancing of self from a thorny or an apparently insoluble matter and just tossing it into God's hands. It is a recognition that divine intervention is possible everywhere and anywhere, every time and any time, with everyone and anyone. Further, EoC companies tell stories all the time because they believe it's quite likely that there will be some future connected event to the story. (2014, 153)

Who are the protagonists of development? Does guidance for the direction of a business or development project flow from top-down experts, or does it emerge from grassroots insights? Within the varieties of EoC experience, the answer is not only both, and not just a synthesis. By placing a priority on relationships of communion, and by opening themselves to divine intervention, the protagonist becomes, in a certain sense, the life of communion itself.

2. Interests in Tension: Beyond Altruism

A second tension in development work is the struggle to articulate shared *interests*. Stated in the broadest terms, it is difficult to imagine and articulate how the interests of people with social and legal control over material resources might fully align with the interests of those who lack the material resources needed for social and economic development. It is not that people with resources are not engaged in shifting the balance, but that this shift is perceived as requiring them to pull against their own interests and to sacrifice something valuable.

Karol Wojtyla captured well the core conundrum at the heart of economic theories in which a good exists in "in isolation from the good of the others and from the common good."

> In this system, the good of the individual has the quality of being opposed to every other individual and his good. This kind of individualism is based on self-preservation and is always on the defensive . . . "The others" are for the individual only a source of limitations and may even be opponents and create polarizations. (Clark 2016, xi–xii)

Echoing Paul VI and John Paul II, in his 2009 encyclical *Caritas in Veritate*, Pope Benedict also issued a strong critique of *homo economicus* as an incomplete anthropology. As Kenneth Himes summarizes:

To reduce human motivation and thought to that of
a rational maximizer of self-interest is to truncate
the nature of the human and to misread the aim of
authentic human development. Human beings, of
course, do demonstrate self-interest in their attitudes
and behaviors. Yet humans are complex beings who act
for a variety of reasons, and a more adequate market
economy will make room for a wider range of human
motivations to be considered. (Himes 2012, 32)

In order to address a challenge of this magnitude, it is not
enough simply to recover a framework of commitment to the
whole. The work, according to Charles Taylor, is to find sources
of meaning outside of the self, but that also resonate with the
self. We need categories that can help us, again in Taylor's
terms, to grasp "an order which is inseparably indexed to a
personal vision" (Uelmen 2012, 66–67).

Italian economist Luigino Bruni, whose groundbreaking
work has provided theoretical foundations for the Economy
of Communion project, highlights the historical contribution of economic theorists less tainted by the polarities of
individualism. As Bruni summarizes, in the work of Antonio
Genovesi, "love of self and love of others are two dimensions
that are both present in the person, and the dynamics of human
action are explainable on the basis of the interplay between
these two basic forces." For Genovesi, the "diffusive force" of
love for others "was not simple benevolence or, as we would
say today, altruism; it has more to do with interpersonal relationships, and its basic element is the capacity for friendliness
. . . an indelible characteristic of our nature—which explains
that great majority of human actions in both small and large
societies" (Bruni 2012, 65). This in turn provides a foundation
for interests to align.

Profound theological support for alignment of interests
is also evident in Pope Benedict's reflections on the relational
dynamic at the heart of the Trinity in *Caritas in Veritate*: "God

desires to incorporate us into this reality of communion as well: 'that they may be one even as we are one'" (John 17:22). In this light, we understand that "true openness does not mean loss of individual identity but profound interpenetration" (§54).

With a strong conceptual grounding in this anthropological vision, the Economy of Communion project offers a laboratory for reconceptualizing shared interests. For Focolare founder Chiara Lubich, the hermeneutical key to what she termed the "culture of giving" was to discover all the ways in which these everyday acts of openness to others were *not* in the order of a heroic pull against one's own interests.

> Unlike the consumer economy based on a culture of having, the Economy of Communion is the economy of giving. This could seem difficult, arduous, heroic. But it is not, because the human person, made in the image of God who is love, finds fulfillment precisely in loving, in giving. This need to love lies in the deepest core of our being, whether we are believers or not. (Lubich 2007, 25; cf. Uelmen 2010, 38)

When the culture of giving or of communion is lived in all of its power and depth, participants in these projects break through the tension at the heart of zero-sum game theories of altruism in which service to others is pitted against one's own interests. Instead, through a Trinitarian lens, calls for sacrifice or generosity make little sense if a sharing of material goods is simply an expression of one's own identity, as a member of the universal human family (Uelmen 2010, 38). To paraphrase Lubich, service to others may *seem* arduous and heroic, but *it is not* because such a stance is precisely what leads to personal fulfillment as well.

Some interpretations of the story of the Good Samaritan emphasize the Samaritan's selfless capacity to set aside his own interests and fears in order to help a stranger in need. Through the anthropological lens of communion, the very concept of interests is expanded to embrace the personal fulfillment that emerges from a lifestyle based on loving others. In other words, if I fail to recognize the humanity and the needs of others, the question becomes not only what will happen to marginalized and discarded people, but also what will happen to me—to my own identity, to my own humanity? (Uelmen 2017, 1410–14).

In his own reflections on what the charism of unity has to offer the Church and the world, Pope Francis summarized the dynamic with the catchphrase "the spirituality of the we."

> The charism of unity is a providential stimulus and a powerful support for experiencing this evangelical [mysticism] of "the we," that is, walking together in the history of the men and women of our time as "of one heart and soul" (cf. Acts 4:32), discovering and loving concretely those "members of one another" (cf. Rom 12:5). Jesus prayed to the Father for this: "that they may all be one as you and I are one" (cf. Jn 17:21), and in himself he showed us the way, up to the complete gift of all in the abyssal emptying of the cross (cf. Mk 15:34; Phil 2:6-8). It is the spirituality of "the we." (2018)

It is very important to note that this "we" is not a uniform agglomeration without identity or a flattening collective of a merely sociological nature. Instead, it is better understood as the result of the concrete practice of the Pauline motto "you are one in Christ Jesus" (Gal 3:28), perhaps best expressed with the more literal translation from Greek: "you are one person in Christ Jesus." The "we" in this sense ultimately points to the experience of the Trinitarian God in human flesh (cf. John Paul II 2001, 16–28).

As Pope Francis explained, this is what saves us from every form of egoism or egotistical self-interest. "It is not only a spiritual fact, but a concrete reality with formidable results—if we live it and if we authentically and courageously affirm its various dimensions—at the social, cultural, political, economic levels. . . . Jesus redeemed not only the individual person, but also social relations" (2013, §178). Taking this fact seriously means "molding a new face of the city of men according to God's loving plan" (2018).

It is also helpful to read this against the backdrop of *The Joy of the Gospel*:

> Though it is true that this mission demands great generosity on our part, it would be wrong to see it as a heroic individual undertaking, for it is first and foremost the Lord's work, surpassing anything which we can see and understand. . . . The real newness is the newness which God himself mysteriously brings about and inspires, provokes, guides and accompanies in a thousand ways. This conviction enables us to maintain a spirit of joy in the midst of a task so demanding and challenging that it engages our entire life. God asks everything of us, yet at the same time he offers everything to us. (2013, §12)

In *Laudato sì* Pope Francis further opens out how the capacity to give of oneself with a dynamic life of communion is a hallmark of human maturity:

> The human person grows more, matures more and is sanctified more to the extent that he or she enters into relationships, going out from themselves to live in communion with God, with others and with all creatures. In this way, they make their own that trinitarian dynamism which God imprinted in them when they were created. Everything is interconnected, and this invites us to develop a spirituality of that global solidarity which flows from the mystery of the Trinity. (2015, §240)

This is the dynamic cultural anthropology at the heart of the Economy of Communion, and also at the heart of the Pope's call to reimagine our participation in "the Lord's work," including in the various aspects of social, cultural, political, and economic development (2013, §178). To recognize and work to creatively address the needs of others is not so much a matter of reaching beyond my own interests, but the logical consequences of an *ontological claim* about what it means to be human—that is, to acknowledge how my own identity is grounded in my fundamental connection to other human beings and their needs (Uelmen 2017, 1410–11).

3. Prophetic Economy: Reconciling (Personal) Charity and (Structural) Justice

The cries of the poor and the cries of the earth also urgently call for reflection on large scale projects to address the structures of systemic injustice. In a true reconciliation of opposites, a grounding in and appreciation of *el pueblo fiel* and work to overcome the zero-sum game frameworks for personal commitment and action, in no way devalues thoughtful and critical engagement with economic, financial, legal, and policy *systems*.

In fact, a discussion that limits itself to personal incentives and individual action would still beg the important question of at which level to address economic and social inequality. Do the deepest solutions emerge through an emphasis on freely chosen personal commitments to economic justice; or through adjustments to regulatory schemes that mandate structural change and re-distribution of economic costs and benefits?

Here too, the answer of course is "both." But in his February 2017 discourse, Pope Francis also warned: The Good Samaritan is "not enough." Particularly when engaging interdisciplinary projects at the nexus between theological reflection and business models, the pope encourages EoC participants to pay close attention to the deeper and more structural questions that may permeate the incidents and contexts that lead to accidents, violence, or other forms of injury. The problem with a myopic focus on individual action is that it may obfuscate the occasions when the root of our most difficult problems should also be attributed to structures and systems that foster injustice (cf. John Paul II 1987, §36–39).

Further, we also need to pay close attention to how our work is embedded in *social and legal systems* that tend to "produce" marginalized and "discarded" people. As Pope Francis explained:

> Capitalism *continues to produce discarded people* whom it would then like to care for. The principal ethical dilemma of this capitalism is the creation of discarded people, then trying to hide them or make sure they are no longer seen. A serious form of poverty in a civilization is when *it is no longer able to see its poor*, who are first discarded and then hidden. (2017)

What might it mean to explore a vision of justice that pushes beyond *individual* attention to those who are "discarded"? Pope Francis exhorts:

> We must work toward changing the rules of the game of the socio-economic system. Imitating the Good Samaritan of the Gospel is not enough. Of course, when an entrepreneur or any person happens upon a victim, he or she is called to take care of the victim and, perhaps like the Good Samaritan, also to enlist the fraternal action of the market (the innkeeper)....But it is important to act above all *before* the man comes across the robbers, by battling the frameworks of sin that produce robbers and victims. An entrepreneur who is only a Good Samaritan does half of his duty: he takes care of today's victims, but does not curtail those of tomorrow. (2017)

What kinds of frameworks, or better *paradigms*, could change the rules of the game so that the socioeconomic system no longer produces discarded people? What kind of corrective might help to remedy the problem of no longer being able to even *see* the poor?

Reflections on this topic could of course be encyclopedic. Here we note just three ways in which the Economy of Communion project is poised to contribute to reflection at this level. First, it has helped to spearhead a project entitled "Prophetic Economy." As Jeffrey Sachs reflected at the first Prophetic Economy gathering in 2018:

> We need a worldwide effort to face the ecological and the social exclusion. We are a rich, technologically advanced and scientifically sophisticated world; but the world economy does not produce justice. It does not ensure social inclusion, and it certainly does not protect creation. Therefore we can't depend on market forces or what economists call the "invisible hand" to protect us, to save us from ourselves. For that, we need a moral commitment; we need a diplomatic framework; we need a common plan for the world. (Sachs 2019)

Recognizing the enormity of the challenges posed by structural injustice and outdated aid policies, the Prophetic Economy project aims to connect and network the people and communities around the world who "believe passionately in human development and sustainability" and who are "working tirelessly to change the rules and demand justice" (EoC Website, "Prophetic Economy").

Second, since its inception the Economy of Communion project has valued academic work in all of the disciplines that engage social and economic life, probe the roots of systemic injustice, explore the potential for a paradigm shift, and propose creative alternatives (EoC Website, "Study and Research," "Publications").

But perhaps one of the greatest challenges in our current climate is generating an imaginative vision of how our work for social and economic justice is connected in a vital way.

Activists and academics may have different roles and tasks, but they need each other if we are to address complex systemic problems with both vigor and depth. Similarly, children, teenagers, young adults, and those who have been already engaged in their professions for many years, may have different perspectives on how to solve current problems. But we need this variety of perspectives to generate a fully engaged vision for the future. And so for every form of difference: ethnic, geographic, religious, and so on.

For this work, the charism of unity can illuminate how every relationship, every human connection, and every form of commitment to the good can be charged with meaning. As Chiara Lubich reflected in 1959:

> In this world we are all brothers and sisters and yet we pass each other as if we were strangers. And this happens even among baptized Christians. The Communion of Saints, the Mystical Body exists. But this Body is like a network of darkened tunnels. The power to illuminate them exists; in many individuals there is the light of grace, but Jesus did not want only this when he turned to the Father, calling upon him. He wanted a heaven on earth: the unity of all with God and with one another; the network of tunnels to be illuminated; the presence of Jesus to be in every relationship with others, as well as in the soul of each. This is his final testament, the most precious desire of a God who gave his life for us. (2007, 99)

When the darkened tunnels that connect the human family are illuminated, we not only see each other, but also respond to each other's needs as members of a body.

The various dimensions of the Economy of Communion project are one way to cultivate these ways of seeing and being, which in turn can inform in-depth reflection on systems and methods to embody structural change.

4. Viewing Projects to Humanize the Economy through a Non-Ideological Lens

We save the most difficult question for last. As we noted at the outset, we believe that one of the most formidable obstacles to the broader reception of the challenge launched by Pope Francis to develop new economic models lies in currently intense levels of social, political, and ecclesial polarization, including the tendency to interpret his proposals through an ideological lens. As Cardinal Peter Turkson, prefect of the Dicastery for Promoting Integral Human Development, explained, Pope Francis's reference to a social economy "is not to be confused with the socialist economy." He noted: "This is a problem we often find in the United States when we go to present the message of the Holy Father. Many accuse him of being socialist or communist" (Harris 2019). The interpretive debate undoubtedly precedes the pontificate of Pope Francis (Finn 2012, 105–113, Lucas 2018, 124–125; Zamagni, 2019). Nonetheless, one might argue that the debates have become especially heated, perhaps also exacerbated by increasingly levels of political and cultural polarization. Thoughtful scholars have been probing the potential for the reception of Pope Francis's challenge to both the right and the left (Cloutier 2015).

Might the Economy of Communion project offer any insight into this challenge, or solace regarding steps toward healing? An analogy to a recent television commercial helps to illustrate the potential. In April 2017, the Heineken beer company launched its "Worlds Apart" advertising campaign. Footage of its social experiment involved ordinary people (not actors) who when they met for the first time were asked to assemble together a piece of furniture and to complete a questionnaire. The assembled result was, of course, a bar, and once they were seated together at the bar they viewed a short film that captured their partner exposing in no uncertain terms a political view that ran counter to their own. At this point they are given a choice: to leave, or to "stay and discuss your differences over a beer." All six choose to stay and converse respectfully about their views (Hunt 2017; Segarra 2017).

We will not venture to guess whether there is no political gap that cannot be bridged over a beer. And as discussed above, the relationships in many Economy of Communion settings are *much* thicker than anonymous strangers coming together for a one-time random and somewhat banal cooperative effort. Nonetheless, just as the shared project of constructing a piece of furniture generates a much greater possibility that otherwise-polarized citizens might sit together at the same table, the concrete *project* of the Economy of Communion offers a potential platform for people to come together to build something constructive, notwithstanding their strong ideological differences.

To illustrate: Within the Focolare communities in the United States and Canada, some people have been involved with the Economy of Communion project since its inception, in 1991. If one were to attempt a survey of the political leanings of those present at the annual North American EoC conference, even in 2019 it might be difficult to discern who in the group was a Republican and who was a Democrat. Certainly, contrasting ideas about the role of the state, the role of religion in the public square, and preferred political models for social action and change would come up in conversations. But for the most part, the common commitment to a concrete project in service to the poor and the unemployed or underemployed, together with a shared conviction that Gospel values could inform an approach to business life, helped to forge the kinds of deep non-ideological bonds that greatly relativized political affiliations.

To be clear, Focolare communities in the United States and elsewhere have *not* been immune to the political polarization that is currently so intense. And more broadly, those who dedicate themselves to living a spirituality of unity, whether in business projects or other settings, are certainly not immune from the conflicts that emerge from differences of opinion or in perspectives on how to proceed with the concrete dimensions of their work together.

In fact, when gathered with the Focolare's Loppiano community near Florence in May 2018, Pope Francis went out of his way to explicitly encourage community members not to shy away from the hard work involved in facing and working through conflict. Commenting on the account of the wedding feast at Cana, he noted the creative tension between Jesus and Mary regarding the appropriate timing to initiate his public ministry. Notwithstanding what could be interpreted as a kind of rebuff or correction ("Woman, what does this have to do with me? My hour has not yet come"), Mary nonetheless acts to prepare the way for the miracle: "His mother said to the servants, 'Do whatever he tells you'" (Jn 2:4–5). Pope Francis challenged the community to draw on Mary's example: "Mary speaks and intervenes. . . . Always look to this, this lay woman, Jesus' first disciple, how she reacted in all the conflicting episodes of her son's life. It will really help you" (Francis 2018).

The daily life of any business venture or any community-based project offers numerous occasions for the reconciliation of opposites. In our current political climate, it can be difficult for everyone, even those who try to live a spirituality of unity, to get traction for a system based on the unity of opposites: Energy and commitments seem to gravitate toward the poles. Nonetheless, it may be helpful to reflect further on how the *witness* of a *shared project* might light a candle in the dark.

It is through concrete projects, through the "incarnation," that we can receive the invitation to be protagonists, and also to appreciate the precious contribution of others, even in the midst of contrasting ideas and conflicts. For this process, the perspective of Pope Francis is especially helpful and encouraging:

> Community conflicts are inevitable: in a certain sense they need to happen, if the community is truly living sincere and honest relationships. That's life. It does not make sense to think of living in a community in which there are brothers who are not experiencing difficulties in their lives. Something is missing from communities where there is no conflict. Reality dictates that there are conflicts in all families and all groups of people. And conflict must be faced head on: it should not be ignored. ... Covering it over just creates a pressure cooker that will eventually explode. A life without conflicts is not life. (Francis 2013b, Catholic Herald translation)

Conclusion

Humanity is at a crossroads, and it is no small feat to discern the path forward. Pope Francis invites us to move into spaces fraught with tension and conflict in order to discover together the new paradigms and paths that could lead to greater justice and a sustainable future for our planet. As the pope himself noted, economy and communion are "two words that contemporary culture keeps separate and often considers opposites." The Economy of Communion's efforts to unite these realms over the course of more than twenty-five years now offers to the church and civil society a locus for deeper reflection on the path forward. And while the project may demand, in the words of Pope Francis, "great generosity on our part," its greatest strength is in the realization that it is not "a heroic individual undertaking" (Francis 2013, 12). Communion—itself a sign of the unity of opposites—is also the life-giving protagonist and source of insight and strength for the journey ahead.

Bibliography

Allen, John. L., Jr. 2009. "Pope Greets Obama: Encyclical Precedes Historic Visit," *National Catholic Reporter* (24 July).

Argiolas, Giuseppe. 2017. *Social Management: Principles, Governance and Practice.* Switzerland: Springer International Publishing.

Benedict XVI, Pope. 2009. *Caritas In Veritate.* http://www.vatican. va/content/benedict-xvi/en/encyclicals/documents/hf_ben-xvi_enc_20090629_caritas-in-veritate.html.

Borghesi, Massimo. 2018. *The Mind of Pope Francis.* Collegeville, MN: Liturgical Press Academic.

Bruni, Luigino. 2012. *The Wound and the Blessing: Economics, Relationships, and Happiness.* New York: New City Press.

Bruni, Luigino and Amelia J. Uelmen. 2006. "Religious Values and Corporate Decision Making: The Economy of Communion Project." *Fordham Journal of Corporate & Financial Law* 11, 3: 645–680.

Christiansen, Drew. 2015. "The Economy of Grace and the Church of the Poor: Paper Responses to the Financial Crisis." *Journal of Catholic Social Thought* 12, 2: 189–206.

Clark, Charles. M.A. 2016. "Foreword." In *The Wound and the Blessing* by Luigino Bruni. New York: New City Press.

Cloutier, David. 2015. "Pope Francis and American Economics," Theological Roundtable with Charles Clark, Mary Hirschfield and Matthew Shadle. *Horizons: the Journal of the College Theology Society* 42: 122–155.

Congregation for the Institutes of Consecrated Life and Societies of Apostolic Life. 1994. La vita fraterna in comunità: "Congregavit nos in unum Christi amor." Milan: Paoline.

Duncan, Bruce. 2017. "The Economics Behind the Social Thought of Pope Francis." *The Australiasian Catholic Record* 92, 2: 148–166.

Economy of Communion. 2018. "2018 EoC Report." http://edc-online. org/en/poverta-e-oltre/rapporto-edc/report-eoc-2018.html.

_____. 2019. Website (International). http://www.edc-online. org/en/.

Finn, Daniel. K. 2012. *The Moral Dynamic of Economic Life: An Extension and Critique of Caritas in Veritate.* New York: Oxford University Press.

Francis, Pope. 2013. *Evangelii Gaudium.* http://www.vatican. va/content/francesco/en/apost_exhortations/documents/ papa-francesco_esortazione-ap_20131124_evangelii-gaudium.html.

_____. 2013b. Ai Superiori Generali (November 29, 2013). Translation: "Key quotes from the Pope's meeting with the Union of Superiors General." *Catholic Herald* UK, (January 4, 2014).

_____. 2015. *Laudato Sì.* http://www.vatican.va/ content/francesco/en/encyclicals/documents/papa-francesco_20150524_enciclica-laudato-si.html.

_____. 2017. *Address to Participants in the Meeting "Economy of Communion," Sponsored by the Focolare Movement* (February 4, 2017). http://www.vatican.va/content/ francesco/en/speeches/2017/february/documents/papa-francesco_20170204_focolari.html.

_____. 2018. Pastoral Visit to Nomadelfia to Meet the Community Founded by Don Zeno Saltini; and to Loppiano to Visit the International Centre of the Focolare Movement (May 10, 2018). http://www.vatican.va/content/francesco/en/ travels/2018/inside/documents/papa-francesco-nomadelfia-loppiano_2018.html.

_____. 2019. *Letter sent by the Holy Father for the Event 'Economy of Francesco,'* Assisi 26-28 March 2020. http://www. vatican.va/content/francesco/en/letters/2019/documents/papa-francesco_20190501_giovani-imprenditori.html.

Frémeaux, Sandrine and Grant Michelson. 2017. "The Common Good of the Firm and Humanistic Management: Conscious Capitalism and Economy of Communion." *Journal of Business Ethic* 145: 701–709.

Gallagher, John. B. 2014. "Communion and Profits: Thinking with the Economy of Communion about the Purpose of Business." *Revista Portuguese de Filosofia* 70, no. 1: 9–27.

Gallagher, John and Jeanne Buckeye. 2014. *Structures of Grace: The Business Practices of the Economy of Communion*. Hyde Park, NY: New City Press.

Gold, Lorna. 2010. *New Financial Horizons: The Emergence of an Economy of Communion*. Hyde Park, NY: New City Press.

Gomez, P.Y., A. Grevin & O. Masclef. 2015. *L'entreprise, une affaire de don. Ce que révèlent les sciences de gestion*. Editions Nouvelle Cité, Collection GRACE.

Grassl, Wolfgang. 2011. "Hybrid Forms of Business: The Logic of Gift in the Commercial World." *Journal of Business Ethics* 100:109–123.

Guitián, Gregorio. 2010. "Integral Subsidiarity and Economy of Communion: Two Challenges from *Caritas in Veritate*," *Journal of Markets & Morality* 13, no. 2: 279–295.

Ivereigh, Austen. 2014. *The Great Reformer: Francis and the Making of a Radical Pope*. New York: Picador.

Harris, Elise. 2019. "Top Vatican Official Says Americans Misunderstand Pope's Social Agenda." *Crux* (May 15, 2019).

Himes, K. 2012. "Benedict's View of the Person." In *The Moral Dynamic of Economic Life: An Extension and Critique of Caritas in Veritate*, edited by Daniel Finn, 31–33. New York: Oxford University Press.

Hunt, Elle. 2017. "That Heineken ad: brewer tackles how to talk to your political opposite." *The Guardian* (US Edition) (April 27, 2017).

John Paul II, Pope. 1987. *Sollicitudo Rei Socialis*. http://www.vatican. va/content/john-paulii/en/encyclicals/documents/hf_jp-ii_ enc_30121987_sollicitudo-rei-socialis.html.

_____. 2001. *Novo Millennio Ineunte*. http://www.vatican.va/ content/john-paul-ii/en/apost_letters/2001/documents/hf_jp-ii_apl_20010106_novo-millennio-ineunte.html.

Lafont, G. 2017. *Brief Essay on the Time of Pope Francis*. Bologna: EDB.

Lubich, Chiara. 2006. *A New Way: The Spirituality of Unity*. Hyde Park, NY: New City Press.

_____. 2007. *Essential Writings: Spirituality, Dialogue, Culture*. Hyde Park, NY: New City Press.

Lucas, Brian. 2018. "The Not-for-Profit Sector: A Roman Catholic View." In *Research Handbook on Not-for-Profit Law*, edited by Matthew Harding, 108–129. Cheltenham and Massachusetts: Edward Elgar.

Masters, Thomas & Amelia Uelmen. 2011. *Focolare: Living a Spirituality of Unity in the United States*. Hyde Park, NY: New City Press.

McCann, Dennis. 2012. "The Principle of Gratuitousness: Opportunities and Challenges for Business in *Caritas in Veritate*." *Journal of Business Ethics* 100: 55–66.

Miller, Michael M. 2014. *Film: Poverty, Inc*. Directed by Michael Matheson Miller.

Sachs, Jeffrey. 2019. "Global Problem Solving," (March 2019). https://www.edc-online.org/en/eventi-e-news/prophetic-economy/15037-global-problem-solving.html. Also published in *Living City Magazine* (March 2019) pp.10–11.

Segarra, Lisa Marie. 2017. "Heineken Ad Pairs Up Strangers With Opposing Views on Transgender Rights, Climate Change and Feminism." *Time Magazine* (April 27, 2017).

Sophia University Institute Website. 2019. http://www.sophiauniversity.org/en/.

Stubley, Peter. 2019. "Extinction Rebellion: Activist Greta Thunberg, 16, tells protesters they are 'making a difference.'" *Independent* (21 April 2019).

Theobald, Christoph. 2016. *Fraternità*. Magnano (Bi): Sympathetika-Qiqajon.

Uelmen, Amelia. J. 2010. *"Caritas in Veritate* and Chiara Lubich: Human Development from the Vantage Point of Unity." *Theological Studies* 71, 1: 29–45.

_____. 2012. "Resources for Receptivity to a Transcendent Vocation." In *The Moral Dynamic of Economic Life: An Extension and Critique of Caritas In Veritate*, edited by Daniel Finn. New York: Oxford University Press.

_____. 2017. "Where Morality and the Law Coincide: How Legal Obligations of Bystanders May Be Informed by the Social Teachings of Pope Francis." *Seattle University Law Review* 49, 4: 1359–1415.

Voce, Maria. 2012. "Spirituality and Trinitarian Theology in the Thought and Life of Chiara Lubich," *Claritas: Journal of Dialogue & Culture* 1, 2: 21–29.

Vatican Press Release. 2019. "The Economy of Francesco: Young People, A Commitment, the Future. Pope Francis invites young economists and entrepreneurs of the world to Assisi to change the economy as it is today and give a soul to that of the future." May 11, 2019.

Zamagni, Stefano. 2010. "Catholic Social Thought, Civil Economy, and the Spirit of Capitalism." In *The True Wealth of Nations: Catholic Social Thought and Economic Life*, edited by Daniel K. Finn, 63–93. Oxford University Press.

Zanghì, Giuseppe M. 2015. *Leggendo un Carisma: Chiara Lubich e la cultura*. Rome: Città Nuova.

Chapter 10

A Person-Centered Theory of the Firm:
Learning from the Economy of Communion

Celeste Harvey

Abstract: In this essay the Economy of Communion model of business practice is explained by situating it in context with other traditional theories of the firm, the purpose of business, and other socially concerned entrepreneurship models. Harvey argues that the Economy of Communion model of doing business represents a "Person-Centered Theory of the Firm," drawing on two empirical studies of EoC enterprises. She explains the unique features of the EoC model of doing business by first comparing it to the stakeholder and stockholder approaches, and then by comparing and contrasting it with forms of social entrepreneurship and other models such as B Corps.

Introduction

Business is one of the most powerful institutions in the modern world. The majority of us will spend the majority of our life—in terms of sheer time and productive energy—in the service of its agendas and aims, with our time and many of our relationships determined by its demands. So the question of the purpose of business is not an idle one. What owners, entrepreneurs, managers, and employees take to be the purpose of business will have an inescapable effect on how those of us engaged with the for-profit business sector spend our lives and our energies. And how we spend our lives, of course, contributes a fair amount to how well our lives are ultimately lived.

There are two dominant theories of the purpose of the firm: stockholder theory and stakeholder theory. This essay outlines a third possibility for thinking about the purpose of business and makes the argument that this alternative—the person-centered theory of the firm—gives us a better way of thinking about business and its purpose, potential, and place in society. This person-centered theory of the firm comes from the business practices of entrepreneurs, owners, and managers associated with the Economy of Communion, or EoC for short. Drawing on the empirical research into the business practices of EoC businesses completed by John Gallagher and Jeanne Buckeye (2014) and Lorna Gold (2010), this essay will argue that the person-centered theory of the firm offers a significantly different way of thinking about the purpose of business than what we have on offer with the two dominant theories of the firm currently taught in most business schools, stakeholder and stockholder theories.

Furthermore, although the EoC shares much in common with other contemporary movements seeking to re-envision business as a force for good in the world—corporate social responsibility, social entrepreneurship, and B Corps, for example—the Economy of Communion also differs from these other movements in important ways. What this means is that, despite their similarities, firms associated with the Economy of Communion cannot be totally understood through the lenses of these other popular movements.

There are two parts to this paper. The first part will explicate a person-centered theory of the firm (in contrast to stakeholder and stockholder theories) by drawing on two empirical research studies into the business practices of EoC companies. These studies suggest that what we find in the EoC is a distinctive way of thinking about the purpose of business, and that this way of thinking about business is different enough that it can be considered a rival to the two dominant theories of business. The second part will compare and contrast the Economy of Communion with other recent movements that have sought to harness the power of business for social good and describe what makes EoC different from some of these other initiatives.

The Purpose of the Firm

There are two theories of business that predominate in business school education. These are theories about the purpose for which business exists and the objectives for which managers ought to aim. The first is commonly known as "stockholder theory" or "shareholder theory." Popularized by the Nobel Prize-winning economist Milton Friedman, stockholder theory says that the purpose of business is to maximize value for owners, which is to say that the purpose of business is profit maximization (Friedman 1970). By contrast, stakeholder theory says the purpose of business is to create—or possibly maximize—value for all stakeholders in the business, not only the stockholders. In the broadest conception, a "stakeholder" is anyone whose interests are affected by the success or failure of the firm or who can themselves affect the success of the firm (Freeman 1984, 46). Owners, employees, customers, suppliers, and financiers obviously have a significant stake in the success or failure of the firm. In a lesser, but still quite real, way, local communities; competitors; employee's families; federal, state, and local governments; and maybe even the environment can be said to have a stake in the success or failure of the firm.

The debate between advocates of stockholder and stakeholder theories of business is ongoing, and it's not necessary to dig into the mire of that debate here, but we might note a few key points. The difference between the two might not be as great as it appears at first glance. After all, how could a business reasonably expect to increase profitability while ignoring or neglecting the interests of customers or workers or other stakeholders? A large business with a strong market position might ride rough-shod over stakeholder concerns for a while and pursue strategies that maximize profits at their expense, but this is not a viable long-term strategy for success. Small and medium-sized businesses will have an even shorter window of "success" with such a strategy. Some major advocates of the stakeholder approach, emphasizing just these points, have strongly resisted the opposition of stakeholder theory to stockholder theory. Instead they have insisted that the entire basis of profitability in a business rests on stakeholder relationships. For this reasons some major advocates of stakeholder theory insist that the stockholder view "is compatible with stakeholder theory. After all, the only way to maximize value sustainably is to satisfy stakeholder interests" (Freeman et al. 2010, 12). This perspective takes stakeholder theory to be the best strategy for sustainable profitability.

Those who see these two views as more opposed than aligned stress that businesses have obligations to their stakeholders for their own sakes. And these obligations demand more of managers than mere instrumental concern for stakeholder interests, contingent upon their ability to impact profits. This way of reasoning suggests stakeholder theory as something like a moral framework in business that requires managers to consider the interests of stakeholders for their own sakes, and not simply as instrumental to profit (Donaldson and Preston 1995).

For all of the differences between stakeholder and stockholder theories, what they share in common is more important for our purposes here: These two dominant theories of the purpose of business fail to integrate business as an economic activity into a wider theory of life. Neither of these theories touches on or even attempts to answer the question of the purpose of business by situating business in the wider context of a good human life. Both treat business as an instrument for creating profit and neither attempts to answer the question: What is the purpose of the profit that we seek? The stockholder theorist's view is that this profit belongs to stockholders, while the stakeholder theorist believes that the company's profitability must promote the interests of all stakeholders, or at least be pursued with full consideration of the interests of stakeholders. But given that many stakeholder theorists think that stakeholder theory should be followed because it leads to greater success (financially) as a company, it is obvious that profit remains the primary motive, even for most stakeholder theorists (van der Linder and Freeman 2017). Whether the business pursues profitability for the sake of stockholders or stakeholders, simply specifying the beneficiaries leaves the question of the purpose of profit unanswered.

Cut off from a wider vision of the purpose of life, the pursuit of profit as an end in itself (for whomever that may be) has a tendency to alienate those engaged in the activity from themselves and from others. The problem with making profit for its own sake the ultimate goal is that it locks people in a rat race. It's almost always possible for an endeavor to be more profitable, so if profit is the aim, then no matter how much profit one earns, one might always have more, and thus one's life might be better if one had more. But this is the rat race run on a wheel that never stops. No matter how fast you run, you never reach the end. Even if one is successful and enjoys the social respect, prestige, power, and lifestyle that can come with such success, in the end, it's not uncommon to wonder, what has been the point of it all? In the Economy of Communion, we find a theory in which the purpose of business and the purpose of profits are given a place in a wider theory of life.

Origins of the Economy of Communion

The Economy of Communion began in Brazil as a pragmatic response to poverty on the part of the Focolare, an ecumenically minded but predominantly Catholic faith community (see Gold 2010, chaps 4 & 6; Masters and Uelmen 2011). A hallmark of Focolare spirituality is unity and solidarity with all people, but particularly the poor, and as members of a like-minded global community, the Focolare in Brazil had long been active with the poor inside and outside their faith community. But in São Paulo, where the initiative began, there was a depth of poverty that no amount of charity seemed capable of addressing. Out of this overwhelming need came the inspiration for the Economy of Communion project: Operating profit-generating enterprises would expand the limited resources available for sharing. These businesses would be owned and operated by independent entrepreneurs—competent people with business acumen and a certain expertise—who would voluntarily join the association and share the profits of their enterprise to advance a common mission to make sure that the basic needs of all people can be met and that all people have the resources necessary to support a life worthy of the dignity of the human person. EoC entrepreneurs see themselves as creating a "new economy" founded on these ideals of unity and solidarity, an economy oriented around a "culture of giving" rather than a "culture of having," and one that places the person at the center of the enterprise.

The Person-Centered Theory of the Firm

The founding vision of the Economy of Communion was to use the potential inherent in for-profit enterprise to provide for basic human needs through the sharing out of the profits generated by for-profit enterprise in the market economy.

From its founding, the EoC has espoused a three-part vision of the purpose of profits: 1) direct assistance to the poor, 2) re-investment to grow the business, and 3) spreading "the culture of giving" though education about the project.[1] But this commitment to the idea of a purpose for profits has proved to have far-reaching implications and has transformed the practice of business inside EoC firms. This way of doing business consistently challenges EoC business leaders to "put the person at the center" of the enterprise because it is the needs of persons which enterprise serves. The business does this by creating goods and providing services that meet genuine needs and improve the quality of life for individuals and communities, giving an outlet to the basic human need to create and have meaningful work in which to invest oneself, and connecting individuals to wider networks of reciprocity and gratuity through the communion made possible by market exchange.

While the business is an economic institution organized for the production and distribution of goods and services with economic value, the EoC shows how—even working within a competitive market economy—the purpose of the firm need not be a narrow economizing one. Understanding the true potential of business requires that we see the firm as a social institution as well as an economic institution and the market within which the firm operates as a "meeting place" for persons. This vision of the purpose of business offers us a genuine alternative to the dominant theories of business put forward in stakeholder and stockholder theories.

In Lorna Gold's study of EoC companies, published as *New Financial Horizons* in 2010, she synthesizes her findings from many interviews with EoC business owners around the

---

1.   EoC, "The 'Identification Card' of the EoC," Economy of Communion: EdC Online, http://www.edc-online.org/en/chi-siamo-it/documento-di-pre-sentazione.html.

world. Gold finds that a central way EoC business owners think of their businesses is in terms of creating a "new economy," an economy that embodies genuine relationship between economic actors, one based on the principles of fraternity, gratuity, and reciprocity between people (Gold 2010, 88, 103). The business is an economic institution, but it is also a social institution, a place to form relationships with employees, customers, suppliers, and even competitors.

As an example, consider the case of a Brazilian EoC company in the medical supply industry.[2] Cutthroat competition and sharp dealings with competitors are quite common in the medical supply industry in Brazil. The director of this firm relates the following incident: "There was a competitor who tried to attack us on every corner . . . creating a very difficult situation for our business. Then, at a certain point, the law in Brazil changed and it was a very important change" for the industry as a whole. "In order to help this business, we faxed this news to them. The business owner was so struck by our gesture that he not only wanted to re-establish his friendship with us, but he offered to help us in areas that we find difficult. It was through him that we had the idea of getting in a consultancy—the best decision we ever made" (Gold 2010, 145). Thus a formerly aggressive relationship was completely transformed.

What the director of the Brazilian firm demonstrates is a not-uncommon experience in EoC businesses. These businesses operate in a competitive context, but the EoC experience has been that relationships are possible even with competitors, and the cultivation of such relationships can have unpredictable domino effects on the firm. In the Brazilian firm, the consultant they brought in at the suggestion of their competitor "was

---

2. The following cases are drawn from two empirical research studies into the business practices of the Economy of Communion: Gallagher and Buckeye's *Structures of Grace* (2014) and Lorna Gold's *New Financial Horizons* (2010).

so impressed by how we run our business that he goes out of his way to help us in whatever way he can." In the director's mind the connection is not coincidental: "This all started through responding to the aggression of our competitors with a different attitude" (Gold 2010, 145).

The perspective of the EoC is that the market is more than just a place for economic transactions, the impersonal buying and selling of goods. Though this is how it is often presented, in reality, the market is a "meeting place," a forum for the development and cultivation of human relationships. In Gallagher and Buckeye's study of EoC companies in the U.S, *Structures of Grace*, they point out that "Going beyond a purely transactional view of economic activity, the EoC understood communion or unity to be the true objective of business activity; markets were valuable not for buying and selling alone, but more importantly as places for interpersonal encounter and relationship" (2014, 21).

The EoC recognizes that an economy overly pre-occupied with values of efficiency, profit, and unconstrained desire-satisfaction can produce systems, processes, and institutions that are ultimately dehumanizing. In the EoC understanding, "humanizing" the economy is done by consistently privileging relationships over profit-maximization as well as by putting profits in common and using them to address acute social needs and concerns. It also means "humanizing" the policies and practices of business so that they express respect for the inherent dignity of each person (Gallagher and Buckeye 2014, 14).

This way of thinking about business and the market challenges EoC business leaders to continually put the person at the center of the enterprise. That person might be an employee whose economic welfare depends directly on the business, or a competitor with whom a relationship involving reciprocity or gratuity seems impossible according to dominant economic norms. In Gold's study, "over half of the businesses said that the EoC had changed the relationship with their competitors.

In most cases, the aim was to create an open relationship in which competition did not degenerate into bad feelings" (Gold 2010, 145).

Consider next the case of Netuitive and the financial crisis of 2008. Netuitive, Inc., is a software company, providing algorithm-based software to help large organizations monitor their internal electronic systems (e.g. systems for online credit card payments, for purchasing plane tickets in a travel business, etc.). Netuitive's software enables IT departments to diagnose and fix problems before the systems fail. Netuitive is a privately held C-corp with 78 percent of Netuitive stock owned by outside investors. The CEO is committed to managing by EoC principles, but not all of the company's investors share the EoC vision. The CEO tells the following story of how the company was affected by the financial crisis of 2008 when orders from large banks—their biggest customers at the time—in his words, "evaporated."

> After trying every possible cost reduction measure such as salary freezes, cuts in bonus, marketing and in travel, etc. . . . we had come to the conclusion that the only way to save the company and to balance our budget was a reduction in force (30% of total). We had been very transparent about the economic situation of the company all along. . . . We involved each manager in defining the decision criteria/selection process on who to make redundant and every decision was truly a group decision. The most important discussion was on how we would treat the personnel made redundant. We [the managers at all levels] unanimously agreed to size severances at the high end of the possible range, way above industry standards, even if it meant reducing the now-more-than-ever-precious cash on hand for the company. We wanted to put the people first. When I presented the plan to the board, it raised some

eye-brows; I feel that they allowed us to go ahead with it because they saw how responsible we were being in trying to salvage the company. (Gallagher and Buckeye 2014, 170–71)

With this reduction in their workforce and some other changes to their business model, the company survived the financial crisis. Reflecting back on the event, the CEO calls it a "moment of truth." He describes it as "an opportunity to stick to our corporate values and demonstrate to ourselves and to all employees that we were true to them." According to the CEO, *the way* the process was carried out "turned the existing and former employees of Netuitive into even stronger supporters of the company" and its values. As evidence of this, he points to the fact that employees terminated in that round of layoffs have gone on to refer new hires to the company in the years since (Gallagher and Buckeye 2014, 172–73). This is hardly something one would expect of a former employee who felt mistreated or taken advantage of.

But of course, there is no guarantee that an unorthodox business decision will pay such positive returns. Consider a different case: Sofia Violins was founded in 1988. With headquarters in Indiana, Sofia "maintains a global group of master violinmakers in a vertically integrated production-sharing structure" (Gold 2010, 112). The company has a foreign subsidiary in Bulgaria and had been associated with another foreign subsidiary as well, but the relationship with the latter was terminated after a series of troubles. The problems began when the local manager of this subsidiary stopped sending financial reports, leaving the parent company in the dark about the financials, while the subsidiary continued to receive thousands of dollars every month for rent, salaries, taxes, and other expenses. For obvious reasons this was unacceptable, and Sofia responded by firing the manager. In retaliation, the manager broke into the workshop after hours and stole $45,000 in finished product. According to the owner, "Because of a rather corrupt legal system there was no recourse possible to recover the instruments. We quickly made the decision to exit [country name redacted]" (Gallagher and Buckeye 2014, 163). This would eliminate the risk of any such future incidents. But was it possible to resolve this risk without punishing the other employees and jeopardizing their future livelihoods?

> We attempted to do it in a way that would give our employees the possibility of continuing their work. We gave them all of the company's equipment and years of cured production wood material. We told them that we could be their largest customer. (We called it a "Happy Birthday ESOP.") (Gallagher and Buckeye 2014, 163)

However, it became clear rather quickly that this arrangement was not going to work. The owner describes what happened next: "In response employees immediately began contacting our customers to see if they could get them away from us. In doing so, they blatantly infringed on our trademark. For us, that was the end of any contact with them" (163). On this rather unhappy note, Sofia ended its relationship with this foreign subsidiary.

Part of what we learn from this story is that putting the person at the center does not give carte blanche to any behavior, as though it required supporting or endorsing a person's behavior no matter what. Just like other businesses, EoC businesses uphold standards for employee performance and failure in one's basic responsibilities is regarded as grounds for termination. And as with all relationships, betrayal can be their undoing.

But this story also highlights what both research teams found in their study of EoC firms: a strong sense of responsibility for the well-being of employees. Given the manager's theft and the lack of legal protection, Sofia concluded that the current form of relationship with their foreign subsidiary was not sustainable. The initial response, gifting machinery and production materials for what might have been the start of a totally independent company, neutralized the future risk from the legal environment beyond Sofia's control, but it also provided a path for the remaining employees to continue to make a livelihood as highly skilled luthiers.

For the EoC, responsibility for employee well-being entails, at a minimum, paying a fair wage, but especially in the Brazilian companies interviewed by Gold, it often means more. Some Brazilian companies reported contributing to the housing expenses and schooling fees of their employees in addition to the standard employee wages. The way this reduces profits for sharing is obvious, but the Brazilian directors reported a sense of obligation to their employees as their nearest neighbors in need (Gold 2010, 110–11).

Balancing the desire, on the one hand, to produce profits for sharing with, on the other hand, the needs of other parties inside the firm raises many difficult questions about how the benefits of enterprise should be distributed. Putting the person at the center in those companies operating in countries where the employees are extremely poor poses serious challenges for the owners as they have to make difficult decisions about how to help and whom to help. What is clear from the research is that different EoC owners balance competing claims in different ways. Some regard the needs of those nearest them as the most serious and pressing, while for others there is a strong conviction that there are distant others in still greater need of help.

What the researchers found to be widely shared is the conviction that the profits to be shared must be "clean" and generosity must be exercised pragmatically. The express goal of EoC businesses is to generate profits to share with those in need, but EoC business owners recognize strong limitations on this goal based on both ethical and prudential considerations.

Lorna Gold draws attention to the ethical boundaries placed around the goal of creating profits to share: "Since at its heart the Focolare seeks to create spaces where relationships are founded on love . . . the businesses had to reflect this spirit in everything they did. Profit therefore could not be the result of efficiency savings borne out of exploitation, coercion or corruption—they had to be the result of a new relationship . . . among the people within the businesses" (Gold 2010, 117). So profits cannot be the result of underpaying employees, taking unfair advantage of competitive contexts or other such unethical or illegal means, such as tax evasion. In Gold's surveys, 59 percent of respondents "reported a change in their attitude toward legal authorities and in particular toward taxation, through their participation in the EoC" (Gold 2010, 149). As one director put it, the profits to be given had to be "clean" (Gold 2010, 118).

The demands felt by the business owners to do more for their own employees or for distant others through profit sharing are potentially limitless, but the owners and directors also recognized strong pragmatic limits on their generosity. The researchers found a strong and shared sensibility among the North American business owners that to give everything away or to give too much away at any one time would be reckless (and ultimately futile) if doing so endangered the financial stability or future viability of the business or if giving now meant the business would be forced to borrow later (Gallagher and Buckeye 2014, 150). The research revealed a shared language for talking about such limitations, suggesting a commonly developed and communally approved pragmatism. As one director put it, "We can't become the needy" (150). To give in ways that would undercut the viability of the business in the long-run would be self-defeating. Gallagher and Buckeye characterize the general EoC approach as "pragmatic generosity" (153).

A Rival Theory of Business

Some may wonder why EoC businesses cannot be considered profit-maximizing firms who simply have different ideas for how to allocate profits. After all, when all is said and done, EoC businesses are for-profit organizations. They are not charities or nonprofits. (There are a few exceptions.) They are privately held companies which operate within the framework of market exchange. They pay their employees and sell their goods and services at prices which make them competitive and profitable in their particular context. They pay taxes. They actively pursue profitability.

Why then shouldn't these businesses be understood under the stockholder theory of the firm? Primarily because, while they do pursue profit, this is not their ultimate purpose. These businesses see profit as a means to ends beyond profit itself. The business is itself an avenue for living out a spiritual vision of building relationship, or "communion" between people. Profit is a means for providing for people, eliminating barriers between the "haves" and the "have nots" and participating in a culture of giving. Thus EoC businesses see the purpose of business within a wider theory of life and are explicit about the wider ends that business serves when it is profitable. It has been said that profit is like food (Dicastery 2018, §56). In the Economy of Communion profit feeds the life of the enterprise-engaged community.

If stakeholder theory is a managerial strategy for maximizing firm value, then obviously the same reasoning applies to what we might call strategic stakeholder theory. Might EoC be understood as a kind of stakeholder firm committed to giving due consideration to all stakeholders for their own sakes, and not merely as instrumental to profit-driven ends?

This kind of stakeholder firm comes much closer to the person-centered EoC ideal than does the strategic stakeholder theory or the stockholder theory. This kind of stakeholder firm takes into consideration the well-being of the people affected by and dependent on the business as it pursues its economic activities. It sees the personal dimension of economic activity and doesn't reduce consideration of persons to mere instruments to an ulterior end. This kind of stakeholder theory knows about justice. But it does not know about reciprocity or gift.

Business can be a social institution that enables its members to live out the dimension of gift in the economic sphere. And the person-centered theory of the firm expresses this. The business is a place to give the gift of oneself and to receive the gift of others. Speaking to EoC entrepreneurs in Rome, Pope Francis commented that "The first gift of the entrepreneur is of his or her own person: your money, although important, is too little" (Pope Francis 2017). Those involved with the business bring their talents, their resources, their time, and also their needs as gifts. The immediate purpose of the firm is the production of goods and services with economic value, but the deeper purpose of the firm is to live out the spiritual vision that animates and gives meaning and purpose also to the rest of life. It says that business can bring unity between people, and it can be a space for reciprocity, gratuity, and gift.

Speaking about the need for a new model of economic development, Vera Araùjo notes that "there is a need for a kind of person who could be called *homo donator*, who is capable of giving rise to the category of *gift* or sharing within public activities and, in particular, within economic ones" (Araùjo 2002, 22). The activities of this kind of person can give rise to a new kind of culture.

> This culture can be called a *culture of giving*. It is not about being generous or benevolent or practicing philanthropy, nor it is about embracing the cause of charity. Rather, it is about learning and living out the dimension of gift, and giving oneself as an integral part of human existence. (Araùjo 2002, 22)

The relationships created and maintained to sustain the economic function of the business are also a place to bring to life a culture of giving. Within the Economy of Communion, drawing from the Focolare spirituality, it is not only those with material resources who contribute to the culture of giving. There is no scope or need for giving if others do not contribute their need. On this way of seeing, the need of the poor is also a gift contributed to the culture of giving. In practicing the culture of giving and in working to realize communion in and between those involved in the business, the business is itself a space to live out the spirituality which animates and gives meaning to life outside of business as well. The Economy of Communion gives us a vision of the purpose of the firm which is in this way consistent with an ethic of life that goes beyond the firm.

Comparing Other Initiatives

How does the EoC compare to other recent initiatives in the realm of business that advocate for the creation of profits with a purpose? If EoC firms operate outside of the stakeholder/stockholder paradigms, can they be understood under the lens of other recent initiatives in the world of business? The EoC has definite similarities with corporate social responsibility (CSR), B Corps, and social entrepreneurship. What all of these ventures share in common is a motive to re-think the purpose of business or to use the power of business for higher ends and purposes. While there are a number of important similarities, EoC does not entirely fit the mold given by CSR, B Corps, or social entrepreneurship.

Corporate Social Responsibility

CSR is, today, firmly established in mainstream business culture. Corporate social responsibility (CSR) has a long history in the business community, especially if one considers the business philanthropy of the nineteenth century and the "corporate citizenship" model of the early and mid-twentieth century to be the precursors of today's CSR (Carroll 2008). Many firms, both large and small, have corporate social responsibility programs. Corporate philanthropy is a mainstay of such programs, but the concept is a broad one, encompassing a panoply of business activities and initiatives. For example, CSR might include coordination of employees engaging in community service events, donations of goods or services to worthy causes, affirmative action in hiring, ethics codes, efforts to ethically source materials and labor, ridding the supply chain of slave and child labor, improved workplace environment and employee benefits, and environmental sustainability, just to name a few. If there is anything that unites CSR initiatives, it might be the attempt by the corporation to go above and beyond the requirements of the law in order to be responsive to issues of broad social concern. As Carroll (2008) notes, surveys of CSR issues in the early 1970s identify "minority hiring," "concern for environment" and "hard-core [unemployed] hiring" as among the most prevalent corporate social responsibility activities listed by the firms surveyed (100 percent, 95 percent, and 79 percent respectively) (33). In the twenty-first century, the intense social concern with long-term unemployment that marked the 1970s has diminished, but businesses continue to initiate programs aimed at demonstrating their responsiveness to the social concerns of the day. While environmental sustainability remains a core component of many CSR programs, more recently, many large, publically traded corporations have promised to increase female and minority representation on their corporate boards. Some are being required by law to do so (Green et al. 2019).

Corporate social responsibility is an important way for business to broaden its perspective and recognize the power, significance, and impact that business operations can have, directly and indirectly, on society. One possible way of understanding the Economy of Communion is as an exercise in corporate social responsibility. EoC businesses engage in philanthropy by sharing a significant portion of their profits with the poor in their community and with EoC ventures worldwide. Similar to corporations with strong, thorough-going CSR programs, EoC businesses often place a significant emphasis on creating good workplace environments and taking care of employees through benefits programs. Furthermore, EoC businesses may make a concerted effort to be good corporate citizens, donating services or encouraging employees to volunteer in the community, and many also exhibit strong environmental concern in their production processes.

However, there are important differences between the business philosophies of EoC and CSR. Corporate social responsibility exists within the dominant paradigm of the purpose of business, and it does not fundamentally challenge that. The CSR paradigm accepts that the purpose of business is profit. It is for this reason that it is not at all uncommon for businesses to feel compelled to justify CSR initiatives on strategic grounds, for example, as good for public relations and therefore good marketing, or important for employee morale and therefore reducing employee turnover. The evidence of whether CSR does benefit the bottom line is decidedly mixed (Kurucz et al. 2008, 84). That this is the paradigm for CSR is evident from the business literature on it. According to Keith Davis, CSR "refers to the firm's consideration of, and response to, issues beyond the narrow economic, technical and legal requirements of the firm" (Davis 1973, 312). This conceptualization of CSR defines "socially responsible" actions as those actions not directly related to the profit-generating activities of the firm, thus reinforcing the idea that the "socially responsible" actions of the firm are extrinsic to the "business" of the firm. Thus, CSR accepts and exists within the idea that the purpose of business is profit.

Because the directors of EoC businesses see the purpose of business as broader than profit and see the profits of the firm as a means to sustaining authentic human goods made available by the activity of business, while EoC firms may undertake many initiatives traditionally associated with corporate social responsibility (and in the US context, EoC owners may even use the language of corporate social responsibility to describe the firm's activities), these initiatives within an EoC company do not have the same status and are not truly comparable. Because profits are in service to a higher set of ends and values, the generation of those profits cannot be manifestly inconsistent with the higher ends and values those profits are intended to serve. The profits themselves must be "clean." This means that the socially responsible initiatives are not extraneous to the core business functions, but essential to it. For EoC businesses, *the way* profit is generated is as important as *that* profit is generated.

Certified B Corps

The Certified B Corp is a relatively new movement. Certified B Corps are businesses that have applied for and received certification from the nonprofit B Lab which seeks to encourage the use of "business as a force for good" by assessing, verifying, and certifying the positive social and environmental impact of for-profit businesses. Every Certified B Corp is given an "Impact Score" based on an assessment of its overall social benefit. The total Impact Score is based on five broad areas of social impact: governance, workers, community, environment, and customers. According to B Lab, the Certified B Corp is a "new kind of business" that is purpose-driven, not merely profit-driven, and creates benefit for all stakeholders, not just shareholders. In their statement of purpose, B Lab says this: "By harnessing the power of business, B Corps use profits and growth as a means to a greater end: positive impact for their employees, communities, and the environment" (B Lab).

A number of well-known firms, long-recognized as leaders of corporate social responsibility, such as Patagonia, Ben and Jerry's, and Stonyfield Farm have sought B Corp certification. However, status as a Certified B Corp goes beyond the norms of corporate social responsibility and recognizes only those businesses that use the tool of for-profit business to accomplish a purpose with recognizable social value. The purpose of these firms is not strictly profit maximization. This sets B Corps apart from other kinds of businesses, even those with strong CSR platforms.

Like B Corps, EoC businesses have a clear sense of the value of the goods and services that they provide to their clients and customers, as well as how the work they do contributes to the common good by, for example, tutoring struggling students, crafting high-quality violins, providing environmental evaluations and geological surveys, fashioning durable employee uniforms, or producing non-toxic and sustainably sourced cleaning products. And like B Corps, EoC businesses operate in the context of a competitive market economy. Maybe most importantly, B Corps and the Eoc share a vision of a wider transformation of the economic system, creating a "new economy" based on businesses that use the power of profit to sustain other human goods.

An important difference between EoC businesses and Certified B Corps is the EoC view that an important part of this new economy are the relationships created by the business, and the underlying spirituality that motivates the EoC. Certified B Corps are businesses with a goal to improve the world by the products and services they provide as well as *the way* that those goods and services are provided. *But EoC companies aim to be more than a group organized around a product or service.* In her study of EoC businesses, Gold captures this idea well:

EoC businesses are understood "not simply as a mean to an end, but as an end in itself, as a 'social space'" (Sorgi 1991). Within this social space, the goal of making a profit is paralleled with that of creating an atmosphere of caring among all those who participate and through promoting a more socially and environmentally sustainable world. (Gold 2010, 192)

The EoC idea is that the business itself creates and sustains a new space for relationship. And this is intimately connected and in no way divorced from the underlying spirituality that drove the creation of the EoC. "In the EoC, far from being viewed as a simple means to an end, the business itself became the central focus for living out the spirituality. The directors interviewed regarded their businesses as playing a critical role in transforming modern society into one that is more equitable and just" (Gold 2010, 127–128). In his address to the EoC, Pope Francis captured the EoC approach to living spirituality through business this way:

> With your life you demonstrate that economy and communion become more beautiful when they are beside each other. Certainly the economy is more beautiful, but communion is also more beautiful, because the spiritual communion of hearts is even fuller when it becomes the communion of goods, of talents, of profits. (Francis 2017)

It is in and through the economic activity of the business that people have an opportunity to live the spirituality that inspires them. And it is not only a one-way street, with spiritual values "taming" business pursuits, but the activity of the business also enriches the spiritual life. None of this is to say that EoC companies are incompatible with B Corps ideals. There may be EoC companies that would find B Corp Certification valuable, but in the EoC there is an added dimension of doing business in a person-centered way that isn't captured by the B Corps model.

Social Entrepreneurship

Social entrepreneurship is an increasingly influential way of approaching social change. Especially in the US context, this term is closely related to "social enterprise." This is how one dictionary of business terms describes the relationship: "Social entrepreneurship describes the discovery and sustainable exploitation of opportunities to create social and environmental benefits.... The social entrepreneurship process can in some cases lead to the creation of social enterprises" (Hockerts 2010). On this conception, social enterprises are what social entrepreneurs create.

The term "social entrepreneurship" has taken on a broad and diffuse usage. There are at least three distinct uses of the term. "Social entrepreneurship" is commonly used to describe mission-driven businesses that intentionally seek to contribute to the common good through their business. These businesses have a purpose beyond profit, but they use the power of the for-profit model to produce goods and services with real social value in a financially sustainable way. These businesses may take a "triple bottom line" approach or measure their success in terms of the value of social benefits generated in addition to revenue. The businesses that seek and receive B Corps certification can be seen as paradigm cases of social entrepreneurship in this sense. Call this "social entrepreneurship Type 1."

A second way of using the term moves social entrepreneurship out of the traditional sphere of for-profit enterprise and into what has been the sphere of nonprofit and charity work. It is not uncommon to find creative new ways of approaching what has long been known as "charity work" in the nonprofit sector as "social entrepreneurship." These organizations find ways of funding traditional charity work with a for-profit enterprise—the hospital auxiliary thrift is a classic example of this kind of work—or they create new ways to provide the goods and services that have traditionally been provided by charity, but in a financially self-sustaining way—Grameen Danone Foods Ltd.'s mission to supplement the diets of malnourished children with essential nutrients through their yogurt is a good example of this kind of social entrepreneurship (on Grameen Danone see Kiviat 2010). In the case of Grameen Danone, the initiative required philanthropic funding to get started, but the goal is to grow to a point where the production can be financially self-sustaining.

Rupert Scofield's *The Social Entrepreneur's Handbook* (2011) is good example of this usage of the term. The organizations that Scofield describes are indistinguishable from traditional charities, except that in addition to seeking donations and grants, they may also have a profit-generating subsidiary as another leg of their financial stool, and they may make use of the more rigorous financial tracking methods common in for-profit business to track things like cash flow, personnel performance, and non-monetary metrics of organizational success. In a classic in the scholarship of social entrepreneurship, William Dees calls these organizations "enterprising nonprofits" (Dees 1998). Call this "social entrepreneurship Type 2."

A third and more restrictive concept of "social entrepreneurship" focuses on innovative approaches to social problems that have the potential to drive wide-scale change. In *Getting Beyond Better*, Sally Osberg, president and CEO of the Skoll Foundation, and her co-author Roger Martin argue that what distinguishes social entrepreneurs from other actors seeking to improve society, such as social service providers and social activists, is that social entrepreneurs have a vision and drive to create wide-scale social change and they take direct action to drive that change. Social entrepreneurs effectively change the existing system or the prevailing conditions which create the problem, whereas social service providers tend to work within the existing systems and social activists lobby others for ameliorative measures, but again, within the existing system (Martin and Osberg 2015, 7–10). Call this "social entrepreneurship Type 3."

Pratham is an example of social entrepreneurship recognized by the Skoll Foundation for its pioneering work in literacy education in India. The organization's Teaching at the Right Level (TaRL) approach to literacy helps kids learn to read by targeting literacy interventions on the basis of current literacy level rather than age or grade level. Under Skoll's definition, Pratham is an example of social entrepreneurship because rather than working within the existing framework for helping students learn to read (e.g., tutoring struggling students using traditional literacy methods), or attacking the problem indirectly (e.g., by lobbying the government for more adequate funding and more accountability for teachers), it created a new program to directly remedy the problem of illiteracy in school-aged children (skoll.org).

While many B Corps presumably would not count as social enterprises by this definition, Skoll sees B Lab, the organization behind B Corp Certification, as an important example of social entrepreneurship. Essential to their recognition by Skoll is the fact that B Corp certification has the potential to drive large-scale social change. By offering a rigorous certification process, B Lab has pioneered a path to encourage socially responsible business. When it comes to the environment, government can regulate extractive processes or industrial pollution, providing a baseline beneath which business is not allowed to operate, but law is not an effective mechanism for enforcing ideals, and the competitive nature of markets tends to push competitors toward a lowest common denominator that discourages sustainable business practice. So B Lab has created a mechanism for encouraging environmental standards that neither government regulation nor the market can reliably enforce. By providing public recognition and third-party validation, B Lab has given conscientious consumers a way to "vote every day" for environmentally conscious business practices, and this has the potential to drive wide-scale change.

Social entrepreneurship obviously has much in common with the Economy of Communion. Along with the Economy of Communion, all forms of social entrepreneurship seek to use the power of business and the profits it generates to serve a purpose beyond profit itself. Does Economy of Communion fit into one of the three types of social entrepreneurship?

B Corps are a paradigm case of Type 1 social entrepreneurship. Having already compared EoC businesses to B Corps, the same similarities and differences would apply to Type 1 social entrepreneurship. This means that while there will be substantial similarities, the EoC is also different from Type 1 social entrepreneurship in important ways.

The origins of the Economy of Communion, with its goal to establish profit-generating businesses so as to meet the needs of the poor, make it similar to Type 2 social entrepreneurship. Type 2 social entrepreneurship typically involves using the power of for-profit business to fund a cause that has traditionally been the province of government or charity. The international association of the Economy of Communion is in fact a nonprofit organization that orchestrates the distribution of shared profits to projects oriented toward poverty alleviation around the world. Both the EoC and Type 2 social entrepreneurship see business as a tool to promote important social ends and objectives that are not currently being met by traditional mechanisms of charity and government funding. Both movements encourage individuals to think creatively about how the free-market enterprise system might be marshaled to meet unmet human need. This connection is clearly rooted in Chiara Lubich's challenge to the Focolare community in São Paolo to go beyond philanthropy to meet the needs of the poorest for the long haul and in a sustainable way.

One thing that makes the EoC different is that the businesses that were established to fund this objective do not have the typical relationship of Type 2 social enterprises to their parent organizations. Social enterprises are generally profit-generating subsidiaries of the parent nonprofit, but EoC businesses are not legally connected to or controlled by the association. EoC businesses are independent entities that voluntarily choose to contribute to the EoC mission. Additionally, and this point was made previously, their purpose goes beyond sharing profits. It is also to realize a new person-centered way of doing business and to humanize the economy.

Given that part of the vision of EoC businesses is to humanize the economy, to "give a new soul" to the economy, EoC might best be understood along the lines of Type 3 social entrepreneurship. While the movement is small in absolute terms, the vision of the movement includes wide-scale transformation of the economy as such. The goal is to transform those aspects of the market economy that contribute to alienation, exploitation, and poverty into a sphere for communion oriented toward meeting the needs of all. As one business owner expressed it:

> What motivates me in the EoC is the possibility of giving a new soul to the economy, a new vision. Not just the distribution of profits, which is one of the important points . . . but above all, this motivation for a new society, for these new relationships that are built. I feel that this is the most revolutionary aspect of the EoC. (Gold 2010, 130)

Type 3 social entrepreneurship is about driving wide-scale change to create a new social equilibrium around a pressing social problem, thereby moving to a more optimal and more just situation. While there are certainly obstacles to the adoption of the EoC ideal on a wide scale, there is no question that this has the potential to radically transform our economic reality.

Are EoC companies social enterprises? If so, in what sense? The broader vision of transforming the market economy makes EoC companies most similar to Type 3 social enterprises, and yet EoC companies are not in any sense charities—the paradigm cases of Type 2 and Type 3 social enterprises are what traditionally have been called charities, though they will often have some revenue-generating capacity and hence some degree of financial sustainability. EoC companies, by contrast, are financially self-sustaining organizations that provide goods and services with economic value in a competitive market economy, and they do not rely on grant funding or donations to sustain their enterprise, which many Type 2 and Type 3 social enterprises do in order to achieve their mission. This means that on a practical level, EoC businesses are more like Type 1 social enterprises. Of course, the original motivation of many entrepreneurs for joining the association and aligning their business as an EoC company was to be able to contribute the profits of the business to more effectively address the needs of the poor, and this makes EoC businesses similar to Type 2 social enterprises, which are established to provide a funding source for a social cause. So the EoC doesn't exactly fit any of the major models of social entrepreneurship, but it shares characteristics of all of them. Maybe we can call EoC companies Type 6 social enterprises, since 1 + 2 + 3 equals 6!

Social entrepreneurship is a broad and—in many ways—amorphous concept used to describe a number of different kinds of organizations, and the Economy of Communion overlaps in significant ways with the kinds of things commonly labeled "social entrepreneurship." Yet the Economy of Communion puts these elements together in uncommon ways, combining elements from the different types of social entrepreneurship in a way that makes the EoC a unique kind of movement.

Conclusion

The person-centered theory of the firm operative in Economy of Communion businesses makes a substantial contribution to our understanding of the potential of business as a force for good in the world and to our imagination about the possibility for persons of conscience and good will to be fully invested in the realm of business without bifurcation into a "private self" and a "business self." Understanding this alternative to the dominant theories of the purpose of business offered by stockholder theory and stakeholder theory is important because the dominant theories of the purpose of business create a narrative about the way the world is and the way the world inevitably must be that leaves many in business with the decisive impression that if they want to be successful, they will have to partition their lives and set their personal values aside when it comes to making business decisions. This plays itself out in business education as well. As Michael Naughton has so memorably expressed it: When it comes to business education at liberal arts colleges, students often come away with the sense that they are receiving two types of education: "one that makes them more human and one that makes them more money" (Naughton 2009, 31). By contrast, by putting the person at the center, the practices and principles of the EoC offer us a vision of business where we can—through the practice of business—become more human, and in and through the way we practice business, humanize the economy.

Putting the person at the center of the firm is a way of recognizing that through our creative and productive efforts we meet our own needs as well as the needs of others; we can give the gift of self and receive the gift of others; and productive enterprise even within a competitive market economy can be more than a transactional space. It can also be a place to build relationships that facilitate reciprocity, gratuity, and gift between persons.

Bibliography

Araùjo, Vera. 2002. "Personal and Societal Prerequisites of the Economy of Communion." In *The Economy of Communion: Toward a Multi-Dimensional Economic Culture*, edited by Luigino Bruni. Translated by Lorna Gold, 21–30. Hyde Park, NY: New City Press.

B Lab. n.d. "About B Corps." https://bcorporation.net/about-b-corps. Accessed May 1, 2023.

Carroll, Archie B. 2008. "A History of Corporate Social Responsibility: Concepts and Practices." In *The Oxford Handbook of Corporate Social Responsibility*, edited by Andrew Crane, Abagail McWilliams, Dirk Matten, Jeremy Moon and Donald Siegel, 19–46. Oxford: Oxford University Press.

Davis, Keith. 1973. "The Case for and Against Business Assumption of Social Responsibilities." *The Academy of Management Journal* 16, no. 2: 312–322.

Dees, J. Gregory. 1998. "Enterprising Nonprofits." *Harvard Business Review* (Jan-Feb): 55–67.

Dicastery for Promoting Integral Human Development. 2018. *Vocation of the Business Leader: A Reflection*. St. Paul, MN: University of St. Thomas Press. https://www.stthomas.edu/media/catholicstudies/center/ryan/publications/publicationpdfs/vocationofthebusinessleaderpdf/FinalTextTheVocationoftheBusinessLeader.pdf.

Donaldson, Thomas, and Lee E. Preston. 1995. "The Stakeholder Theory of the Corporation: Concepts, Evidence, and Implications." *Academy of Management Review* 20, no. 1: 65–91.

Francis, Pope. 2017. *Address of His Holiness Pope Francis to Participants in the Meeting 'Economy of Communion', Sponsored by the Focolare Movement*. Available online at https://w2.vatican.va/content/francesco/en/speeches/2017/february/documents/papa-francesco_20170204_focolari.html.

Freeman, R. Edward. 1984. *Strategic Management: A Stakeholder Approach*. Boston: Pitman.

Freeman, R. Edward, Jeffrey S. Harrison, Andrew C. Wicks, Bidhan Parmar, and Simone de Colle. 2010. *Stakeholder Theory: The State of the Art.* Cambridge: Cambridge University Press.

Friedman, Milton. 1970. "The Social Responsibility of Business is to Increase Its Profit." *New York Times*, September 13: 33.

Gallagher, John and Jeanne Buckeye. 2014. *Structures of Grace: The Business Practices of the Economy of Communion.* Hyde Park, NY: New City Press.

Gold, Lorna. 2010. *New Financial Horizons: The Emergence of an Economy of Communion.* Hyde Park, NY: New City Press.

Green, Jeff, Hannah Recht, and Mathieu Benhamou. 2019. "Wanted: 3732 Women to Run American Companies." *Bloomberg Businessweek*. March 21, 2019. https://www.bloomberg.com/graphics/2019-women-on-boards/.

Hockerts, Kai. 2010. "Social entrepreneurship." In *The A to Z of Corporate Social Responsibility*, edited by Wayne Visser, Dirk Matten, Manfred Pohl, & Nick Tolhurst, 2nd ed. Hoboken, NJ: Wiley.

Kiviat, Barbara. 2010. "Danone's Cheap Trick." *Time*, August 23, 2010. http://content.time.com/time/magazine/article/0,9171,2010077,00.html.

Kurucz, Elizabeth C., Barry A. Colbert, and David Wheeler. 2008. "The Business Case for Corporate Social Responsibility." In *The Oxford Handbook of Corporate Social Responsibility*, edited by Andrew Crane, Dirk Matten, Abigail McWilliams, Jeremy Moon, and Donald S. Siegel, 83–112. Oxford: Oxford University Press.

Martin, Roger and Sally Osberg. 2015. *Getting Beyond Better: How Social Entrepreneurship Works.* Boston: HBR Press.

Scofield, Rupert. 2011. *The Social Entrepreneur's Handbook: How to Start, Build, and Run a Business that Improves the World.* New York: McGraw Hill.

Skoll.org. "About the Organization: Pratham." Available at https://skoll.org/organization/pratham/. Accessed April 25, 2020.

Sorgi, Tommaso. 1991. *Costruire il sociale.* Rome: Città Nuova.

van der Linden, Bastiaan, and R. Edward Freeman. 2017. "Profit and Other Values: Thick Evaluation in Decision Making." *Business Ethics Quarterly* 27, no. 3: 353–379.

Chapter 11

The Business of Business: Recapturing a Personalist Perspective

Rev. John McNerney, PhD,
The Catholic University of America

Abstract: The business of business properly understood is necessarily personalistic. The human person acting as an entrepreneur or working in business is not merely froth and bubble in the stream of history but is a freely acting person motivated toward specific ends. The businessperson can be seen as an exemplar of what it means to be a human being. The Economy of Communion project is an attempt to regain and promote the personalist nature of business. In this perspective commercial life is not seen an end in itself since it creates a space in which we can realize our personal dignity in creative action. As human persons we live in an existential tension searching to become who we are. The drama of business life is a part of a greater whole, of a reality that unfolds who we are as human beings.

We begin with the words:

> It was the best of times, it was the worst of times, it was the age of wisdom, it was the age of foolishness. . . . We had everything before us, we had nothing before us. . . . (Dickens 1859)

You may recognize these words as taken from Charles Dickens's *A Tale of Two Cities*, which is set against the background and turmoil of the French Revolution. Dickens and many other authors, through literary form, also gave a profound social analysis of the hard times endured by workers and children during the industrial revolution. In *Oliver Twist*, the undertaker Mr. Sowerberry declares:

> I wish some well-fed philosopher, whose meat and drink turn to gall within him; whose blood is ice, whose heart is iron; could have seen Oliver Twist clutching at the dainty viands that the dog had neglected. I wish he could have witnessed the horrible avidity with which Oliver tore the bits asunder with all the ferocity of famine. There is only one thing I should like better; and that would be to see the Philosopher make the same sort of meal himself, with the same relish. (Dickens 1839)

Indeed, as we can see from these literary but nonetheless genuine accounts, the business of business was and can be a very nasty business. It was Fredrich Engels and Karl Marx who famously provided the theoretical basis for a critique of capitalism. In the *Economic and Philosophic Manuscripts* Marx describes economic conditions in which human persons have lost their "experiential substance" (Walsh 1990, 138). He opposes the "hollow shell" of the work experience that Engels gathered materials on in *The Condition of the Working Class in England in 1844*. Engels describes Manchester's worker districts in heart-wrenching detail. He speaks of the "filth and disgusting grime . . . which contain unqualifiedly the most horrible dwellings which I have yet beheld" (Tucker 1978, 580). Engels goes on:

> And such a district exists in the heart of the second city of England, the first manufacturing city of the world. If anyone wishes to see in how little space a

human being can move . . . how little of civilisation
he may share and yet live, it is only necessary to travel
hither. . . . The industrial epoch alone enables the
owners of these cattlesheds to rent them for high
prices to human beings, to plunder the poverty of
the workers . . . in order that they *alone*, the owners,
may grow rich. (Tucker 1978, 584)

You cannot but sense Marx and Engel's spiritual aspiration
of the sigh of the oppressed human being who can no longer
bear the weight "of a senseless form of existence" (Walsh
1990, 138). In the analysis of the business of business in
his own time Marx uses almost personalistic language. He
says that you can dream all you like about some "fictitious
primordial condition" in order to explain economic reality,
but this simply will not do (Tucker 1978, 71). The inherent
experience of alienation is, according to Marx, a necessary
consequence of the capitalistic system. He describes the
depersonalizing nature of work in which the human person

becomes an ever cheaper commodity the more commodities he creates. . . . The product of labour is labour
which has been congealed in an object, which has
become material: it is the *objectification* of labour. . .
. The *alienation* of the worker in his product means
. . . that it exists *outside him* . . . as something alien
to him . . . it means that the life he has conferred on
the object confronts him as something hostile and
alien. (Tucker 1978, 72)

The human person is therefore *unpersoned* in the business
of this production process. The Marxist solution is that in
changing the material circumstances you go to the heart of
the resolution of the human predicament of the alienation
experienced. But the core of the problem lies much deeper; it
concerns "rather how we relate to one another, even somehow
despite the circumstances" (McNerney 2003, 127). Karol

Wojtyła, having lived through communism, insightfully explained that any economic system must be evaluated in the light of this basic criterion:

> Do [the structures] create the conditions—for this is their only real function—for the development of participation? Do they enable and help us to experience other human beings as other *I*'s? Or do they do just the opposite? Do they obstruct participation and ravage and destroy the basic fabric of human existence and activity, which must always be realized in common with others? The central problem of humanity in our times, perhaps in all times, is this: *participation or alienation?* (Wojtyła 1993, 206)

It was Milton Friedman who was quoted as rather controversially saying that the "business of business is business" (Friedman: 1970). Now, given what we outlined in terms of the existential experiences of alienation in the industrial business process demonstrated in the Marx-Engels analysis, Freidman's view seems very unenlightened. If he is correct we could conclude with Dickens that we are therefore living in "the worst of times." But this is not the whole story, nor is it necessarily the meaning Freidman intended. Neither does it give us the full significance of human action in business. If we read Friedman's reasoning in its fuller context we get a better sense of what business is actually about. In *Capitalism and Freedom* Friedman wrote "There is one and only one social [ethical] responsibility of business—to use its resources and engage in activities designed to increase profits" (Friedman 2002, 133). He goes on to say in the same passage that the profit motive must stay in what he calls the rules of the game, that is, "to engage in free competition, without deception or fraud" (Friedman 2002, 133). This means economic activity occurs within a given moral framework or human perspective. In this regard I find it interesting how on the occasion of the hundredth anniversary of Friedman's birth, economic journalist Kevin Williamson wrote an appraisal of Friedman's approach, saying it

> was based on an economics of love: for real human beings leading real human lives with real human needs and real human challenges.... He loved human freedom ... because it allowed for human flourishing on all levels.... He didn't argue for capitalism in order to make the world safe for the Fortune 500, but to open up a world of possibilities for those who are most in need of them. The real subject of economics isn't simply supply and demand, but people, and to love liberty is to love people and all that is best in them. And it is something that can only be done when we are free to choose. (Williamson 2012)

Friedman is commonly understood as a purely free-market rugged-individualist thinker. But Williamson's insight on his approach is very interesting. Friedman is also often taken as having a rather negative interpretation of human freedom leading to prohibition of making moral judgments in the marketplace. But Friedman's perspective on human freedom is, I contend, much more nuanced than this. A free society is "a more productive society than any other." It actually "releases the energies of people, enables resources to be used more effectively, and enables people to have a better life" (Friedman 2017, 184). But this is not the fundamental reason Friedman values freedom as such. His explanations are actually much more human-centered than imagined. Friedman believes that the real case "*for a free society and for freedom is ignorance*—[because] we cannot be sure we are right (Friedman 2017, 185)." He says that "the basic virtue in a free society and *the basic justification for a free society is humility*, a willingness to recognize no matter how strongly one may believe he is correct, he cannot be sure" (Friedman

2017, 186). St. Benedict, who lived during the fifth and sixth centuries and was a keen observer of human nature, equally spoke of the need for humility in our human interactions. He realized that most times people in their actions simply just fail. Even abbots! Indeed, this is the story of most entrepreneurial and business ideas. In *The Rule of St Benedict*, Benedict says the abbot must "distrust his own frailty." He stressed the importance of the person and the relationship of persons living and working together. He equally respected the freedom of the human person, urging that the abbot "arrange everything [so] that the strong have something to yearn for and the weak nothing to run from" (Benedict 1982, 88).[1] Milton Friedman is well known for his views on the role of business, namely, profit maximization alone. Nonetheless, we can retrieve in his writings and those of other economists emergent personalistic perspectives not necessarily envisaged by the writers. Thus, there is need among economists and philosophers to recapture these personalistic traces.

A Personalist Manifesto Unfolded: Toward Economic Personalism

The term "personalism" was originally coined by the German philosopher and theologian Friedrich Schleiermacher (1768–1834) (Williams and Bengtsson 2014). There are various currents and schools of personalism which we will not discuss in this paper. European thinkers predominate, with various approaches like Jacques Maritain's Thomistic personalism, Gabriel Marcel's "existentialist" approach, and Emmanuel Mounier's "communitarian personalism." It was from British and more specifically Scottish personalism that the personalist school of thought came to North Amer-

---

1.   See also chapter seven of *The Rule* on humility, 32ff.

ica. The term "American personalism" was created by Walt Whitman (1819–1892) in his essay "Personalism," which was published in *The Galaxy* in May 1868 (Williams and Bengtsson 2014). The founder of North American personalism was Borden Parker Bowne who, even before Mounier, Maritain, and Marcel, had connections with British personalism and German Idealism (Bowne 1908). Bowne was a Methodist pastor and taught in the department of philosophy at Boston University. The Boston personalist tradition emerges from this point, ultimately influencing Dr. Martin Luther King, Jr. King described how personalism was "the theory that the clue to the meaning of ultimate reality is found in personality" (King 2010, 88). In a talk on the philosophy of integration he observed how segregation is opposed to the sacredness of the human person:

> Immanuel Kant said in one formulation of the *Categorical Imperative* that "all men must be treated as *ends* and never as mere *means*." . . . To use the words of Martin Buber, segregation substitutes an "I-it" relationship for the "I-thou" relationship. . . . But man is not a thing. He must be dealt with, not as an "animated tool," but as a person sacred in himself. (King 1986, 119)

Without going into the various strands of personalism, its central insight is the understanding that "the person exceeds the whole by virtue of the capacity to transcend itself on behalf of the whole. Rights and dignity are accorded to persons who are ends-in-themselves beyond the whole" (Walsh 2020, 27). Economic personalism is a further application of this philosophy of the human person to the economic drama of life. While not ignoring the essential questions of efficiency and the necessary technical aspects of economic analysis, economic personalism "focuses upon adjudicating which economic arrangements promote or denigrate human dignity" (Gronbacher 1998, 19). The intellectual progenitors of economic personalism are economists like Wilhelm Röpke and philosophers and theologians such as St. John Paul II, Michael Novak, and Rocco Buttiglione.[2]

Hidden Personalist Roots: The Other as Me in Economic Thought and Business Practice

Believe it or not, going right back to the Scottish philosopher and economist Adam Smith there has always been a consideration of the importance of the *other* in economic and moral thought. If you look at Smith's earlier but little-studied book written in 1759, *The Theory of Moral Sentiments*, you find him referring to the importance of concepts like "sympathy" and "fellow-feeling." We might say, "putting oneself in the other's shoes" in order to make moral decisions. He gives the example of torture and explains that in order to understand the other, "our brother upon the rack," we have to "enter as it were into his body, and become in some measure the same person with him" (Smith 1979, 9). If I have not sympathy "we become intolerable to one another, I can neither support your company, nor you mine" (21). Sympathy is not extrinsic to but constitutive of human nature. In other words, our lives necessarily involve and are directed to others.

Adam Smith also freely refers and admits to the problem of corruption in human life. In fact, we can think of how Fyodor Dostoevsky wrote *Crime and Punishment* reflecting on how the greatest moral challenges are to be found within ourselves. So too, Smith delineates how "there are hypocrites of wealth and greatness, as well as of religion and virtue; and a

---

2. Novak, for example, authored *The Spirit of Democratic Capitalism* (New York: Simon & Schuster, 1982); *Will It Liberate? Questions about Liberation Theology* (Mahwah, NJ: Paulist Press, 1986); and *The Catholic Ethic and the Spirit of Capitalism* (New York: The Free Press, 1993).

vain man is as apt to pretend to be what he is not" (Smith 1979, 64). Smith's antidote to this ongoing human moral challenge is thought-provoking and open to further development. The ambitious who merely envy riches, despise the poor, and are corrupt and corrupting are almost always "most miserably disappointed in the happiness which they expect." Human beings may try to cover up or forget what they have done but "remembrance never fails to pursue him. He invokes in vain the dark and dismal powers of forgetfulness and oblivion . . . and that remembrance tells him that other people must likewise remember it" (Smith 1979, 65). This is to me suggestive of the restorative powers of *anamnesis*. In other words, it seems that an original memory of the good and true is to be found within us. Remembrance or anamnesis is an inner sense, a capacity to recall and recapture the true and good. It is as such constitutive of our reality as human persons.

We can discover within Smith a rich type of personalistic dynamic and language in his reflections on the foundations of our judgments concerning human actions and what he calls "the Sense of Duty" (Smith 1979, 109). He speaks, for example, of the role of the "impartial spectator" who acts like a mirror (the Other as Me), which helps me reflect upon the decisions I should make in human action. He describes how the person can appeal "to a much higher tribunal, to the tribunal of their own consciences, to that of the supposed *impartial and well-informed spectator*, to that man of the breast, the great judge and arbiter of their conduct" (Smith 1979, 130). In taking account of the impartial spectator, we go out of ourselves in deciding *how* to act as human persons. But Smith also says that in the last resort there is also "an appeal to a still higher tribunal, to that all-seeing Judge of the world, whose eye can never be deceived and whose judgments can never be perverted" (Smith 1979, 131). Smith describes how the human person "naturally desires, not only to be loved, but to be lovely; or to be that thing which is the natural and proper object of love. He naturally dreads, not only to be hated, but to be hateful; or to be that thing which is the natural and proper object of hatred" (Smith 1979, 113–14). In *Wealth of Nations* this insight into the significance of the other is furthermore applied to economic life, when the importance of a division of labor and specialization in human action is analyzed, that is, if a society is to develop economically. So, we can see clearly, Smith and others knew that society works better if we facilitate the interdependent dimensions of human reality.

Nonetheless, it is true to say that the human dimension often threatens to become eclipsed from our normal understanding of business and economics. We end up not necessarily knowing *why* we need the *other* or *who* they are even in the world of business. So, they can really remain strangers to us in the whole process. The Great Recession of 2008 is a case in point. This is actually the tenth anniversary of the Lehman Brothers collapse. We may well ask: Has anything been learned from the surrounding economic breakdown? Larry McDonald, in *A Colossal Failure of Common Sense*, writes about the crash:

> It changed me. It stripped away all the careless glances at stock charts I have lived with all my life. The ramifications of those charts have a different meaning now. Where once I stared at the zigzagging lines, and just thought, *Up, down, win, lose, profit, crash, problem, solution, long, short, buy, sell*, now I see mostly people. Because every movement, up or down, has a meaning. I see it because I've been there. Every fraction of every inch of those financial graphs represents hope or fear, confidence or dread, triumph or ruin, celebration or sorrow. There's nothing quite like a total calamity to focus the mind.... And, I say again, it never should have happened. (McDonald and Robinson 2009, 339)

These crises and economic breakdowns unmistakably point to the fact that there is always bias involved in human action, and business life is no stranger to this. We can and do make choices leading to our own personal disintegration and that of others as human persons. Indeed, Borden Parker Bowne used the term impersonalism; this is equally applicable to the world of business in the circumstances where the actual experience becomes corrupted and abstracted from the truth of the human person (Bowne 1908, 223). This possibility is essentially a part of the experience of human beings acting in the economic horizon of life. It is the fragility of the human, and to ignore or to jettison this from our understanding of the economic process occludes the multidimensional reality we are dealing with. Free markets are complex, as are human beings. Different factors like "a lack of perfect knowledge, the limitations of resources, the occasional inability of people to cooperate" can all lead to disequilibrium in the free economy (Gronbacher 1998, 16). But it is important to keep in mind that the bedrock of the free economy is human freedom itself. We are free to be free. The philosopher Eric Voegelin referred to Plato's phrase "a polis is man writ large" and called it the "anthropological principle" (Voegelin 2000, 136–37). This insight, that society is an expression of the kind of people who constitute it can, he claims, be used as "a general principle for the interpretation of society" but it can also be used as "an instrument of social critique" (Voeglin 2000, 137). It can be applied, I believe, equally to our understanding of the economy. The free economy is the human person writ large and *acting* in the economic horizon. The economic and financial scandals and subsequent economic disaster are clear evidence of the need for a proper critique of the model of the human person used in economic theory. The economic personalist apperceives that markets are not abstract realities but are composed of individual human persons. This means that "the flaws and imperfections of these limited persons will be equally evident in the marketplace. In fact, the entire catalog of sins found in the human heart eventually take expression in commercial society" (Wojtyła 2011, 17). This is what I call the "O. S. factor," that is, original sin abides in the business world. We cannot operate or live within an anthropological vacuum, since this is not *who* we are.

Thus, freedom actually entails the reality that the human person is good or evil through his or her acts, otherwise we are not speaking of liberty. He or she is, or rather becomes, good or evil because the act itself not so much *is* but *becomes* so. Karol Wojtyła explains how *"the essence of 'moralitas,'* lies in the fact that *a man* [human person], *as a man, becomes good or evil through the act"* (2011, 17). If we want to speak about duty in this context he suggests it is exactly because of the good or evil possibility involved in human choice that we can become who we are as persons. When I do my duty "it is always a *specific actualization of the spiritual potentiality of a person in act*; that actualization comes out 'for' good and 'against' evil" (2011, 17). To be is to act. Wojtyła explains how the whole range of human action is determined by what the human person does and brings to pass. He observes that "the act per se is a specific manifestation of the principle of human *operari*; in the act and through the act man stands revealed as an individual" (1981, 14). Thus, even in economic life we are dealing with a profoundly personalistic process which of itself is open to different possibilities. So, it is for good or bad that the business of business is personalist in nature.

The Economy of Communion Project: A Personalist Symphony Regained

It is within a personalist framework that we can, I argue, better understand the whole Economy of Communion project founded by Chiara Lubich. In light of our earlier comments on freedom it is noteworthy how the venture is often referred to as the "economy of communion *in freedom.*" The economists Luigino Bruni and Stefano Zamagni outline how the project is about "inviting people to start up new businesses and to transform existing ones, all within the fullness of freedom—actually, the full name of the project is 'the Economy of Communion in freedom'" (Bruni & Zamagni 2004, 91). Zamagni, writing about the contribution of the Economy of Communion to standard economic theory, notes:

> Freedom, in fact, cannot be defined only in terms of self-determination—the notion of "free to choose" put forward by Milton Friedman. . . . It has to be seen also in terms of *personal self-fulfillment,* that is, the concrete opportunity which every person has to choose his or her own plan of life—including the economic one—in accordance with the values in which he or she believes and to which he or she wants to give witness. Freedom does not only have to take into account the freedom of the other—as individualist liberal thought recognizes—but has also to regard the other as a constitutive part of that freedom. (Zamagni 2014, 52)

In Lubich's perspective the human person is not only free *from* but is free *for* initiating a culture of love; she sees this freedom as fundamentally underlying the Economy of Communion project. In an address to British politicians at the Palace of Westminster, London, Chiara spoke of a different type of politics based on communion, but her words apply equally to the Economy of Communion. She observed:

> We know well, *if emphasis falls solely on liberty, it can easily become the privilege of the strongest.* And as history confirms, *emphasis solely on equality can result in mass collectivism.* In reality, many peoples still do not benefit from the true meaning of liberty and equality. . . . How can these be acquired and brought

to fruition? How can the history of our countries .
. . resume the journey towards its true destiny? We
believe the key is in *universal fraternity*, in giving
this its proper place among fundamental political
categories. (Lubich 2007, 258)

The Economy of Communion is essentially about the more of
love set in a business culture. Chiara described how it challenges us "to love all those who are involved in the business."[3]
She sets out what this culture entails: "Let's give a smile,
understanding and forgiveness; let's listen; let's give our intelligence, our will and availability; let's give our experiences
and capabilities" (Lubich 2001). Now these are essentially
the fundamental characteristics of entrepreneurial action
in economic life. There is not necessarily a great divorce
between *who* we are as human acting persons and creative
economic life. But it is important to note Lubich's emphasis
on "in freedom" in all of this, since freedom's use or misuse
can, of course, in Dickens's words, lead to "the best of times"
and "the worst of times."

Chiara Lubich seized exactly upon the personalist dimension of business in her launching of the Economy of Communion in the midst of the seismic poverty she witnessed. The
person-centric aspect is evident in economic and business
life but at times it is like a disappearing stream in economic
history too. There is no doubt a continual forgetfulness about
the uniqueness and truth of human persons in economic and
commercial life. At times this anthropological amnesia can
surely be said to be willful and deliberate, and in other cases it

---

3. The entrepreneurs involved in the EoC project devised The Company
   Cube® as a practical way of remembering the person-centered focus of
   the businesses. This "discovery" of The Company Cube is not just for use
   in small businesses but can also be universally applied to create a new
   culture in even the largest of companies. See http://thecompanycube.org,
   accessed April 7, 2019.

is undoubtedly just lost sight of. The economist Joseph Schumpeter, in investigating the fundamental centrality of creative human action in the free-market process, once said that the occlusion of the importance of entrepreneurial creativity and its function is rather "like *Hamlet* without the Danish Prince" (McNerney 2016, 120). An economic crisis essentially points us to the *crisis of economics*, that is, the continuing danger of the eclipse of the reality of the human person in the whole process.

Luigino Bruni, a member of a new and upcoming group of economists called the Bologna School, points us toward important insights in regaining the essential human elements of the free-market economy. He reminds us:

> The market when it functions properly is a place where innovations and human creativity are favoured and rewarded. It is all too clear that we will never emerge from this crisis [the Great Recession of 2008] without a revival of entrepreneurship. . . . The market, the competition of the market . . . can be seen, that is, if we want to understand it in its totality, as a race to innovate: whoever innovates grows and lives, whoever does not innovate, remains behind and exits from the economic and civil game. . . . The author who has most developed this *virtuous* dynamic of the market (the capacity to innovate is certainly a virtue, because it is an expression of *areté*, of excellence) is the Austrian economist Joseph A. Schumpeter. (Bruni 2012, 1–2)

It is thought-provoking how the economist Wilhelm Röpke called for a new humanism and for us to "adopt a philosophy which, while rendering unto the market the things that belong to the market, also renders unto the spirit what belongs to it" (1998, 116). Although Röpke lived before the launching of the Economy of Communion, there is a profound equivalence between his insights and Lubich's. Röpke emphasized how economics had to be attentive to "the nature of man and the sort of existence that was fitting to that nature" (1998, 229). And this is essentially Chiara's spiritual and intellectual intuition.

In light of this, Zamagni speaks of the urgent need to update the market economy with a more personalistic perspective and observes how "the market . . . can become an instrument which can reinforce social ties . . . and the creation of an economic space in which it is possible to regenerate those values (such as trust, sympathy, benevolence) on which the existence of the market itself depends" (2002, 134).

As a result, the Economy of Communion project can be understood as a way of recapturing the person-centric dimensions of economic action. It is hugely significant that Chiara Lubich, in the face of the great poverty she witnessed in Brazil in 1991, turned not to solutions involving a redistribution of wealth but to the prioritization of the creative and entrepreneurial dimensions of business life. The venture can be understood in its fullness and intricacy only when considered from "the spirituality's viewpoint of the human person and social relationships" (1999). Although not an expert in economics, she said: "I thought that our people could set up firms and business enterprises so as to engage the capabilities and resources of all, and to produce together. . . . They would have to be managed by competent persons who would be capable of making them function efficiently and *derive profits* from them" (1999).

Indeed, Pope Francis sketches out interesting reflections on economic action. He wrote:

> It seems important to observe that no activity goes on by chance or autonomously. Behind every activity there is a human being. That person can remain anonymous, but there is no activity that exists that does not originate in man. The current centrality of

financial activity in relation to the real economy is not random: behind this there is a choice by someone who thinks. (Gentili 2018)

We can discern a correlation between the importance of a focus on human action as being revelatory of the reality of the person and its application in understanding the economic drama. The necessary corollary of this position is that "economic action or work has human significance" (McNerney 2016, 230). Indeed, the Judeo-Christian insight into the human person is very specific in regard to the intersubjective nature and relevance of his or her actions. The fallout effect of this therefore in political, social, and economic life is the challenge to try to understand and act according to the full anthropological measure of the reality of seeing oneself as another. This means the *other* is another *I* and human action, therefore, must measure up to this truth. This might seem very far away from the world of business, but it is not that remote from it; indeed, many economists and commentators are increasingly discovering this.

At the Business, Faith and the Economy of Communion conference held at Creighton University in the fall of 2018, we heard many experiences from different entrepreneurs and business people unfolding how business can be personalist in nature. Charles, for example, an entrepreneur, husband, and father, owns a company in Italy. Out of his sixty employees, around a quarter are non-Italian and some of them have had traumatic past experiences. Charles explains how "our work includes quarrying and recycling construction materials and at the same time considering the environment and the area where we live." Some years ago, the economic crisis hit the business hard. He faced the dilemma: "Should I save the business or the employees?" He explains:

> We made some people redundant. But we carefully discussed it with them and [found] the least painful

solutions. It was a dramatic experience with many sleepless nights of worry.... Even in this great difficulty I knew that I can do my job either well or poorly. I try to do it as best I can. I believe in the positive influence of ideas. A business focused only on monetary profit will not last long. People must be at the center of all we do. I believe in God and am convinced that business and human solidarity is not a dream.

The Economy of Communion focuses on for-profit businesses. Profit is not just of a monetary nature, since it is a fundamental motivator and a tangible sign of a successful human enterprise (McNerney 2016, 155). It communicates whether a business is been run properly and successfully. It also addresses what economists call the "knowledge problem" involved in economic action. Fredrich Hayek describes how the free economy is a subtle communication system in which information is digested and dispersed efficiently. The human person has to use what knowledge they have "not to shape the results as the craftsman shapes his handiwork, but rather to cultivate a growth by providing the proper environment" for the business enterprise to prosper (Hayek 1978, 34). Hayek says it is essentially a lesson in humility recognizing the limits of our human powers and knowledge.

But then as the entrepreneur Charles said, if we just focus on the monetary aspect of profit a business will not last long. Profit communicates that a business is not only financially worthwhile but also humanly successful. Business is *for* the human person; the human being is not just *for* business. As we have seen, the Economy of Communion project is based upon a free invitation made to entrepreneurs and business people to start up new businesses or to transform existing ones into spaces and places where human beings can flourish and be fulfilled as persons. Economy of Communion businesses are based on the free-market economy. Lubich in her writings never critiques commercial society or entrepreneurs as such. To do so would, to use the words of Martin Luther King, Jr., be *"like condemning a robbed man because his possession of money precipitated the evil act of robbery"* (King 1998, 195).

St. John Paul II in *Centesimus Annus* also spoke of what he called "the legitimate role of profit as an indication that a business is functioning well":

> When a firm makes a profit, this means that productive factors have been properly employed and corresponding human needs have been duly satisfied. But profitability is not the only indicator of a firm's condition. It is possible for the financial accounts to be in order, and yet for the people—who make up the firm's most valuable asset—to be humiliated and their dignity offended. Besides being morally inadmissible, this will eventually have negative repercussions on the firm's economic efficiency. In fact, the purpose of a business firm is not simply to make a profit, but is to be found in its very existence as a *community of persons* who in various ways are endeavouring to satisfy their basic needs, and who form a particular group at the service of the whole of society. Profit is a regulator of the life of a business, but it is not the only one; *other human and moral factors* must also be considered which, in the long term, are at least equally important for the life of a business. (1991, §35)

The business of business properly understood is necessarily personalistic. The human person acting as an entrepreneur or working in business is not merely froth and bubble in the stream of history but is a freely acting person motivated toward specific ends. The businessperson can be seen as an exemplar of what it means to be a human being. Commerce is not necessarily, as W. B. Yeats suggested, just about fumbling in the greasy till and adding the halfpence to the pence

(1913). Business is not an end in itself, rather it creates a space in which the human person can realize their personal dignity in creative action. As human persons we live in an existential tension searching to become *who* we are. It is a part of a whole, of who we all are as persons.

Adam Smith observes in *The Wealth of Nations* how we stand in need of continual cooperation and it is because of this human exchange that we attain "from one another the far greater part" of the good (Smith 1981, 26). In this regard Pope Leo XIII, citing Thomas Aquinas, says in *Rerum Novarum*:

> The interests of all . . . are equal. The members of the working classes are citizens by nature and by the same right as the rich; they are real parts . . . which makes the body of the commonwealth. . . . To cite the wise words of St. Thomas Aquinas: "As the part and the whole are in a certain sense identical, so that which belongs to the whole in a sense belongs to the part." (1891, §33)

Pope Francis, speaking in February 2017 to participants attending an Economy of Communion meeting in Rome, said, "The first gift of the entrepreneur is his or her own person" (Francis 2017). So, business life, just like in the realms of social and political life, is challenged to be "guarded by the mystery" of our reality as human persons (Walsh 1999). It is because of this mystery that we can see emergent in the Economy of Communion project a movement toward regaining a more personalist understanding of the true nature of the business of business.

Bibliography

St. Benedict. 1982. *The Rule of St. Benedict*, ed. Timothy Fry, O.S.B.. Collegeville, MN: The Liturgical Press.

Bowne, Borden Parker. 1908. *Personalism*. Boston, MA: Houghton Mifflin Company.

Bruni, Luigino. 2012. "Su imprenditori e concorrenza: Una guida alla lettura nei tempi di crisi." *Nuova Umanità*, XXXIV 199: 1–14 (my translation).

Bruni, Luigino and Stefano Zamagni. 2004. "The Economy of Communion: Inspirations and Achievements." Revue Finance et Bien Commun 20: 91–97.

Dickens, Charles. 1839. *Oliver Twist*. London: Richard Bently. https://www.gutenberg.org/files/730/730-h/730-h.htm.

_____. 1859. *A Tale of Two Cities: A Story of the French Revolution*. https://www.gutenberg.org/files/98/98-h/98-h.htm,

Francis, Pope. 2017. *Address of His Holiness Pope Francis to Participants in the Meeting 'Economy of Communion,' Sponsored by the Focolare Movement*. https://www.vatican.va/content/francesco/en/speeches/2017/february/documents/papa-francesco_20170204_focolari.html.

Friedman, Milton. 1970. "The Social Responsibility of Business is to Increase its Profits." *The New York Times Magazine*. (September 13).

_____. 2002. *Capitalism and Freedom*. Chicago, IL: University of Chicago Press.

_____. 2017. *Milton Friedman on Freedom: Selections from The Collected Works of Milton Friedman*, edited by Robert Lesson and Charles G. Palm. Stanford, CA: Hoover Institution Press.

Gentili, Guido. 2018. "Work, money, Europe, migrants: an interview with Pope Francis." http://www.ilsole24ore.com/art/notizie/2018-09-06/work-money-europe-migrants-an-interview-to-pope-francis-195352.shtml?uuid=AEvWFjlF.

Gronbacher, Gregory M.A. 1998. *Economic Personalism: A New Paradigm for a Humane Economy*. Grand Rapids, MI: Acton Institute.

Hayek, F. A. 1978. *New Studies in Philosophy, Politics, Economics and the History of Ideas*. Chicago, IL: University of Chicago Press.

John Paul II, Pope. 1991. *Centesimus Annus*. http://www.vatican. va/content/john-paul-ii/en/encyclicals/documents/hf_jp-ii_ enc_01051991_centesimus-annus.html.

King, Martin Luther, Jr. 1986. *The Essential Writings and Speeches of Martin Luther King, Jr.* Edited by James M. Washington. San Francisco, CA: HarperCollins.

_____. 1998. "Letter from Birmingham Jail." *The Autobiography of Martin Luther King, Jr.* Edited by Clayborne Carson. New York: Grand Central Publishing.

_____. 2010. *Stride toward Freedom: The Montgomery Story*. Boston, MA: Beacon Press.

Leo XIII, Pope. 1891. *Rerum Novarum*. http://w2.vatican.va/content/ leo-xiii/en/encyclicals/documents/hf_l-xiii_enc_15051891_ rerum-novarum.html.

Lubich, Chiara. 1999. "For an Economy based on Communion." https://eocnorthamerica.files.wordpress.com/2015/11/ chi_19990129_en.pdf.

_____. 2001. "Some Aspects of the Economy of Communion." A talk at Castel Gandolfo, (5 April). https://eocnorthamerica. files.wordpress.com/2015/11/chi_20010405_en.pdf.

_____. 2007. *Essential Writings: Spirituality, Dialogue, Culture*. Edited by Tom Masters and Callan Slipper. Hyde Park, NY: New City Press.

McDonald, Larry and Patrick Robinson. 2009. *A Colossal Failure of Common Sense: Incredible Inside Story of The Collapse of Lehman Brothers*. Reading, UK: Ebury Press.

McNerney, John. 2003. *John Paul II: Poet and Philosopher*. London: T&T Clark.

_____. 2016. *Wealth of Persons: Economics with a Human Face*. Eugene, OR: Cascade Books.

Novak, Michael. 1982. *The Spirit of Democratic Capitalism*. New York: Simon & Schuster.

_____. 1986. *Will it Liberate? Questions about Liberation Theology.* Mahwah, N.J.: Paulist Press.

_____. 1993. *The Catholic Ethic and the Spirit of Capitalism.* New York: The Free Press.

Röpke, Wilhelm. 1959. "The Economic Necessity of Freedom." *Modern Age* 3, no. 3: 170–176.

_____. 1998. *Humane Economy: The Social Framework of the Free Market.* Wilmington, DE: ISI Books.

Smith, Adam. 1979. *The Theory of Moral Sentiments.* Edited by D.D. Raphael and A.L. Macfie. Indianapolis, IL: Liberty Fund.

_____. 1981. *An Inquiry into the Nature and Causes of the Wealth of Nations.* Edited by R.H. Campbell, A.S. Skinner and W.B. Todd. Vol. 1. Indianapolis, IN: Liberty Classics.

Tucker, Robert C. 1978. *The Marx-Engels Reader.* New York: Norton.

Voegelin, Eric. 2000. *New Science of Politics.* In *Modernity Without Restraint,* edited by Manfred Henningsen. *Collected Works of Eric Voegelin,* vol. 5. Columbia, MO: University of Missouri Press.

Walsh, David. 1990. *After Ideology: Recovering the Spiritual Foundations of Freedom.* San Francisco, CA: Harper.

_____. 1999. *Guarded by Mystery: Meaning in a Postmodern Age.* Washington, DC: The Catholic University of America Press.

_____. 2020. *The Priority of the Person.* Notre Dame, IN: University of Notre Dame Press.

Williams, Thomas D. and Jan Olof Bengtsson. 2014. "Personalism." In *The Stanford Encyclopaedia of Philosophy* (Spring 2014 edition), edited by Edward N. Zalta. http://plato.stanford.edu/archives/spr2014/entries/personalism.

Williamson. Kevin. 2012. "Milton Friedman: An Economics of Love" *National Review Online.* 30 July 2012. https://www.

nationalreview.com/exchequer/milton-friedman-economics-love-kevin-d-williamson/.

Wojtyła, Karol. 1981. *Toward a Philosophy of Praxis*. Edited by Alfred Bloch and George T. Czuczka. New York: Crossroad. https://www.cairn.info/revue-finance-et-bien-commun-2004-3-page-91.htm#.

_____. 1993. "Participation or Alienation." *Person and Community: Selected Essays*. Edited by A.N. Woznicki. Translated by Theresa Sandok. New York: Peter Lang.

_____. 2011. *Man in the Field of Responsibility*. Translated by Kenneth W. Kemp and Zuzanna Maślanks Kieroń. South Bend, IN: St. Augustine's Press.

Yeats W.B. 2004. "September 1913." In *The Poems*, 55–56. London: Orion Publishing.

Zamagni, Stefano. 2002. "On the Foundation and Meaning of the 'Economy of Communion' Experience." In *The Economy of Communion: Towards A Multi-Dimensional Economic Culture*, edited by Luigino Bruni. Translated by Lorna Gold, 130–140. Hyde Park, NY: New City Press.

_____. 2014. "The Economy of Communion Project as a Challenge to Standard Economic Theory." *Revista Portuguesa de Filosofia* 70, no. 1: 44–60.

Chapter 12

Exploring Subsidiarity:
The Case of the Economy of Communion

Jeanne G. Buckeye, University of St. Thomas, MN

Abstract: This article discusses the meaning and significance of subsidiarity and its companion principles, solidarity and participation, as both principles
of Catholic social thought (CST) and as management
principles. The author provides a brief overview of
the development of CST, particularly with regard to
subsidiarity and principles related to contemporary
management. The discussion of subsidiarity and its
companion principles posits a "culture of subsidiarity"
that indicates the presence of the principle and what
is necessary to sustain it in practice. A short introduction and history of the Economy of Communion
(EoC) and its parent, Focolare, form the basis for an
examination of how subsidiarity works in practice.
The specific example used is the startup of the EoC,
featuring particular actions pointing to the presence
of a spirit of subsidiarity.

Introduction

Why would businesses from different countries and unrelated
markets and industries align themselves with an association
that, on the face of it, contributes nothing to their economic
performance? Join an association that asks leaders to take on
more responsibilities when they already have full agendas?

Join an association that asks them to set aside a significant portion of their profits to support projects for the benefit of others—imposing a constraint on business growth and personal wealth accumulation?

Why, indeed. In the traditional way of viewing business priorities, it is hard to understand the appeal of such an association. But there are many things about the Economy of Communion (EoC) that are hard to understand in the usual way. EoC has anything but a traditional view of business; in fact, it claims to be "out to change the world." How? By "humanizing the economy" through businesses that prize relationships more than transactions, that place communion (i.e., community) on a plane with human dignity—and both of these above prosperity as the purpose of business. The EoC's approach to "changing the world" has nothing to do with insurrection, resurrection, economic dominance, political power, or partisan agendas. It is, in practice, much humbler, reflective of the maxim attributed to Gandhi: "If you want to change the world, start with yourself."

Ghandi's advice very neatly encapsulates a key aspect of subsidiarity. The idea is that change is best begun where the need for it arises first—locally. Change is best achieved when the first to be materially affected by it hold themselves responsible for the decision. Change-making decisions work best when those with the most to gain or lose also have a commitment to follow through. This is the object of subsidiarity: the right ordering of decision making. As a normative principle, subsidiarity applies to individuals, families, communities, institutions, and civil life, and it states that it is unjust to assign to a greater and higher association what a lesser and subordinate organization can do. Isn't this Ghandi's point? It is the EoC's point too. Their plan to "change the world" is to do it locally—one person, one transaction, one relationship, one business at a time.

This paper first discusses the meaning and significance of subsidiarity; then, using the Economy of Communion as a case example, it illustrates how the principle might look like in practice. For some readers subsidiarity will be a new term, though its companion principles—participation and solidarity—may sound more familiar. Subsidiarity is by no means a mainstay in the lexicon of management. But then the Economy of Communion is not exactly a familiar term either. So this is an opportunity to examine two important ideas in one essay, to look for evidence of one in the other, and to ask what it might mean, in practice, to establish and sustain a culture of subsidiarity, thus letting responsibility for decision making contribute to personal and organizational development.

My own introduction to the EoC happened about a decade ago when I worked with John Gallagher on a business case about Mundell & Associates, Inc., an EoC company in Indiana. The business was interesting, of course, but we were both surprised and confused by some of the terms and phrases the owner used to describe his company and its challenges. Stories were peppered with phrases like "spirituality of unity" and "seeing Christ in the other" and "culture of sharing." He talked about international gatherings of members of the "communion" (translated as "community") who owned businesses in South America, Canada, Africa, Europe. He talked about maximizing his employees' educational opportunities. He was also committed to sharing two-thirds of the company's profits—a portion to the poor and a portion to promote EoC outreach—and keeping the rest for the business. But the owner, John Mundell, was not running a charity. This was a competitive enterprise operating in a free market and proud of it. Fascinated with the EoC idea, John Gallagher and I undertook a study of a dozen or so North American EoC companies and published the results in *Structures of Grace: Business Practices of the Economy of Communion*. Many conferences and conversations later, the EoC companies, principles, and employees continue to interest and inspire.

Subsidiarity, Solidarity, and Participation:
A Leadership Trio in Catholic Social Thought

Catholic social teaching addresses the questions and challenges in daily life: e.g., the nature of work, the culture of work environments, management and economic practices, care for the poor, the creation and use of wealth. These principles remind decision makers to consider what is at stake for humanity in a given decision and to be guided by Christian morality directed at a transcendent good. They inspire creativity in identifying new moral solutions to social problems. They work as screens for evaluating the morality of specific options. Key elements of Catholic social teaching are presented as principles applying to multiple venues, including family, community, business, and government. In its own way, each principle reiterates the essential truth of human dignity and points to the goals of human flourishing and the common good.

Contemporary expressions of Catholic social teaching have their roots deep in Church history. But with the publication of Pope Leo XIII's *Rerum Novarum* in 1891 the stage was set for a more intense and continuous look at social changes and moral challenges brought about by industrialization and its accompanying social upheaval. The *Compendium of the Social Doctrine of the Church* calls *Rerum Novarum* "a heartfelt defense of the inalienable dignity of workers" (Pontifical Council 2004, §268). The forces Leo addressed were powerful and complicated: historical events, economic changes, the social displacement of laborers, labor movements, modern philosophies, capitalism, socialism, and Marxism. *Rerum Novarum* marked a renewal of the Church's "commitment to vitalize Christian social life" (§268). Throughout the twentieth century the list of concerns addressed by CST continued to expand: war, fascism, communications, technology, science, education, and postmodern philosophies hostile to Christian culture and to humanity itself. In response Leo's successors in the past century have produced a stream of encyclicals and other reflections that further developed the Church's thinking (Pontifical Council 2004, §87–92).

Within this rich vein of reflections on economics and organizational life are three principles that have unique relevance to the challenges and dynamics of management and business: subsidiarity, solidarity, and participation. Among other things this "management trio" addresses human development and the realization of individual potential. These principles affirm the importance of welcoming ideas and perspectives from all corners of the organization. They simultaneously encourage delegation, personal responsibility, partnership, collaboration, and accountability. The economic and social outcomes for which they aim are widely, if not universally, valued by organizational leaders.

Subsidiarity as a Management Principle

Subsidiarity is concerned with the right ordering of participation in decision making, emphasizing the need to make decisions at the level where consequences are likely to be greatest. The assumption here is that people at all levels of the organization want to be broadly informed and take an active interest in policies and strategies where they have expertise or will be the first to feel the effects. In practice, subsidiarity discourages efforts to reserve for greater and higher levels of association what lesser and subordinate ones can do themselves. Consequently, where authentic subsidiarity is practiced, bureaucracy, centralization, and management by fiat are minimized. Leaders do not so much distribute authority for decision making as acknowledge that the quality of decisions may be higher when they are made closer to the point of implementation, at various locations and ranks within the organization, or connected naturally to places, expertise, and human relationships. So instead of moving outward or downward from central authority, delegation moves from the parts to the center. Underlying themes of duty and moral responsibility associated with the principle have relevance in a variety of institutions, beginning with "the family, as a community of persons [which] is the first human society," (John Paul II 1991, §883) and extending to intermediary communities, business, government, and so on. Subsidiarity points to the goods of human fulfillment and healthy communities. In addition, it opens the way for innovation and meaningful change in organizations, and by its very nature reinforces the need for accountability and a shared vision of the good (Naughton et al. 2015).

In their treatment of subsidiarity in business, the authors of *Respect in Action: Applying Subsidiarity in Business* (2015) link it with an organizational environment of co-entrepreneurial ventures; it is "not a matter of management giving away power but placing power where it belongs the most" (Naughton et al. 2015, 7). In the management context, subsidiarity assumes "that people are an organization's most valuable resource and that a manager's job is to prepare people and to free people to perform" (Drucker and Colins 2008, 239). Leaders in this environment encourage employee engagement and are challenged to be good listeners and observers of people. The resulting culture emphasizes employee competencies, management practices, and trust. In such a culture leaders do not emphasize subordination or encourage dependent subordinates. Instead they foster freedom and encourage meaningful participation, and members recognize their responsibility to contribute from the bottom up. Charles Handy describes a subsidiarity environment as featuring "reverse delegation," important because it makes fresh thinking more likely and sets the stage for new ideas to be tried. People become more willing to engage the unfamiliar, confident that their insights and judgment will be honored. In this way subsidiarity helps individuals discover new interests and their own special abilities; the organization likewise discovers new resources, talents, and opportunities. Subsidiarity, says Handy, avoids the discouragement and indignity employees experience when they are asked to contribute only the minimum (Handy 1999).

The contemporary view of the leader as servant, visionary, and strength builder complements these managerial treatments of subsidiarity. But the concept itself is not new. The idea of subsidiarity has roots in ancient Rome—like much of the language and some of the methods for organizing and leading that management still uses today. *Subsidium* is a Latin word meaning "to assist or to strengthen." It refers to a military leader's role in relation to soldiers on the battle field (Naughton et al. 2015, 2). In battle the Roman commander's task was not primarily to fight but to observe and to be ready to provide the soldiers what *they* needed in order to fight. Yet credit for the concept of subsidiarity as we understand it today belongs less to Caesar and his legions than to the Church of Rome that survived their fall. In the late nineteenth and into the twentieth century, when the social challenges of the industrial revolution and succeeding technological periods created social upheaval and displacement, Church teaching began to explicate the theological principle of subsidiarity. Addressing it in new and more expansive ways, papal encyclicals have used it to affirm the primary responsibility for formation and care of family, to examine the role of work in human development, and to consider in a host of social, political, and economic dynamics the benefit derived from giving local responsibility and local effort priority over central authority and central planning.

Subsidiarity as a Theological Principle

In *Rerum Novarum* (1891) Leo XIII addressed issues raised by socialism, communism, and philosophies promoting the idea of the state's supreme authority. By introducing the idea of subsidiarity and placing it within the family, he made it clear that the state is subordinate to the individual and not vice versa. Twenty-five years later, in *Quadragesimo Anno*, Pius XI (1922–1939), who was the first to call subsidiarity a "social philosophy," extended Leo's logic regarding limiting the power of the state. The state was obliged, Pius said, to let subordinate groups handle matters and concerns of lesser importance. Today the idea of subsidiarity is generally understood to reflect the idea that the state should have a subsidiary function in society, undertaking only those tasks which cannot be done effectively by people at the local level, e.g., within the family or community. The principle points to less rather than more centralized authority in civic and other spheres.

Theologically, subsidiarity begins with respect for the human person and the intermediary communities which together make human flourishing possible—family, locations, governments, and groups that form around various enthusiasms. Subsidiarity rests on the "logic of gift." That is to say, it accepts that human dignity derives from the truth about the individual human life: that each life reflects the Creator, has a purpose, and is endowed with certain gifts, duties, vocations, and missions (Hittinger 2002, 393). This dignity and purpose elevates each person to the level of decision maker. It thus affirms the right for people to have a voice, if not full authority, in those matters for which they are by nature responsible (e.g., self and family) and which directly impact the fulfillment of their lives. Logically, a mature expression of this right to voice and to authority requires discovery, development, and the individual exercise of unique gifts and ultimately, the dispersal of gifts within populations. This diversity and distribution of gifts is, among all living things, unique to humankind.

Gifts are meant to benefit all of humanity. Some gifts—talents, abilities, callings—are apparent early in life. More often, though, they are discovered through experience: learning, performing, and trying new things. Parents, friends, teachers, and leaders may be instrumental in this discovery. They play varying roles in encouragement, attentive nurturing, and opening opportunities for expression. Responsibility for the care and effort needed to bring native gifts into maturity and to use them well lies within the individual person, but family and intermediary groups share in this duty as well. To squander, waste, exploit, commoditize, or take for granted our own gifts or someone else's is an injury and an injustice.

Good, But Not Utopia

It can be said that subsidiarity is present to the degree that a community or organization facilitates participation in decision making. While "all or nothing" may not be the correct measure of subsidiarity in an organization, precisely for the sake of participation, a good measure may be "more is better than less." Why? First, it has the potential to advance the organization beyond the need to manage efficiently and effectively. Good leaders pay attention to individual performance and make decisions in light of these constraints. Subsidiarity adds a new dimension; it assumes that leaders are at their best when they actively draw upon the diverse gifts of all employees. The focus on individuals that this requires not only allows the discovery of gifts and the possibility of developing them, but also, by doing so it reduces the potential for isolation, alienation, and boredom.

A second reason to hold out for subsidiarity is that it faces up to the challenges of hard times. It has the potential to make people stronger. If subsidiarity were only meaningful in good times it would justifiably be seen as shallow, insincere, and even manipulative. Fortunately, subsidiarity challenges people to understand one another, to express themselves honestly, to openly discuss differences, and to do a lot of forgiving and forgetting because there will inevitably be problems and disagreements. Trust, psychological connectedness, and spiritual maturity—key virtues in a culture of subsidiarity—get stronger when tested, when failure and disappointment make it tempting to walk away, but people stay anyway.

Third, innovation moves the organization forward. Because subsidiarity invites the discovery, development, and expression of diverse gifts, rethinking jobs, training, and performance will be a constant. The implications are important. At a minimum this will mean special attention to job design, training and development, decision-making practices, hierarchy, delegated authority, and communications methods. In this way the chances for innovation increase.

Solidarity and Participation

Subsidiarity is no panacea. Leaders have a duty to see and to engage the organization in its entirety. Where subsidiarity is practiced, local interests and local autonomy may begin to take precedence over concern for the common good. The result may be a slide into privatism or self-centered concern for local welfare: "We will do what serves our interests and never mind yours!" Expression of diverse gifts and interests cannot long survive in the face of persistent resistance or resentment. So subsidiarity needs a balancing factor—and solidarity serves that function. Solidarity is a necessary companion to subsidiarity, reducing the chances of runaway localism and strengthening the potential for individual development and the good of the community to advance together.

Solidarity reminds us that sometimes we need to set aside personal interests and submit to the common good, discouraging personal ambition for the sake of dominance. As a theological principle solidarity is a choice to respect human dignity and at the same time to serve the common good. It is a moral virtue, born in the heart of Christ, a human response to his prayer to the Father that "they may all be one" (Hittinger 2002, 196). The whole array of relationships and interdependence of life, from family and friendships to business and economic life, depend on solidarity. It is evident in forgiveness, reconciliation, and sacrifice for the good of another. In Church teaching, solidarity has been called simply "friendship" and "charity." An act of moral imagination, an attempt to empathize, a quest to live by the Golden Rule—these are acts of solidarity at its broadest. When we try to understand the world from another's point of view, that is solidarity. Refusing to be free riders who benefit from the labor of others with no contribution of our own, demonstrates solidarity. Acknowledging the reciprocal bonds and duties of the Christian faith is acting in solidarity. Gratitude for the heroes, wealth, and culture that are part of our heritage is also an act of solidarity. When we express true appreciation for the discoveries, creations, and effort of all kinds shared by men and women from the past and in our midst, we demonstrate solidarity. When we protect and preserve what is good today for the benefit of others tomorrow, that is an expression of solidarity too. Solidarity acts as a sort of compass, orienting an organization to the common good, contributing to the feeling of being part of something meaningful and important. Without solidarity, subsidiarity tends toward social privatism or localism, forgetting to be concerned for the good of others and grateful for their gifts.

Solidarity is no panacea for the challenges of organizational life either. Despite its potential for good, it can devolve, becoming just another version of social assistance, demeaning those in need by insisting on doing for others what they can do for themselves. Too much solidarity tends toward paternalism and centralization (Naughton et al. 2015, 59). A good balance of the two—subsidiarity and solidarity—depends on the third member of the "management trio" of Catholic social principles: participation. It is the indispensable method for the discovery and expression of individual gifts and for the affirmation of the community.

Participation is a foundational principle in management, affirming the need to inform decision making by inviting the

input of multiple perspectives (i.e., stakeholders). It recognizes the importance of honest communication, suggestions,
feedback, and shared responsibility in decisions as a path
to inclusion and engagement, to building community, and
to optimizing the chances for decisions to be implemented
effectively. Too little participation or too much top-down
management creates a kind of dictatorship—benevolent or
otherwise; too much trivializes the importance of voice and
generates cynicism of "death by meetings."

Theologically speaking, participation is not merely a tool. It
is a moral imperative. In Catholic social thought it refers to the
activities through which people, individually or with others,
directly or indirectly, "contribute to the cultural, economic,
political and social life" of the civil communities to which they
belong. It is interesting to note that participation is described
first not as a *right* but as a *duty*: "to be fulfilled consciously by
all, with responsibility and with a view to the common good"
(Pontifical Council 2004, §189). Forms of participation range
from voice, to playing an active role in social life, to affirming
ownership of capital (§281) and one's own labor. In this sense
participation is an aspect of justice at all levels of society. Pope
John XXIII called it "the greatest aspiration of a citizen," and
a pillar of all democratic orders, "one of the major guarantees
of the permanence of the democratic system" (§190). It is more
than self-expression or democratic inclusion. Participation is
oriented toward asserting influence, even if it is only the influence of free assent over matters that concern our lives and
others' as well. It is in this sense that participation is central
to the practice of subsidiarity. When accompanied by prayer-
ful reflection, participation provides the channel through
which the Spirit moves. Thus it is a key aspect of discernment
regarding community life and the common good. Exhibit 1
offers a brief summary of key cultural elements of subsidiarity,
solidarity, and participation.

Exhibit 1:
Managerial "Habits" Supporting Key Elements
Associated with Subsidiarity, Participation, and Solidarity

Subsidiarity:
1. Recognizes that it is wrong to assign to a higher association or unit what a lesser one can do;
2. Encourages problem solving and meaningful participation in decision making by people closest to the problem and capable of solving it;
3. Welcomes local responsibility demonstrated through initiative decision making;
4. Avoids needless bureaucracy, centralization, or management by fiat;
5. Cultivates listening and observation skills, trust, psychological connectedness, and spiritual maturity;
6. Recognizes that individuals have different gifts, and that human gifts are intended to benefit all mankind;
7. Acts with care and effort to bring native abilities to maturity in each person;
8. Avoids squandering, wasting, exploiting, commoditizing, or taking for granted any individual's gifts;
9. Orients culture and community life toward the potential for human flourishing;
10. Affirms voice, if not full authority, over those matters for which persons are by nature responsible and which directly affect the fulfillment of their lives.

Participation:
1. Emphasizes the need to have both a voice and an active role in social life;
2. Allows meaningful contributions to community life and shared tasks;
3. Orients individuals toward asserting influence—even if only free assent;
4. Affirms ownership of one's own labor, ideas, and gifts;
5. Fulfills a duty to serve to the common good.

Solidarity:
1. Emphasizes the importance of friendship, charity, and the Golden Rule;
2. Acts on the need for shared sacrifice and generosity;
3. Seeks healing and restoration through forgiveness and reconciliation;
4. Practices diligence in making personal and local contributions;
5. Expresses gratitude for the faith, culture, institutions, and wealth, and for models of wisdom, heroism, and personal sacrifice bestowed by past generations;
6. Treats expression of unity as a moral imperative;
7. Extends through an array of relationships and interdependence;
8. Protects what is good today for the benefit of others tomorrow.

The Economy of Communion

The EoC is unique, but not simple to understand. The influence of Catholic social principles is evident in the management and culture of both the association and at least some of its individual members. The EoC has, from the first, embodied ideas and practices associated with the principle of subsidiarity and its expression in organizational culture. Though spiritually motivated, the EoC is also very concrete—concerned with economic activity where people have to use their brains, roll up their sleeves, and get to work (Lubich 1999, 286). As a community of businesses the EoC pursues shared objectives, recognizes individuals' unique gifts and potentials, and honors both by emphasizing local decision making and avoidance of unnecessary bureaucracy or centralization.

The EoC philosophy views business positively. It appreciates the value of entrepreneurship, private ownership, and free markets. It recognizes the capacity for business to both meet real needs and open avenues for human achievement and progress. At the same time, the EoC has a vision of the transcendent good—a deeper, broader, and more enduring good—that can be accomplished when a lively faith informs daily life in the practice of business. In this regard they see a need for change. Starting with themselves, the individual businesses of the EoC try to conduct business in ways that model every excellence for the purpose of serving a transcendent good. Businesses of the EoC, though diverse in their products, services, markets, locations, sizes, and organizational structures, are anything but a random group.

Returning to the questions raised at the start of this paper, the pursuit of excellence and a transcendent good go a long way to explaining what attracts businesses owners to the EoC.

Participating businesses come freely into the Economy of Communion. They are likewise free to leave at any time. These two facts are central to the character of the association—whose full name is "The Economy of Communion *in Freedom*." A spirit of unity drives the organization. Like the challenge of living up to twin expectations for person-centered management and for sharing wealth, living in a spirit of unity can only be realized if freely chosen.

As members of the EoC, business leaders envision a new kind of economic culture where building community and sharing abundance with the poor take precedence over market dominance and the accumulation of wealth; where relationships are privileged over transactions; and where profit is valued more than profit-maximizing. The EoC is committed to fostering unity and to creating a culture of giving—for the sake of the Gospel. In the sphere of business worldwide, the EoC is still relatively unknown. None of its participating companies are the equivalent of "Fortune 500" businesses. Yet virtually from its founding, the EoC has been the subject of journal articles, graduate theses, and even several dozen books. Writers have looked at the EoC's philosophy and its theological roots, its impact on various local cultures, especially in poorer parts of the world, and at the principles and business practices that seem to be shared by its members. The Economy of Communion has been mentioned in a papal encyclical (Benedict XVI 2009). Its leaders have been invited to the United Nations to explain the EoC's purposes and ideals. At the EoC's 2017 international conference in Rome, Pope Francis addressed the assembly, as John Paul II and Benedict had done before him.

Each business develops in its own way, shaped, as businesses tend to be, "in response to its experiences, its crises, its celebrations, its failures and its triumphs" and, of course, by the values and perspectives of the founder (Gallagher and Buckeye 2014, 180). So it is with EoC businesses. They look like other businesses of their size and kind wherever they are in the world. In our study of the business practices of EoC companies in North America, John Gallagher and I found no strong evidence that EoC businesses adhere to a uniform set of management practices or that they share anything like a one-right-way mentality. We did, however, see evidence of *patterns* of cultural preferences and management practices. In marketing, for example, the range of concerns for pricing, communicating, etc., were what might be expected anywhere. But we also saw a pattern among the companies that we described as "habitual sensitivity to the needs and wants of customers." As a marketing practice, this took precedence over market research and supported "word of mouth, reputation and relationship marketing" over any other kind of promotion (181). While we observed no consistency in the way that leaders introduced employees to the EoC or fostered a sense of EoC identity, we did see among leaders a "keen awareness of their identity as EoC companies" and an unquestionable commitment to EoC ideals. We saw evidence of a pattern of "hiring for the community," for team decisions in hiring, and for selection based on optimal professional qualifications, but we found nothing that suggested parochial hiring or insider/outsider thinking (184). There were other patterns, as well:

> These companies appear to share similar cultural aspects marked by openness and mutual respect, and they appear to take the development of culture seriously and intentionally.... They strive to be familial and embrace storytelling and celebrations, for example, and do not generally embrace formal mission and vision statements.... [Leaders] demonstrate a preference for action; they are doers first and talkers later.... [They show] a flexibility grounded in their understanding of the business as community. (Gallagher and Buckeye 2014, 185–186)

The EoC's attraction to business participants may also be explained by a well-articulated package of values, grounded in faith and spirituality, e.g.:

1. EoC members see their businesses and the EoC itself as a concrete expression of the "spirituality of unity" and they openly talk about Divine Providence as a factor in organizational life, inviting God to intervene, "even within the hard facts of economic reality" (Lubich 1999, 277).

2. The businesses seek to live out the social teachings of the Catholic Church with a particular focus on solidarity with the poor.

3. Commitment to sharing with the poor includes sharing profits, creating jobs, training, and patient endurance with regard to employee development (Lubich 1999, 276).

4. In the daily activity of business, EoC companies seek to place the person at the center of the enterprise.

5. They share an economic philosophy that emphasizes private ownership and accountability; free market activity; a general commitment to ethical management; establishing "loyal and considerate relationships" with customers, suppliers, government, and even competitors; appreciating employees, involving them, and keeping them informed.

Member companies seek out the EoC, not the other way around. The EoC's reputation spreads by word of mouth rather than promotion (Gallagher and Buckeye 2014, 181). For the leaders of the EoC, whether entrepreneurs or heads of established businesses, the association provides access to a network of business leaders who share their values, opportunities for meaningful discussion (through publications, conferences, internet, etc.), and an ongoing inspiration to integrate faith and work. EoC members "feel themselves part of something much larger" than just being in business or running a business (Lubich 1999, 277). The writings, reflections, and self-reported experiences of EoC business leaders are replete with references to participation, the common good, human dignity, solidarity, respect for creation, and respect for life. This is not surprising, since most businesses come into the EoC by way of the Focolare Movement, the EoC's organizational "parent" and a spiritual model for articulating goals, beliefs, and mission in a way that resonates across cultures.

Focolare: A Brief History

Out of the destruction and loss of life that marked the bombing of so many great cities in World War II came at least one remarkable new creation: the Focolare Movement. The unlikely founder, Chiara Lubich, was little more than a girl. Not only did she cunningly and courageously endure the relentless attacks on her city and home, she triumphed over them. In the manner of young entrepreneurs, she saw a need and set out to fill it. And in the manner of a morally mature Christian—and to paraphrase an idea often attributed to St. Ignatius—she prayed as if everything depended on God, worked as if everything depended on her. She began by sharing her own belongings with those who had lost everything, and others were attracted by her generosity and diligence. Together they created a system to collect from those who were able to share and to distribute to others who needed it. The work became a lifeline for poor in need until the war ended. After the war, it survived, it grew, and lives on now as an official and worldwide work of the Roman Catholic Church (Masters and Uelmen 2011, 33).

The story of Lubich and the Focolare demonstrates the power of subsidiarity. She saw a need. She accepted responsibility for solving a problem. She used the resources available to her, addressed the problem locally, and invited others to join her—with or without a line of direct authority. Focolare thrives today as a work of the "spirituality of unity" in pursuit of universal brotherhood, dedicate to encouraging a culture where *giving* is more important than *having* (Gallagher and Buckeye 2014, 20). Meeting the needs of the poor remains a priority. Lubich continued as Focolare's spiritual leader until her death in 2008. But her written legacy—letters, spiritual reflections, etc.—continues to undergird the Focolare tradition. But Focolare is not Lubich's only institutional legacy; she founded the Economy of Communion as well.

Founding the Economy of Communion

By 1991 Brazil had a large Focolare community representing all parts of the local society. In May of that year Lubich visited. She came knowing about the country's poverty, but nothing had prepared her for the poverty of São Paulo. Thousands of meager dwellings spread across the hills surrounding the city formed the favelas, or slums, where the poor lived on the absolute edge of society, with too little food, little or no paying work, and only the slimmest hope for ever achieving anything more. Not only were the favelas home to the poorest of the poor, Lubich learned, but they were home to many Focolare members too.

In response to this deep poverty, Lubich decided, as she had 50 years earlier, that something must be done (Bruni 2002, 34). She discussed the problem with a handful of other Focolare leaders and together they developed a plan for action. Within days of her arrival Lubich proposed a way forward. In the Focolare there was talent, energy, and faith enough to take on the challenge. The Focolare would create an Economy of Communion to do more than attract charity to fill the gaps in the lives of the very poor. The EoC would actually "increase the communion of goods through giving rise to businesses . . . entrusted to competent people who would be able to run them efficiently so as to make a profit" (15). At the very least these businesses would generate income and enough jobs to address the needs of Focolare members living in Brazil. The crowd received Lubich's idea warmly, eagerly. Lubich herself was surprised by the immediate buzz of enthusiasm. Within days word of the EoC was out among Focolare throughout Brazil, but also in Latin America, Europe, wherever Focolare communities were found (16).

Lubich offered few specifics, but almost from the moment she proposed the plan, prospective EoC business owners were developing, experimenting, and refining the idea and how it could be achieved. The original call was "to increase the communion of goods through giving rise to businesses, which would be . . . [managed] efficiently to make a profit" (Bruni 2002, 15). Some of the profit would go directly to people in the form of charity and jobs that paid a living wage; another part would be reinvested to grow the businesses; a third part would go to spread the word about the project and to inspire others to adopt the model. EoC businesses would look like other competitors in their markets. Their products and services would look the same. Generating revenue and managing expenses—that would be the same too. However, EoC companies would be different from other businesses in at least one essential: They would operate with practices informed by Focolare ideals. Instead of treating net revenue as strictly for the benefit of the businesses or its owners, for EoC businesses, profits would be seen as a gain to be distributed in multiple ways and for multiple purposes. What charitable giving alone had been unable to accomplish for the poor in Brazil and elsewhere, profits from EoC businesses would supply (Gallagher and Buckeye 2014, 22).

In the first four years, almost 500 businesses became part of the EoC, operating businesses of all kinds in multiple economic sectors. Lubich credited early success to the Focolare. The EoC grew, she said, "because it was promoted by people of the Movement [Focolare] shaped by our Ideal" (Lubich 1999, 285). Nearly 30 years later, with new businesses coming and others leaving, the EoC has stabilized at about 850 enterprises worldwide, each managed in its own way and carrying out a shared mission to do business well and to do it in solidarity with the poor. Most, though not all, EoC owners are part of the Focolare. Their businesses ride the same currents of competitive activity as others in their markets. Size and economic success vary. Like the owners of small and medium-sized businesses, especially family businesses, EoC owners today have concerns about succession planning and transitioning ownership to the next generation, both a sign of and a challenge to success.

Several years after the birth of the EoC, Lubich revealed that before visiting Brazil she had come to believe that "God was calling the Movement to something more and something new," but what that was she did not know (Lubich 1999, 275). Nor, apparently, had she connected this calling with the journey to Brazil. Lubich continued to believe in the promise of the EoC, and she clearly understood it as a response to a heavenly calling:

> This is how we should see, how we should understand the Economy of Communion: something built according to the mind of God, a work that will endure not only on this earth but remain in the life to come, where we will have the immense joy of finding it again in the new earth and the new heavens that await us. (Lubich 1999, 289)

Reflections on Subsidiarity and the Economy of Communion

Did Chiara Lubich and the Focolare leaders use subsidiarity as a principle to support the creation and shape of a new way of being in business? I have no specific evidence to share on this question. But whether or not it *consciously* guided their thinking, subsidiarity was there in spirit. In the story of the EoC's founding we see evidence of this spirit, and it helps explain the proposal's immediate appeal. It also sheds light on the EoC's ongoing attraction for entrepreneurially minded business owners: respect in action. A brief reflection on the EoC's founding highlights five observations in support of this point.

First, as the founder of the Focolare talking to a gathering of Focolare members about the extreme poverty experienced by some among them, Chiara Lubich sounded very much like a woman who was taking action as a family member on behalf of her family in the spirit of subsidiarity. It was surely no great stretch for Lubich to relate to the Focolare as a spiritual family, albeit a worldwide one. They were a special community, close knit by virtue of their shared spirituality and ideals; they cared deeply about one another. Lubich's call for a "new economy" was meant to resolve a painful and potentially life-limiting problem facing this family. The proposal was to address the problem for the family and within the family. This ideal is the very heart of subsidiarity. Without the resources or the direction of an outside authority, a family addresses a problem threatening their own survival or undertakes a project to enhance their lives. The family needs no permission to do what is needed to care for its members. Sometimes it must act alone. The stronger and better-equipped members of a family look out for others among them; all members contribute as they are able for the good of the family, especially for those in greatest need. In the case of the EoC, the initial concern was like family concern—by the Focolare for the Focolare. In other words, Lubich and her leadership team were asserting for the assembled group that they had full authority for those matters (poverty among them) for which, in the natural order of things, they held themselves responsible.

Second, at its start the EoC addressed a problem where it arose in the natural order, where solutions would be felt first and most profoundly and, quite literally, locally—where the poor lived and worked. Lubich and the other Focolare leaders could have responded very differently to the poverty they witnessed in São Paulo. It would have been natural, for example, for the founder and spiritual leader of a large and growing organization to try to generate widespread interest in the problem of poverty in a more public way. Lubich might have called on government to do something by admonishing or pleading with national leaders who seemed to have done too little in the past. She might have lectured the city fathers and local clergy. She might have asked for help from international investors and globalists who admired Brazil's natural resources and economic growth but ignored her poor. But she did not. Nor, apparently, did she try to estimate the size of the problem and what it might cost to fix it, and then go out to appeal for public support. She did not suggest the creation of a new "congress" to explore what could be done or to decide what to do. In other words, she did not call on help from outside the Focolare—from the UN, European countries, the US, or even the Church. Lubich's call emphasized initiative, problem-solving, and decision making at the point where the problem originated and where outcomes would be felt the most: another sign of subsidiarity.

Third, any of the strategies just listed could be justified; most had, in fact, been tried before. But, affirming the dignity of the Focolarini present and demonstrating respect for them, Lubich chose instead to invite members themselves to be part of the solution. There was no language singling people out on the basis of wealth or poverty. No effort to use the powerful to rescue the powerless. The call for an Economy of Communion recognized that individuals have different gifts which they could freely use for the benefit of others. If Lubich had asked the Focolare gathered in São Paulo to dig deeply into their own pockets and give what they could, they almost certainly would have responded generously; after all, sharing is at the heart of Focolare spirituality. Instead, she chose the path of subsidiarity, inviting people to solve their own problems, affirming their ability and that they were waiting to help if asked.

Fourth, Lubich was not proposing a theory in São Paulo that day (Bruni 2002, 20), something that others, more intelligent or more able than present company should ponder and/or employ. She was calling for action—for discrete steps and concrete outcomes generated by capable individuals who would use their own gifts to help solve their own problem. It was as though she was saying, "We do not need to turn this over to the experts. The time to solve this is now. Your participation will mean something. We are a community who can be responsible and take care of itself." And so was born the EoC, or, as Lubich described it, "a unique manifestation of a free economy based on solidarity" (Lubich 1999, 274) and originating in a call to action expressed in the spirit of subsidiarity.

Fifth, Lubich did not call for the creation of an organization to accomplish what she knew could be accomplished by the Focolare. She did not declare herself the leader of this endeavor. But neither did she ask for the intervention of a higher authority, i.e., Church or state, though she did apparently act having been advised and affirmed by trusted leaders. Having accepted the idea of sharing as a Christian duty, she needed no one's permission to act. Lubich's call to action was a classic example of respect for human persons and an expression of the need for human flourishing. By claiming for anyone who wanted to participate the *right* to participate, she affirmed their gifts, demonstrated trust, and connected psychologically with both "haves" and "have nots" in an act of spiritual maturity.

Conclusion

Reflection on the meaning and characteristics of subsidiarity, particularly as presented and developed in Catholic social thought, provides a basis for looking for the evidence of that principle in a business culture. To the extent that a culture of subsidiarity is present in any organization, one might expect to see a commitment to participation and solidarity and evidence that these values reach outside bounds of the organization. Subsidiarity would be evident in relationships with clients, customers, suppliers, and even competitors. Business activities would be inspired by a commitment to ethics and legality. Attention would be given to the working environment and to the natural environment because both are important for workers' well-being. Above all, persons and giftedness would be valued. A shortcoming of this paper is that it deals with subsidiarity in the founding of the EoC but not in the daily activities of EoC businesses as they pursue their individual missions and objectives. Exhibit 2 is an effort to respond to this shortcoming by citing examples of current and regular EoC practices that support a culture of subsidiarity, solidarity, and participation. Most of these practices would not be priorities for non-EoC businesses: moving ideas from the edges to the center; preferring local decision making and responsibility; emphasizing employee gifts and development; creating a person centered businesses. Unusual, yes. But from a human perspective, they make all the difference.

Exhibit 2:

EoC Practices Reflect a Culture of
Subsidiarity, Solidarity, and Participation

1. Annual regional meetings of EoC business leaders (with locally created agendas) that include education, spiritual reflections, discussion of worldwise EoC concerns, encouragement, and formation of future EoC members.

2. Semi-annual global meetings for the purpose of discussing the EoC project as a whole, for spiritual reflection, for education, for connecting with fellow EoC business owners from around the world.

3. A preference for in-person meetings, visiting other EoC businesses, reaching in solidarity to work in locations around the world where entrepreneurial activity is needed but resources are low.

4. Ongoing efforts to connect and to communicate with the Church and with spiritual leaders.

5. Inclusion of academics with scholarly interest in the EoC but no direct involvement in its work, and whose questions, observations, and participation in discussions become part of a learning and reflective environment.

6. Ongoing involvement in educational opportunities—conferences, publishing, formation of university programs, etc.

7. Creation of educational and professional development exercises for young men and women interested in the EoC.

8. Publication and development of EoC websites appealing to various audiences and highlighting trends and concerns within the organization worldwide.

9. Ongoing efforts to encourage EoC participants and supporters to communicate concerns, local problems, personal experiences, successes, failures, difficulties, innovations, and so on; "storytelling" (highly valued) that sometimes becomes "legend" and reinforces values around person-centered management, lessons learned, the work of the Divine, the rewards of sharing, etc.

10. Creation of symbols and tools to communicate and reinforce shared EoC values.

Bibliography

Benedict XVI, Pope. 2009. *Caritas in Veritate*. http://www.vatican. va/content/benedict-xvi/en/encyclicals/documents/hf_ben-xvi_enc_20090629_caritas-in-veritate.html.

Bruni, Luigino, ed. 2002. *The Economy of Communion: Toward a Multi-Dimensional Economic Culture*. Hyde Park, NY: New City Press.

Dicastery for Promoting Integral Human Development. 2018. *Vocation of the Business Leader: A Reflection*. Rome/St. Paul: University of St. Thomas. https://www.humandevelopment. va/en/risorse/documenti/vocation-of-the-business-leader-a-reflection-5th-edition.html.

Drucker, Peter and James C. Collings. 2008. *The Five Most Important Questions You Will Ever Ask about your Organization*. New York: Leader to Leader Institute.

Gallagher, Jim. 1997. *Chiara Lubich: A Woman's Work: The Story of the Focolare Movement and Its Founder*. Hyde Park, NY: New City Press.

Gallagher, John and Jeanne Buckeye. 2014. *Structures of Grace: The Business Practices of the Economy of Communion*. Hyde Park, NY: New City Press.

Handy, Charles B. 1999. *The Hungry Spirit: Beyond Capitalism: A Quest for Purpose in the Modern World*. New York: Broadway Books.

Handy, Charles B. 1999. "Subsidiarity Is the Word for It." *Across the Board*. 36, 6: 7–8.

Hittinger, Russell. 2002. Social Pluralism and Subsidiarity in Catholic Social Doctrine," *Annales Theologici* 16: 385–408.

John Paul II, Pope. 1991. *Centesimus Annus*. http://www.vatican. va/content/john-paul-ii/en/encyclicals/documents/hf_jp-ii_ enc_01051991_centesimus-annus.html.

Leo XIII, Pope. 1891. *Rerum Novarum*. http://www.vatican. va/content/leo-xiii/en/encyclicals/documents/hf_l-xiii_ enc_15051891_rerum-novarum.html.

Lubich, Chiara. 1999. *Essential Writings*. Michael Vandelene, ed. Hyde Park, NY: New City Press.

Masters, Thomas and Amy Uelmen. 2011. *Focolare: Living a Spirituality of Unity in the United States*. Hyde Park, NY: New City Press.

Naughton, Michael J., Jeanne G. Buckeye, Kenneth E. Goodpaster, and T. Dean Maines. 2015. *Respect in Action: Applying Subsidiarity in Business*. St. Paul, MN: University of St. Thomas.

Pius XI, Pope. 1931.   *Quadragesimo Anno*. http://www. vatican.va/content/pius-xi/en/encyclicals/documents/hf_p-xi_enc_19310515_quadragesimo-anno.html.

Pontifical Council for Peace and Justice. 2004. *Compendium of the Social Doctrine of the Church*. Washington, DC: USCCB Publishing. https://www.vatican.va/roman_curia/ pontifical_councils/justpeace/documents/rc_pc_justpeace_ doc_20060526_compendio-dott-soc_en.html.

Chapter 13

The Economy of Communion
As An Exercise of Prophetic Imagination

John Gallagher, Maryville College

Abstract: This paper seeks to consider the purpose and meaning of the Economy of Communion (EoC) movement in the context of totalism. It makes the claim that the EoC is an exercise of prophetic imagination as that idea has been articulated by Walter Brueggemann. The paper proceeds by first explicating the significant dimensions of prophetic imagination at work, then assesses the EoC in light of that explication. We then consider the engagement of EoC entrepreneurs in prophetic ministry and conclude by returning to the question of the EoC as an alternative proposal for economic life and culture.

On March 15, 2019, hundreds of thousands of students across the globe staged a protest by staying out of school for the day. With this Global Climate Strike, young people were protesting the inaction and apathy of the world's leaders toward climate change. The day-long strike was an outgrowth of an effort begun by a 16-year-old student, Greta Thunberg of Sweden, who, in August of 2018, first stayed out of school in a call for our public servants and corporate leaders to act to mitigate global warming. The Climate Strike protesters minced few words in their signs and their speeches, clearly conveying their conviction that world leaders are squandering this next generation's future. In their eyes, world leaders are suggesting that today's young people don't matter—and these young people want an end to such injustice.

While the immediate focus of the strike was the issue of climate change and its threat to the well-being (perhaps the very existence) of future generations, many of the same signs and speeches carried a criticism of the economic and political system of which climate change is a symptom. The young people understand climate change to be attributable to human economic activity. As such the Global Climate Strike is not just a protest against inaction. It is an indictment of an economic and political system that requires significant extractive, industrial, and consumption activity and the environmental degradation that accompanies such, and lays the burden on the young and others without power or voice who will have to confront the full consequences (Gold 2019, 64–65). Protests against global warming and climate change are arguably manifestations of deeper social, cultural, and economic concerns.

There is broad recognition that the current economic system creates, as a by-product, serious social ills that might generally be characterized as inequalities in wealth, power, and access to significant material and development needs like education, food, security, water, employment, and health care. In the United States alone, we might consider the student debt crisis, the dominance of corporate agribusiness, municipal water crises, wage inequalities between men and women, and the number of families unable to afford health care as evidence for these social ills. The human suffering and despair that accompanies these ills is significant and arguably systemic. Pope Francis describes these systemic social ills as the forces behind the creation of marginalized, excluded, and otherwise "discarded people" (Pope Francis 2017). Indeed, it is not hard to imagine that the young climate strikers feel quite like discarded persons; not simply ignored, but essentially written off by those of us with economic wealth and political power.

Walter Brueggemann describes this state of affairs as "totalism" (Brueggemann 2018, 127); a socio-ideological arrangement dominated by a hegemonic ideology that is, in this case, variously and loosely labeled as consumerism, globalization, free-market capitalism, or democratic capitalism. As Brueggemann elaborates, it is an unapologetic ideology the outcome of which is "the monetizing of all social relationships, the commoditization of all social possibilities, and the endless production of dispensable persons who have no legitimate membership in the totalism" (131); to wit, Francis' discarded people. Francis, accordingly, views this creation of discarded persons as the "principal ethical dilemma of . . . capitalism" (Pope Francis 2017).

This paper seeks to consider the purpose and meaning of the Economy of Communion (EoC) movement in the context of this totalism. In this consideration, the paper makes the claim that the EoC is an exercise of prophetic imagination as that idea has been articulated by Walter Brueggemann. The paper proceeds by first explicating the significant dimensions of prophetic imagination at work, then assesses the EoC in light of that explication. We then consider the engagement of EoC entrepreneurs in prophetic ministry and conclude by returning to the question of the EoC as an alternative proposal for economic life and culture.

What Is the Economy of Communion?

The very existence of the EoC is evidence that the challenge of totalism is more than an abstract intellectual concern. Additional evidence takes the form of other movements and projects designed to address the hegemony of our dominant culture of consumerism. Among these are cooperatives, microcredit and microfinancing institutions, B Corporations, social enterprises, forms of collaborative consumption, and various "occupy" movements. These have been variously, and collectively, described as the "New" economy (Alperovitz 2011), the "generative" economy (Kelly 2013), and/or the "circular" economy (Thunberg 2019). All of these terms refer to ideas and practices aimed at more humane economic practices and political policies. Clearly, the economic and political policies our young people are going out on strike against have very real consequences. This indeed may be the salient economic and political crisis of our time. In many ways, in the midst of this crisis, stands the Economy of Communion.

The EoC itself was created in São Paulo, Brazil, in 1991, by Chiara Lubich, the founder of the Focolare Movement, in response to the prevailing social injustice and economic inequality in Brazil. Economic inequality was such that for many people, particularly participants in the Focolare community, serious material poverty was a continuing way of life with little hope of mitigation. The original vision of the EoC, as described by Chiara, was that talented Focolare members

> could set up businesses that could tap their expertise and resources to produce together wealth for the benefit of those in need. They would have to be managed by competent persons capable of making them function efficiently and deriving profits from them. These profits would then be put in common. (Lubich 2007, 275)

The pooling of profits was understood as a three-part distribution: one part to reinvest in the growth and sustainability of the business, one part to provide for the direct needs of the poor, and a third part to support the development of a culture of giving, or of a community such that the initiative could be sustained (Lubich 2007, 275). The EoC was a proposal aimed at addressing material poverty, economic inequality, and diminished hope. The EoC looked to skilled, experienced businesspeople to start (or continue with) businesses, manage them profitably, and then invest those profits, or wealth, in specific ways.

In founding the EoC, the Focolare were looking to the private sector to operate within a market economy, generating products and services, selling those products and services, and earning profits: businesses creating wealth through their interactions in the marketplace (Haughey 2006, 92). Part of that wealth would be pooled and shared as a direct effort to reduce poverty by meeting the material needs of a particular people. Entrepreneurs would manage legitimate private sector businesses that rely on a market economy, buying from suppliers in a market economy, hiring employees in a market economy, and producing goods and services in a market economy, selling those to customers, and generating material wealth, all while operating in a market economy.

It is a very deep and rich idea, yet in some ways, it is so concrete that it is immediately accessible to people. The practice of business and the common understanding of profit-making is so familiar that the core idea of pooling profits to help others is quite intuitive. At this level, it is quite easy to become an EoC practitioner and/or participant. But the EoC is a richer idea than just profit sharing. That richness affords an opportunity for sustained reflection on the meaning and implications of the EoC. Much has been written about the multiple, specific, profound ways in which the EoC understands economic activity and the possibilities of economic activity. As Chiara Lubich herself noted:

> In proposing it, I was certainly not thinking about a theory. I see, however, that it has caught the attention of economists, sociologists, philosophers and scholars of other disciplines who find in this new experience . . . grounds for further study that go beyond the Movement in which it has historically been developed. (2007, 278)

The Idea of Prophetic Imagination

It is important at the outset to mention that Brueggemann is concerned in *The Prophetic Imagination* with the need for change in the contemporary church, particularly a need for the church to confront the dominant culture in the United States of "the American ethos of consumerism" (2018, 1). Certainly the need for change was suspected in 1978 and, as the foreword to the anniversary edition claims, that need has not diminished. The problematic features that Brueggemann "diagnoses in the social situation have not faded into the past…" (2018, xvi), and the global climate strike and attendant issues are evidence for that.

Brueggemann characterizes prophetic imagination as making possible a "consciousness and perception alternative to the consciousness and perception of the dominant culture around us" (2018, 3). For Brueggemann, "prophetic imagination" is manifest most clearly in the scriptural record of prophecy in the life of Israel from the time of Moses through the ministry, eventual death, and resurrection of Jesus Christ. The prophetic imagination instantiates an alternative to the dominant culture. The alternative arises from within its own "experience and confession of faith," and not from external imposition or sources.

The prophetic imagination is a call to live out the truth that we know in a dominant culture that would rather not acknowledge such truth because that truth is a proclamation that the dominant culture does not have all the answers. It has only temporal (and temporary) power to prescribe reality. The dominant culture seeks to perpetuate itself through its rules, its exercise of power, its insistence on what matters or what is important because it imagines that things will always be the way they are at present. This is an apt description of contemporary consumerist culture, where increasing consumption of goods and services is not only understood as an important driver of economic growth and therefore economic policy, but consumption is arguably the primary means of general well-being and happiness (Araùjo 2002, 25). Brueggemann makes the point that the reality we experience living in the dominant culture is itself imaginative and therefore prophetic imagination pronounces an alternative (2018, 3) that serves to both criticize the dominant culture and energize the prophetic community to live in the alternative imagination (2018, 4). This alternative imagination is nothing less than the "imagination of God" (2018, 6).

Brueggemann begins his exposition of prophetic ministry (what I am calling the exercise of prophetic imagination) with Moses and Israel's escape from Pharaoh and flight from Egypt. He then traces the prophetic ministry from Moses, through Jeremiah, to Jesus. Early on, the dominant culture is Egyptian culture under the rule (and imagination) of the pharaoh. This leads Brueggemann, in the original edition, to characterize the dominant culture as "royal consciousness." That is to say that the dominant culture serves the royal state, the pharaoh, or the king (the extension to Solomon). In the anniversary edition, Brueggemann insists that a more contemporary description for what he means by the dominant culture would be "totalism," as we have mentioned, which is a term meant to describe "a socio-ideological arrangement in which hegemonic ideology takes up all the social spaces and allows to no alternative possibility. Its claim is 'total'" (Brueggemann 2018, 127). Consider again our consumerist culture and in particular the synergistic interaction in contemporary times between technology and consumption. The nexus of smartphones, digital assistants, smart appliances, and social media makes virtually all things available, accessible, and shareable—in essence, consumable, at all hours of the day, every day, across time and space. Consumption can become the primary way of relating to not only the things in our world, but also to each other.

It is important to recognize that one of the aims of the dominant culture is self-perpetuation. In the imaginative self-understanding of the dominant culture, it will always be dominant. It sees itself as providing meaning and explanation to the community and will always be thus. The dominant culture, therefore, and by definition, is a "politics of oppression and exploitation" (Brueggemann 2018, 7). The prophetic imagination counters this with a "politics of justice and compassion" (6). The dominant culture always marginalizes some members of the community through oppressive social policy such that the dimension of the prophetic imagination that provides the critique of totalism originates in grief (27). The oppression and marginalization that is partly constitutive of the dominant reality engenders grief, mourning, and anguish at the numbness and insensitivity to the plight of many in the community (46). The prophetic imagination goes beyond the mere recognition that something is not right to a proclamation, a presentation of an "alternative consciousness" that energizes the community to new vitality (59). It provides hope in place of despair. "As the prophetic cry loosens the grip of dominant ideologies, it also energizes and empowers a community out of indifference into action" (Hankins 2018, xiii). It demonstrates the imagination of God and provokes amazement at the sheer generosity and inclusion—the reality in the imagination of God. "YHWH has a specific will and purpose . . . that lies outside the totalism of the day and that will not be mocked or countermanded by the practice of that totalism" (Brueggemann 2018, 128).

An exercise of the prophetic imagination bears these marks. It must "nurture, nourish, and evoke a consciousness and perception alternative to the consciousness and perception of the dominant culture around us" (Brueggemann 2018, 3). The key question is not whether the "alternative is realistic, or practical or viable," but "whether it is imaginable" (39). The alternative consciousness serves to criticize the dominant culture, arising from and expressed as grief, but simultaneously energizing through a promise of a better time and situation in the future. The alternative must arise from within its own experience and confession of faith. It is not new, per se, but it may seem new. But it arises from within—in this sense it is a recovery of a perception that has been, or is co-opted—or better, overwhelmed—by the dominant culture.

The Economy of Communion as the Exercise of Prophetic Imagination

There are arguably four distinctives that support the claim that the EoC proposes a consciousness that is an alternative to the dominant hegemonic ideology. First, it is a practice of abundance. Not only does it operate with a "logic of abundance" (Haughey 2006, 87) but it is a realization of abundance. The logic of abundance is pervasive in Christian theology. This finds expression in multiple ways, but the central idea is that not only does God provide, but that God intends creation to be sufficient to meet our needs—all our needs; not just economic needs (Pontifical Council 2005, §182). The dominant hegemonic ideology of capitalism operates according to a logic of scarcity (Clark 2006, 29). This is the same dominant ideology that Brueggemann refers to as "the American ethos of consumerism" (2018, 1), and what the EoC refers to as the "culture of having" (Lubich 2007, 280). It is what both Brueggemann and Francis decry as a culture that creates "dispensable" or "discarded" persons. Indeed, as John Haughey asserts, "Forgetful of God's logic, humans enthrone self-providence over an economic world in which the logic of scarcity is worked out as 'dog eat dog' and 'every man for himself'" (Haughey 2006, 88–89).

The EoC is a practice of abundance because it is about creating and distributing a set of economic and social goods toward the end or goal of well-being for all persons involved. It would be a mistake to understand abundance in a strictly economic sense. Certainly the creation and distribution of wealth is a core concern, but when the goods and services

produced are *good* goods (Dicastery 2018, §42), when employment is created and sustained, when each business becomes a
communion (a set of valued and valuable relationships), when
subsidiarity is practiced inside the business, when the market
exchange is also an authentic encounter with the other, this
is abundance—well-being that goes beyond mere economic
wealth creation and distribution. When created wealth is
invested in the "culture" of nurturing and development of a
culture of giving, this is abundance. So, the EoC is a practice
of abundance of well-being, where wealth creation and distribution are but one dimension.

Second, as an alternative consciousness, the EoC proposes
the market as a place of authentic encounter with other persons and not merely a place of exchange of goods and services.
Exchange in fact is the means of encounter: Every good and/
or service produced or consumed is the outcome of human
creativity, time, and labor and thus is a tangible marker of a
particular relationship between two or more persons. This is
in keeping with the EoC's insistence on the primacy of relationships. The market in fact is not only a means to connect
persons, even when there is no personal connection, but it also
permits connections between people across time and space.
Goods and services produced in the past and in a particular
location can be consumed by other persons at different times
and in different places.

Further, the EoC understands markets as mechanisms for
the exchange of more than just goods and services. It is also
a mechanism for the exchange of needs. So, markets play a
critical role in the EoC practice of abundance. When markets
are viewed as places of encounter, they can clearly be beneficial
and constitutive, at least in part, of the common good. Additionally, markets are broadly understood to be indispensable
in terms of wealth creation and distribution—one facet of
abundance. To say that the EoC views the market as a place
of encounter as well as exchange is to recognize the primacy
of persons and the presence of community.

And the same for markets; to say the EoC views the market as a place of encounter is to recognize that markets create relationships. At the very least, however distant might be the physical relationship between, say, an employee of a company and the eventual user of that company's product made (in whole or in part) by that employee; they may never know or meet one another personally but they are nevertheless in relationship. It might be fleeting, it might be persistent, but they are in relationship even across time, distance, and space.[1]

Third, as an alternative consciousness, the EoC clearly understands the profit of business as a means to a defined, multidimensional purpose. Profit is not an end unto itself. Profit is not the exclusive private property of the business owner, but rather is covered by what John Paul II called a social mortgage (1987, §42). The owner's claim on the profit of the business is not absolute. Accordingly, the EoC proposes three legitimate uses for business profits: one is for reinvestment in the business to insure vitality, growth, and sustainability; a second use is to directly alleviate the material needs of persons; and the third use is to invest in the cultivation, nurturing, and dissemination of this alternative consciousness.

Fourth, and finally, as an alternative consciousness, the EoC understands the purpose of business activity to be the creation of communion, and not any narrower understanding of business purpose such as maximization of profit or shareholder value. Indeed, Pope Francis recognized this in his address to the EoC:

---

[1]   This sentiment, or a similar sentiment, was given voice on one occasion by Steve Jobs, founder of Apple, when he said, "You make something with love and with care, even though you probably will never meet ... the people that you're making it for, and you'll never shake their hand, by making something with care, you are expressing your gratitude to humanity, to the species" (Bradshaw 2019; accessed July 3, 2019).

You see the entrepreneur as an agent of communion. By introducing into the economy the good seed of communion, you have begun a profound change in the way of seeing and living business. Business is not only incapable of destroying communion among people but can edify it and promote it. With your life you demonstrate that economy and communion become more beautiful when they are beside each other. Certainly, the economy becomes more beautiful, but communion is also more beautiful, because the spiritual communion of hearts is even fuller when it becomes the communion of goods, of talents, of profits. (2017)

This vision of business activity as communion-creation is seen in the EoC in multiple ways. First of all, the EoC recognizes that a business is a de facto communion. What this means is that, by definition, an EoC entrepreneur creates a set of relationships that would otherwise not exist. Customers, employees, suppliers, competitors, and others are united by the very activities of the business: by consuming products and services and by participating in the production of those products and services even in the smallest of ways. Secondly, it recognizes that beyond this, a business is always a communion in formation. That is to say, that each of these relationships may require ongoing nurturing and development. Certainly, each of these relationships brings with it a responsibility for the quality and the sustainability of the relationship, and each relationship could be vastly different in that regard. So, the EoC recognizes the presence of communion, but the business is also called to build communion. Communion is the primary purpose, obligation, and effect of business (Gallagher 2014).

These are the dimensions of the alternative consciousness of the EoC. But what of the other marks of an exercise of prophetic imagination? Is the EoC borne of grief and mourning, and does it function as a criticism of the prevailing order? And does it arise from "inside of its own experience and confession of faith and not through external appropriation from somewhere else" (Brueggeman 2018, 5)? As mentioned, the EoC was a response to social injustice and economic inequality, which is certainly a form of grief. Moreover, its founding story often describes the EoC as a response to the poverty found in the favelas, or slums, of São Paulo, Brazil. Chiara Lubich described her view of São Paulo while aboard her flight as seeing the favelas as a "crown of thorns" surrounding the city (Callebaut 2012, 74).

The grief caused by the experience of deprivation also came with a critique of the injustice that lay at the root of this deprivation. Even though the EoC is so formed and shaped by the spirituality of unity that it looks for ways to bridge differences and distinctions, it often describes the prevailing culture as a "culture of having" distinct from a "culture of giving" (Araùjo 2002, 25). We might note the following from Lorna Gold. The EoC

> ... raises probing questions about the interrelationship between the cultural, the spiritual, and the economic dimensions of life, arguably calling into question the idea that "rational economic man" based on "self-interest" is the only viable principle for a global economy. (Gold 2010, 36)

It is in this way that the EoC is critical.

In the case of the EoC, the alternative consciousness—the practice of abundance, the market as a place of encounter, the legitimate uses for profits, and the purpose of business as communion—certainly arises from the Focolare spirituality of unity. Although we can abstract from its concrete reality to ideas, concepts, and understanding, the EoC principles were not generative. What was generative was the Focolare spirituality and culture. As Masters and Uelmen point out: "A spirituality of unity takes love of neighbor as the measure of everything in life. . . . Building relationships of love and unity constitutes the heart, soul, and driving energy of every Focolare community, project, or activity" (Masters and Uelmen 2011, 40). It is impossible to separate the EoC from the Focolare culture, and from the spirituality of unity. In many respects, the EoC is a lived manifestation of the spirituality of unity, the living out of Jesus' desire and prayer expressed in John 17. If one were to ask how to live the spirituality of unity in business the answer would be the EoC. Chiara Lubich noted:

> This authentic expression of the spirituality of unity in economic life can be understood in its entirety and its complexity only if viewed within the vision this spirituality has of the human person and social relationships. (Lubich 2007, 274)

As discussed above, the EoC grows out of the Focolare culture and spirituality of unity. The Focolare have simply been asking—since their founding—how best to live the prayer of Jesus that we might all be made one, and answering that question with the art of love.

The Economy of Communion as Prophetic Ministry

Exercises in prophetic imagination are more than abstract ideas. In every case, there must be prophets: those persons who are called to engage with the prevailing culture and ideology in prophetic ways. As an exercise of prophetic imagination, the EoC therefore has profound implications for individual business entrepreneurs. These entrepreneurs are among those people that Francis described as "agents of communion" (2017). I have elsewhere referred to the EoC business as a "crucible of formation" (Gallagher 2011).

These refer to two slightly different things, but they are related. As an agent of communion, the entrepreneur realizes that the fundamental mission of his or her business is indeed to create communion. The creation of communion in the context and confines of a market-driven business, subject to the same competitive pressures as all businesses, places significant, weighty, and to many observers, irreconcilable demands on the entrepreneur, and in many cases, on employees involved in the business. EoC entrepreneurs are a prophetic voice.

Business (entrepreneurship) is risky, complex, and demanding. The entrepreneur, even faced with the profit distribution decision, must decide how much to reinvest in the business, how much to contribute to the developing of culture, and how much to send off. These are not easy decisions and one never knows when one has made the correct decision. To that extent, it is shaped by experience in the same way that each of us have our lives shaped by experience. To be sure, it is experience tempered by attention, observation, reflection, deliberation, and renewed action. It is a learning process. It is organic.

When one undertakes to create a company, a business, one takes on a set of relationships that by definition would not otherwise exist, and those relationships can be numerous and qualitatively different. At the same time, one takes responsibility for certain sets of decisions that are presented by the demands of the marketplace and are therefore primarily driven by competition. But these decisions are also guided by law, tradition, and custom.

As mentioned, a business can be conceived as a specific set of relationships that would otherwise not exist. The EoC is prophetic here, calling us to responsibility for a set of relationships we might otherwise overlook or dismiss. When a company is small with no or a very small number of employees or even contract, part-time, or temporary employees, the relationships still exist, of course, but certainly relationships are going to exist with customers, with suppliers, with competitors. They can be fleeting, they can be long lasting, they can be life-changing, they can be challenging and difficult.

They are subject to tension. Can they be effectively managed by policy? Some of those relationships are with other entities and organizations. With another set of relationships—civil authorities, licensing, the law—the other party can be a large organization that might be bureaucratic. And that relationship, no less than any other, demands that we practice unity.

And finally, a relationship exists with the business itself, the company, as an independent entity (Bower and Paine 2017, 57). The entrepreneur has a responsibility to navigate competing demands and needs in regard to the sustaining of the business. When does one put the business ahead of an individual person? This dilemma is perhaps most evident in decisions around the distribution of profits. It is imperative that some part of the profits be devoted to sustaining the business; this suggests investment in tangible as well as intangible assets, and in the repair and maintenance of existing assets such equipment, processes, technology, marketing, branding, and perhaps patents and technology protection.

None of these responsibilities or decisions are necessarily easy. But they are important and necessary in the light of prophetic ministry. And they function both as spiritual discipline and as vehicles of spiritual formation, shaping EoC entrepreneurs in their role as prophetic ministers—indeed, as agents of communion.

The Economy of Communion and the Current Crisis

Chiara Lubich has made the point that the EoC "takes its place alongside the numerous initiatives by individuals and groups that have sought and seek to 'give a human face to the economic system'" (Lubich 2007, 275). The EoC then is in solidarity with many of the ideas, movements, and initiatives described in the opening paragraphs of this paper, and, indeed, in solidarity with the climate strikers and their critique of the prevailing economic system and social culture that, in Brueggemann's words, view persons as dispensable, or in Pope Francis' words, discards them. But given the deep roots of the EoC in the Focolare spirituality of unity and therefore in the Gospel, the EoC calls all of us to prophetic ministry—to a particular spiritual journey (Lubich 2007, 281).

The EoC certainly proposes an alternative consciousness to the dominant culture of consumerism, to the common understanding of markets as exchange mechanisms only, and to the prevailing logic that businesses exist to maximize profits. As a prophetic ministry, the EoC calls us to imagine an economic and political system that places the person at the center of economic purpose, practice, and policy (Lubich 2007, 285); that prioritizes authentic and meaningful relationships over all other ends; that seeks constantly to live out the prayer of Jesus as recorded in John 17, "that all may be one" (John 17:21, KJV). It calls us to a richer imagination than that which has been delivered to us in, as our climate strikers attest, a dehumanizing economy and a possible existential crisis.

Bibliography

Alperovitz, Gar. 2012. "The Rise of the New Economy." *Salon*, May 22, 2012. https://www.salon.com/2012/05/22/rise_of_the_new_economy_movement/.

Araùjo, Vera. 2002. "Personal and Societal Prerequisites of the Economy of Communion." In *The Economy of Communion: Toward a Multi-Dimensional Economic Culture*, edited by Luigino Bruni. Translated by Lorna Gold, 21–30. Hyde Park, NY: New City Press.

Bower, Joseph L. and Lynn S. Paine. 2017. "The Error at the Heart of Corporate Leadership." *Harvard Business Review*. (May–June): 50–60.

Bradshaw, Tim. 2019. "Jony Ive on Leaving Apple, in His Own Words." *Financial Times*, June 27, 2019. https://www.ft.com/content/0b20032e-98cf-11e9-8cfb-30c211dcd229.

Brueggemann, Walter. 2018. *The Prophetic Imagination* (40th Anniversary Ed.). Minneapolis MN: Fortress Press.

Callebaut, Bernhard. 2012. "Economy of Communion: A Sociological Inquiry on a Contemporary Inspiration in Economic and Social Life." *Claritas Journal of Dialogue and Culture* 1, no. 1: 71–82.

Clark, Charles M.A. 2006. "Wealth as Abundance and Scarcity." In *Rediscovering Abundance*, edited by Helen Alford, O.P., Charles M.A. Clark, S.A. Cortright, and Michael J. Naughton, 28-56. Notre Dame IN, University of Notre Dame Press.

Dicastery for Promoting Integral Human Development. 2018. *Vocation of the Business Leader: A Reflection.* Rome/St. Paul: University of St. Thomas. https://www.stthomas. edu/media/catholicstudies/center/ryan/publications/ publicationpdfs/vocationofthebusinessleaderpdf/ FinalTextTheVocationoftheBusinessLeader.pdf.

Focolare. 2020. Focolare Website. https://www.focolare.org/en/.

Francis, Pope. 2017. *Address of His Holiness Pope Francis to Participants in the Meeting "Economy of Communion", Sponsored by the Focolare Movement.* https://w2.vatican.va/ content/francesco/en/speeches/2017/february/documents/ papa-francesco_20170204_focolari.html.

Gallagher, John. 2011. "The Crucible of EoC Entrepreneurship." Presented at The International Economy of Communion Assembly, Mariapolis Ginetta, Brazil. http://www.edc-online. org/en/home/events-in-brazil/brazil-2011/1606-the-crucible-of-eoc-entrepreneurship.html.

Gallagher, John. 2014. "Communion and Profits: Thinking with the Economy of Communion about the Purpose of Business." *Revista Portuguesa de Filosofia* T. 70, no. 1: 9–27.

Gallagher, John and Jeanne Buckeye. 2014. *Structures of Grace: The Business Practices of the Economy of Communion.* Hyde Park, NY: New City Press.

Gold, Lorna. 2010. *New Financial Horizons: The Emergence of an Economy of Communion.* Hyde Park, NY: New City Press.

Gold, Lorna. 2019. *Climate Generation: Awakening to Our Children's Future.* Hyde Park, NY: New City Press.

Hankins, Davis. 2018. "Foreword." In *The Prophetic Imagination* (40th Anniversary Ed.), xiii–xix. Minneapolis MN: Fortress Press.

Haughey, John. 2006. "A Pauline Catechesis of Abundance." In *Rediscovering Abundance*, edited by Helen Alford, O.P., Charles M.A. Clark, S.A. Cortright, and Michael J. Naughton, 87–101. Notre Dame IN, University of Notre Dame Press.

John Paul II, Pope. 1987. *Sollicitudo Rei Socialis.* http://www.vatican.va/content/john-paul-ii/en/encyclicals/documents/hf_jp-ii_enc_30121987_sollicitudo-rei-socialis.html.

Kelly, Marjorie. 2013. "Toward a Generative Economy." *Open Democracy*, May 30, 2013. https://www.opendemocracy.net/en/opendemocracyuk/toward-generative-economy/.

King James Version of the Bible. 1611. London: King James. https://www.kingjamesbibleonline.org/.

Lubich, Chiara. 2007. *Essential Writings.* Hyde Park, NY: New City Press.

Masters, Thomas and Amy Uelmen. 2011. *Focolare: Living a Spirituality of Unity in the United States.* Hyde Park, NY: New City Press.

Pontifical Council for Justice and Peace. 2005. *Compendium of the Social Doctrine of the Church.* http://www.vatican.va/roman_curia/pontifical_councils/justpeace/documents/rc_pc_justpeace_doc_20060526_compendio-dott-soc_en.html.

Thunberg, Greta. 2019. "You Did Not Act In Time." *The Guardian*, April 23, 2019. https://www.theguardian.com/environment/2019/apr/23/greta-thunberg-full-speech-to-mps-you-did-not-act-in-time.

Notes on Contributors

Greg Beabout is a professor of philosophy at St. Louis University, where he has taught for decades. He has published widely on topics related to Catholic social thought, personalism, ethics, and professional ethics, including *The Character of the Manager: From Office Executive to Wise Steward* (Palgrave MacMillan, 2013) and *Beyond Self Interest: A Personalist Approach to Human Action* (Lexington Books, 2002).

Jeanne Buckeye is an associate professor in the Department of Ethics and Business Law at the University of St. Thomas, Opus College of Business, in Minnesota. Her research interests lie primarily in examining how faith commitments affect managerial practice. She is co-author of *Structures of Grace* (New City Press, 2013), a study of American EoC companies, as well as *Respect in Action: Applying Subsidiarity in Business* (UNIAPAC, 2015).

David Cloutier teaches moral theology at The Catholic University of America, in Washington, DC, and is author of the award-winning *The Vice of Luxury: Economic Excess in a Consumer Age* (Georgetown University Press, 2015), *Walking God's Earth: The Environment and Catholic Faith* (Liturgical Press, 2014), and *Reading, Praying, Living Pope Francis's Laudato Si'* (Liturgical Press, 2015).

Luca Crivelli is Director of the Department of Business and Social Sciences at the University of Applied Sciences and Arts of Southern Switzerland as well as Titular Professor of Economics at the Universita della Svizzera Italiana, Deputy Director of the Swiss School of Public Health, and Visiting Professor at Sophia University Institute. He is an active policy analyst and advisor in Switzerland, and has published books and articles on the Economy of Communion.

John Gallagher is emeritus professor of management at Maryville College in Maryville, TN. He has been deeply involved in studying the EoC and is the author of various articles on the EoC and business as well as co-author of *Structures of Grace: The Business Practices of the Economy of Communion* (2013), which examines a number of EoC companies in America.

Andy Gustafson is an EoC entrepreneur, rehabbing and renting out properties in midtown Omaha. He is also a professor of business ethics and society at the Heider College of Business at Creighton University, where he teaches classes on business ethics and business and faith and runs the Business, Faith and the Common Good Institute. Andy has published on business ethics, British utilitarianism, business and the common good, and the Economy of Communion.

Celeste Harvey is an associate professor of philosophy at the College of St. Mary (Omaha, NE) where she teaches ethics and philosophy and is active in the Economy of Communion. She has published on ethics, the Economy of Communion, and feminism, and is currently working on the topic of the vice of luxury.

Chiara Lubich (1920–2008) was the founder of the Focolare Movement in Italy during World War II, and she later helped found the Economy of Communion in 1991. She oversaw the growth of both movements to make a worldwide impact.

Rev. John Simon McNerney, PhD, is an elected international fellow of the Institute for Human Ecology, Washington, DC. He was the first Michael Novak Distinguished Visiting Scholar in the Busch Business School at The Catholic University of America, Washington, DC. His books include *Wealth of Persons: Economics with a Human Face* (Cascade Books, 2016) and *John Paul II: Poet and Philosopher* (UNKNO, 2004). His

Myself as Another: Reflections on Who I Am, published by New City Press, is forthcoming, as is *Crossing the Threshold: A Philosophical-Aesthetic Reflection on Becoming a Human Person.* He is a faculty member at Theological College in The Catholic University of America.

Jesús Morán was elected co-president of the worldwide Focolare Movement in 2014. He is a Spanish philosopher and theologian who has devoted most of his life to the Focolare Movement.

Angus Sibley is an actuary and former member of the London Stock Exchange. Among his publications are *The "Poisoned Spring" of Economic Libertarianism* (Pax Romana, 2011), *Catholic Economics: Alternatives to the Jungle* (Liturgical Press, 2015), and many papers and articles on economic, theological, and cultural topics.

Amy Uelmen is a lecturer on religion and professional life, and a Special Advisor to the Dean at Georgetown Law School, and a Senior Research Fellow at the Berkley Center for Religion, Peace and World Affairs. She is a member of the Focolare and has written extensively on the Economy of Communion.

Index

Topics

FOCOLARE MEDIA

Enkindling the Spirit of Unity

The New City Press book you are holding in your hands is one of the many resources produced by Focolare Media, which is a ministry of the Focolare Movement in North America. The Focolare is a worldwide community of people who feel called to bring about the realization of Jesus' prayer: "That all may be one" (see John 17:21).

Focolare Media wants to be your primary resource for connecting with people, ideas, and practices that build unity. Our mission is to provide content that empowers people to grow spiritually, improve relationships, engage in dialogue, and foster collaboration within the Church and throughout society.

Visit www.focolaremedia.com to learn more about all of New City Press's books, our award-winning magazine *Living City*, videos, podcasts, events, and free resources.

NCP
NEW CITY PRESS

www.ingramcontent.com/pod-product-compliance
Lightning Source LLC
Chambersburg PA
CBHW031806190326
41518CB00006B/219